J. O. Francis, Realist Drama and Culture, Place and Nation

Writing Wales in English

CREW series of Critical and Scholarly Studies
General Editor: Professor M. Wynn Thomas (CREW, Swansea University)

This *CREW* series is dedicated to Emyr Humphreys, a major figure in the literary culture of modern Wales, a founding patron of the *Centre for Research into the English Literature and Language of Wales*, and, along with Gillian Clarke and the late Seamus Heaney, one of *CREW*'s original Honorary Associates. Grateful thanks are due to the late Richard Dynevor for making this series possible.

Other titles in the series

Stephen Knight, *A Hundred Years of Fiction* (978-0-7083-1846-1)
Barbara Prys-Williams, *Twentieth-Century Autobiography* (978-0-7083-1891-1)
Kirsti Bohata, *Postcolonialism Revisited* (978-0-7083-1892-8)
Chris Wigginton, *Modernism from the Margins* (978-0-7083-1927-7)
Linden Peach, *Contemporary Irish and Welsh Women's Fiction* (978-0-7083-1998-7)
Sarah Prescott, *Eighteenth-Century Writing from Wales: Bards and Britons* (978-0-7083-2053-2)
Hywel Dix, *After Raymond Williams: Cultural Materialism and the Break-Up of Britain* (978-0-7083-2153-9)
Matthew Jarvis, *Welsh Environments in Contemporary Welsh Poetry* (978-0-7083-2152-2)
Harri Garrod Roberts, *Embodying Identity: Representations of the Body in Welsh Literature* (978-0-7083-2169-0)
M. Wynn Thomas, *In the Shadow of the Pulpit: Literature and Nonconformist Wales* (978-0-7083-2225-3)
Linden Peach, *The Fiction of Emyr Humphreys: Contemporary Critical Perspectives* (978-0-7083-2216-1)
Daniel Westover, *R. S. Thomas: A Stylistic Biography* (978-0-7083-2413-4)
Jasmine Donahaye, *Whose People? Wales, Israel, Palestine* (978-0-7083-2483-7)
Judy Kendall, *Edward Thomas: The Origins of His Poetry* (978-0-7083-2403-5)
Damian Walford Davies, *Cartographies of Culture: New Geographies of Welsh Writing in English* (978-0-7083-2476-9)
Daniel G. Williams, *Black Skins, Blue Books: African Americansand Wales 1845–1945* (978-0-7083-1987-1)
Andrew Webb, *Edward Thomas and World Literary Studies: Wales, Anglocentrism and English Literature* (978-0-7083-2622-0)

J. O. Francis, Realist Drama and Ethics
Culture, Place and Nation

Writing Wales in English

ALYCE VON ROTHKIRCH

UNIVERSITY OF WALES PRESS
CARDIFF
2014

© Alyce von Rothkirch, 2014

All rights reserved. No part of this book may be reproduced in any material form (including photocopying or storing it in any medium by electronic means and whether or not transiently or incidentally to some other use of this publication) without the written permission of the copyright owner except in accordance with the provisions of the Copyright, Designs and Patents Act 1988. Applications for the copyright owner's written permission to reproduce any part of this publication should be addressed to the University of Wales Press, 10 Columbus Walk, Brigantine Place, Cardiff CF10 4UP.
www.uwp.co.uk

British Library Cataloguing-in-Publication Data
A catalogue record for this book is available from the British Library.

ISBN 978-1-78316-070-9
e-ISBN 978-1-78316-071-6

The right of Alyce von Rothkirch to be identified as author of this work has been asserted in accordance with sections 77, 78 and 79 of the Copyright, Designs and Patents Act 1988.

THE ASSOCIATION FOR
WELSH WRITING IN ENGLISH
CYMDEITHAS LLÊN SAESNEG CYMRU

Typeset by Mark Heslington Ltd, Scarborough, North Yorkshire
Printed by CPI Antony Rowe, Chippenham, Wiltshire

Contents

General Editor's Preface   vii
Acknowledgements   ix
List of Tables   xi
Introduction   1
    J. O. Francis and a Welsh Ethics of Place
    J. O. Francis's Life
    Cultural Background, Themes and Ideas
    J. O. Francis and the Land Ethic

1   A Son of Wales Enters the Stage   24

2   J. O. Francis and Amateur Theatre in Wales, 1920–40   38
    The Ethics of Amateur Theatre
    Amateur Drama in Wales
    Amateur Drama Competitions

3   Place, Politics and the Possibilities of Realism   60
    Change (1912)
    Cross-Currents (1922)
    The Beaten Track (1924)
    Howell of Gwent (1932)
    The Devouring Fire (1953?)

4   Poachers in Little Villages   97
    The One-Act 'Play of Welsh Life'
    The Poacher (1912)
    The Dark Little People (1922)
    Tares in the Wheat (1942) / *The Sheep and the Goats* (1951?)
    The Bakehouse (1912) and *The Sewing Guild* (1943)
    Little Village (1928)

5   A Pilgrim to St David's   122
    First Journey: London – Newport – Cardiff – Rhondda
    Second Journey: London – Brecon – Llanidloes –
    Aberdovey – Aberystwyth
    Third Journey: Into the Heart of the Nation

Afterword   141

List of Works by J. O. Francis   144
    1   Published Plays
    2   Published Plays: Translations
    3   Unpublished Plays
    4   Published Essays and Other Non-Fiction
    5   Work for Radio

List of Performances of Plays by J. O. Francis   150

Notes   157

Bibliography   180

Index   195

General Editor's Preface

The aim of this series is to produce a body of scholarly and critical work that reflects the richness and variety of the English-language literature of modern Wales. Drawing upon the expertise both of established specialists and of younger scholars, it will seek to take advantage of the concepts, models and discourses current in the best contemporary studies to promote a better understanding of the literature's significance, viewed not only as an expression of Welsh culture but also as an instance of modern literatures in English worldwide. In addition, it will seek to make available the scholarly materials (such as bibliographies) necessary for this kind of advanced, informed study.

M. Wynn Thomas
CREW (*Centre for Research into the English Literature and Language of Wales*)
Swansea University

Acknowledgements

Many people have helped me during the time it took me to research and write this book. In no particular order, I would like to thank:

M. Wynn Thomas, Malcolm Ballin, Amanda Smith (Samuel French Ltd), Brian Owen (Curator, Royal Welch Fusiliers Museum), Kirsti Bohata for involving me in the Mapping Writing Project, Sarah Lewis and Helgard Krause at the University of Wales Press, the anonymous reader for their constructive comments, Meic Stephens, Jamie Rees and Margaret Ormrod (Neath Little Theatre), Edward Hull (London Gliding Club), the Department of Adult Continuing Education at Swansea University for supporting me by means of a sabbatical, the staff at Swansea Central Library, the staff at the Hugh Owen Library, Aberystwyth University, the staff at the Victoria and Albert Theatre Archive, the staff at the National Library of Wales, the Research Institute for Arts and Humanities at Swansea University, and the Richard Burton Centre at Swansea University.

All reasonable efforts have been made to find the copyright holders for Francis's published and unpublished work.

List of Tables

1	Number of performances and opinion pieces in the sample	42
2	Performances and language	43
3	Relative popularity of authors, 1920–36	49
4	Plays most often performed	50
5	Drama companies and attendance at competitions	56

Introduction

Almost 100 years ago a week of historic performances took place in the New Theatre, Cardiff. Between 11 and 16 May 1914, the Welsh National Drama Company performed six plays in Welsh and in English: J. O. Francis's *Change* and *The Poacher*, D. T. Davies's *Ephraim Harris* and *Ble Ma Fa?*, R. G. Berry's *Ar y Groesffordd* and T. E. Ellis (Howard de Walden)'s *Pont Orewyn*. Owen Rhoscomyl, the business manager of the venture, made sure that it received sufficient media attention, and both Howard de Walden and George Moore gave speeches in support of it. Rhoscomyl's greatest coup was to persuade Lloyd George to attend performances: the Chancellor saw *Pont Orewyn* on Friday and Francis's *Change* on Saturday. The support of such an illustrious personage who, as the editorial of the *Western Mail* observed, 'represent[ed] a section of the Welsh public, a social and religious section, which ha[d] hitherto looked askance at the drama and held aloof from the theatre', was of crucial importance when it came to establishing 'the Welsh drama . . . as an important form of national literature, and the Welsh stage . . . as an important form of national art'.[1]

J. O. Francis was thus part of a theatrical revolution. The plays performed at the National Drama Week were to 'assist in the movement for the establishment of a national theatre', described by the *Western Mail* as 'a great instrument of national culture [which] enriches literature, . . . expands life, . . . gives to human intercourse an intellectual stimulus which is the greatest of pleasures'.[2] It was, as Rhoscomyl insisted, not 'a sort of amateur movement', although the 'directors of the Welsh National Drama [hoped] that, as a result of their labours, Wales [would] one day be covered with amateur companies from end to end',[3] a prophecy that was shortly to come true in ways Rhoscomyl perhaps did not expect. Instead, the plays were to be presented by professionals, without, however, replicating what he thought were the 'bad traditions and false conventions in acting' of the London stage. Actors were 'to stick to the real atmosphere of actual life',[4] thus introducing a realism to the Welsh stage that was truly innovative.

J. O. Francis was perhaps the most famous of the group of playwrights whose work was performed at the National Drama Week. *Change* certainly received the most media coverage out of the six plays. It was hailed as a great work of national and even international importance. Indeed, as a writer for amateur drama companies, his writing career spanned decades and only came to an end with the decline of amateur theatre itself in the 1950s.

Francis's career and substantial body of work repays closer study for a variety of reasons. First, it is impossible to get a sense of the historical development of Welsh theatre without taking into account the crucial role of amateur theatre before the growth of a literary professional theatre in the 1960s.[5] Francis occupied a key role in the amateur sector and his work should be considered within the greater body of Welsh- and English-language drama of the period as well as within the context of the drama that inspired him – mainly contemporary English and Irish drama. Secondly, he provides a unique link to an Edwardian/pre-First World War writing style and cultural sensibility in Wales that is not represented in that other foundational text of Welsh writing in English, Caradoc Evans's *My People* (1915). Indeed, Francis occupies a niche of his own: his work lies somewhere between the romances of Allen Raine and Owen Rhoscomyl and the realistic school of industrial writing, whose most famous exponents wrote in the 1930s (Lewis Jones, Jack Jones etc.).[6] In tone and style, Francis is perhaps closer to Welsh women writers such as Hilda Vaughan and Elizabeth Inglis Jones, who published their most well-known work in the 1930s. Francis's humour is similar to that of valleys writers like George Ewart Evans and Gwyn Thomas, but they, too, wrote much later. Thirdly, Francis deserves to be read because he brings to the stage the central social conflicts of his day without providing easy solutions. And finally, although the *Western Mail* was perhaps overly cautious when it emphasized that the plays of the National Drama Week were 'of a wholesome tendency, good alike for mind and morals',[7] it is undoubtedly true that Francis's plays are ethical in intent: they express what can be considered a specifically Welsh ethics of community and place.

J. O. FRANCIS AND A WELSH ETHICS OF PLACE

J. O. Francis and contemporary writers of Welsh drama brought two main innovations to the Welsh stage when they began writing and producing original plays from 1912 onwards, thus setting the course for what appeared on the Welsh amateur stage for decades to come: first, they adopted features of the socially committed English new drama and transplanted it to Wales, thus creating the authentic, equally socially committed 'play of Welsh life'. Secondly, they promoted a particular type of one-act play – often a comedy – taking their cue from the realistic Irish comedies written for the Abbey Theatre in Dublin by Lady Gregory and others. Both types of play are realistic in form and deeply rooted in place, which makes them particularly amenable to an analysis based on an ethical literary criticism of place. This involves an examination of the relationship between characters and place, the ideological commitments of authors and potential effects on audiences.

Recent years have seen an 'ethical turn' in literary criticism.[8] Arguments for the validity of ethical literary criticism pointedly written against aspects of postmodern and poststructuralist theory, like Wayne Booth's *The Company We Keep* (1988), are now rare. Instead, debates are more likely to be about exactly how literature can yield examples for philosophical enquiry, such as the Aristotelian scholar Martha Nussbaum's *Love's Knowledge* (1990) or Noël Carroll's and Gregory Currie's discussions of how readers/audiences gain ethical knowledge when reading fictional text.[9] Particularly Emmanuel Lévinas's ethical writings have influenced critics like Robert Eaglestone, who accuses Nussbaum of reading literary texts in the same way as philosophical texts, thus ignoring ambiguities and indeterminacies in meaning.[10]

While I agree with aspects of Eaglestone's detailed criticism of Nussbaum's reading of literature, I do not think that *all* of her philosophically inspired reading of prose fiction is reductive or that her approach itself is flawed. This book claims that an ethical approach that is broadly based on Aristotelian virtue ethics is fruitful when considering J. O. Francis's work because notions of the good,[11] of how human beings should live if they are to be virtuous,[12] underpin all his work, most obviously the socially engaged serious plays but also the comic plays.[13] Moreover, Francis's work shows that he was, like Aristotle, 'committed to thinking that the highest developments of human nature . . . would fit together with the more ordinary life of civic virtue'.[14] In other words, conceptions of an ethically good life feed into notions of civic, national identity.

Aristotelian virtue ethics focuses on ethical actions, such as those aiding a temperate life, maintaining friendships, and developing one's wisdom. Virtuous actions, in turn, allow one to live the good life. The final goal of such virtuous living is what Aristotle has called *eudaimonia*, and which is usually translated as 'happiness' or 'flourishing'.[15] 'Aristotelian virtues are not just the disposition to do the right thing, or to come to the right conclusion. ... [T]hey are settled states of character. They have an affective side: to have virtue is to have one's relevant motivation habituated and trained in the right direction'.[16] All of Francis's plays and some of his creative non-fiction deal to some degree with the development of a good, that is a virtuous, character. John Price's tragic flaw in *Change*, for instance, is that he does not possess the virtues of temperance, magnanimity and proper ambition, while Gareth Parry's character is on his way to *eudaimonia* because, after a considerable inner struggle, he prefers the life of contemplation to the life of action.[17]

The Aristotelian virtues emerged from a particular cultural, social and geographical context, but they are often presented – not least in textbooks on ethics – as timeless, placeless and unchanging.[18] It is precisely this universalism, the notion that some ways of thinking are simply true, that has been successfully challenged by postmodernist theory.[19] How does an analysis of Francis's work, which has Aristotelian virtue ethics at its heart, escape those charges of universalism? Modern ethicists have responded to the charge of universalism differently. Martha Nussbaum argues that the Aristotelian virtues were conceived as more general descriptions of good actions. The 'particular choices that the virtuous person ... makes will always be a matter of being keenly responsible to the local features of his or her context ... [A] good rule is a good summary of wise particular choices and not a court of last resort'.[20] An awareness of 'local features' does not mean that Aristotelians are moral particularists, however. They do have 'a deep interest in the universal and in the universalizability of ethical judgments'.[21] But that does not mean that these universal templates are simply applied to any ethical problem anywhere and at any time.

Alasdair MacIntyre goes further. While indebted to the Aristotelian school of thought, he is a little further down the road to moral particularism by arguing that Aristotle gave 'an account of the good which is at once local and particular – located in and partially defined by the characteristics of the *polis* – and yet also cosmic and universal'.[22] In other words, there are universal aspects to Aristotelian virtues but each culture determines what precisely those virtues mean in its own context: '[t]he exercise of the virtues is itself apt to require a highly determinate attitude to social and

INTRODUCTION 5

political issues; and it is always *within some particular community with its own specific institutional forms* that we learn or fail to learn to exercise the virtues'.[23] While not abandoning the idea that central aspects of the virtues are universal, MacIntyre contends that the interpretations of those virtues through the ages have changed considerably.

To what extent does an individual's moral thinking reflect that of her cultural context? Peter Levine agrees that the way individuals think about the virtues is largely but not totally culturally determined:

> To have a 'culture' is not to make a few basic assumptions from which everything else follows; it is rather to possess a large set of biases, experiences, beliefs, and commitments; examples, archetypes, vocabularies, and role models; styles of representing the world; and repertoires of reasoning skills. Everyone has a different set. Even if there are two people in the world who are so dissimilar that they perceive and judge *every* situation differently, other people share some views with each. In short, human beings are not divided into a set of distinct 'cultures,' each of one with its own worldview or foundation (. . .). Rather, we normally relate to people who are somewhat similar and somewhat different.[24]

Rather than seeing people entirely dominated by the worldviews expressed by one, somehow hermetically sealed, culture, Levine asks us to imagine individuals as existing in a network of connections between other individuals. We are likely to have more in common with those who share cultural assumptions but some universal values may cross cultures. Our allegiances are not automatic but require an act of choice, of imagination. This point is particularly important when reading Francis's work as he, as a London Welshman, wrote from a position outside the centre of the culture of his allegiance. Thus, an approach that is broadly Aristotelian may be alive to the ways in which historical and cultural location interprets the notion of the good and the realization that the individual has some freedom to consciously align herself with certain ideas of the good but not others.

My main criticism of ethical literary criticism is that it tends to focus on ethical relationships between fictional characters, and between (implied) author, characters and (implied) reader.[25] What is lacking in many critical works of this kind is the recognition that characters are, in Edward Casey's term, 'implaced' in a particular environment, which contributes its share of meaning.[26] As Shields argues, 'the spatial has an epistemic and ontological importance – it is part and parcel of our notions of reality, truth, and causality'.[27] Taking account of the spatial is especially important in the case of Francis, who wrote his plays out of a deep commitment to the indissoluble link between community, place and language.[28] Indeed, it seems to me to be profoundly unethical to ignore the way meaning is created in texts by situating characters and plot in a particular place as well as to discount the way readers and audiences, who, of course, are 'implaced' in turn, understand such texts.

As Casey points out, a study of ethics is always already connected to place as the etymology of the word 'ethics' comprises not only 'ethos', meaning *character*, but also 'ethea', meaning *accustomed place* or *habitat*.[29] I conceive of an ethical literary criticism of place, or an ethics of place for short, as critically examining three aspects of literature/drama and performance: first, it looks at the way characters are located in the intersections of cultural, geographical and socio-political place. Secondly, it examines how characters interact with place, how they derive pleasure, meaning and identity from place and, conversely, what their attitude towards place is. In short, it describes the ethical effect of place on people and also of people on place. This is also the moment when morality can but need not enter the equation:[30] does a character's close relationship with a place make her virtuous? Is the close and meaningful relationship of J. O. Francis's incorrigible poacher characters Dicky Bach Dwl and Twm Tinker with nature more virtuous and hence morally better than that of the landowner Venerby-Jones, who has virtually no meaningful relationship with the land and who egotistically wants to keep nature's bounty to himself? Thirdly, an ethical examination extends its purview to take in the (implied) author and the (implied) reader/audience, asking whether the (implied) author perhaps pursues an agenda. And, if, as in J. O. Francis's case, a certain interpretation of the idea of the nation lies behind the creation of fictional place, what type of national idea can be identified and how is it meant to affect the audience? Is the audience meant to engage cognitively and critically or is it meant to be carried along on a wave of patriotic sentiment? Thus the devastating effect on communities caused by rural out-migration, which is presented in Francis's *The Beaten Track*, is clearly meant to affect audiences emotionally but it may also be designed to spur them into action, perhaps leading to their considering moving 'back to the land' themselves.

J. O. FRANCIS'S LIFE

Francis left virtually no personal papers and not many details of his life are known. It is worth spending time discussing the available evidence as his experiences as a young man around the turn of the twentieth century shaped his conceptions of identity, place and the ethics of communal living, and these, in turn, found expression in his writing. Born in Dowlais, Merthyr Tydfil, on 7 September 1882, Francis was part of the generation of progressives growing up around 1900, a generation that included, among others, the scholar, poet, critic and playwright W. J. Gruffydd (1881–1954), the poet, scholar and translator T. Gwynn Jones (1871–1949) – a friend of Francis's – and the Calvinistic Methodist minister, poet and social reformer R. Silyn Roberts (1871–1930), who also translated some of Francis's plays into Welsh. The self-conception of these men was shaped by the example and the teaching of figures like O. M. Edwards, the anthropologist H. F. Fleure, the Cymru Fydd movement, and its several eventual heirs: progressive Liberalism, Christian socialism, Labour socialism and later the cultural nationalism of the early Plaid Cymru. J. O. Francis and his generation helped shape a post-Victorian Wales whose culture had not yet fragmented into two different linguistic communities.

Francis was the second child of David and Dorothy Francis. His elder sister Lilian Dora died in infancy, leaving him the eldest son of the family that later included his brother Edwin and his sisters Queenie and Margaret. David Francis was a 'Shoeing Smith' (farrier) from Merthyr who owned his business. Dorothy originally came from Ystradfodwg Cottage in Ystrad in the Rhondda Fawr Valley. She worked as a dressmaker and milliner and, after David's early death, became head of the household and also ran the family business. It is therefore not surprising that Francis's plays are filled with strong, competent women, who run their households with a firm yet loving hand (*Change*), keep the family together (*The Beaten Track*), successfully run their own business (*Tares in the Wheat/The Sheep and the Goats*), and whose menfolk are frequently absent (*The Sewing Guild*) or dead (*Cross-Currents*, *Hunting the Hare*).

Francis's plays tend to be set either in the urban south Wales valleys or in an unspecified rural Welsh location. As a man who never lived there himself, his sympathy with rural lifestyles may at least partly derive from the fact that his grandfather had come to Merthyr from Carmarthenshire. Francis's obituary in the *Merthyr Express* refers to 'the fact that J. O. Francis's family were just one generation off the land', which 'probably gave his pen its sure touch in creating the delightful rural Welsh atmosphere' in his plays.[31] On the other hand, one may not need to invoke familial experience of rural life: as an adult Francis visited different parts of Wales frequently and his many Welsh friends will have given him a sense of rural culture.

It is unclear whether Francis grew up in an English-speaking or in an at least partly Welsh-speaking environment. As a child Francis seems to have had at least a smattering of Welsh: the census of 1891 records David, Dorothy, the eight-year-old John Oswald and the two-year-old Edwin as being bilingual. However, by 1901 the only bilingual member of the family is Dorothy and the children are recorded as monolingual speakers of English. Evidence of Francis's proficiency in Welsh is ambiguous, however: a profile of Francis published in *Y Ddinas* asserts that he had not 'been reared to speak Welsh' as 'his father spoke no Welsh', which contradicts the census information.[32]

The reason for the loss of whatever Welsh he had had was probably mostly due to his school education. He went to St David's National School, the first intermediate school to open in Merthyr Tydfil, 'on the day that the school was officially opened'.[33] He gained the Senior Certificate in 1898, was awarded the Manager's Scholarship in 1899 and left school to go to the University College of Wales, Aberystwyth in 1900, having won a £40 County Scholarship. The importance of the intermediate school system for the life chances of men and women of Francis's generation and class background cannot be overstated. The schools were put in place in areas of high population density that had been badly served by the mix of voluntary and state provision that had characterized the Welsh education system until the Welsh Elementary Education Act 1870 and the Welsh Intermediate Education Act 1889. These new schools provided an excellent education and offered people like Francis the opportunity to go to university and follow a career of his choice. But unfortunately, contrary to the intentions of the Welsh Intermediate Education Act, schools often 'slavishly imitated the ethos and the curriculum of English grammar schools and . . . neglected subjects which were relevant to the local economy and community'.[34]

Francis regretted not having grown up to speak Welsh and learnt the language as an adult. During his military service 'he spent this time while on guard duty . . . practising the mutations'.[35] He became fluent but seems not to have written in Welsh, although the dialogue in his plays betrays the influence of the language on the English spoken by his characters. Indeed, he suggested in a review of Richard Hughes's *A Comedy of Good and Evil* (1922) that a truly realistic portrayal of Welsh people was not possible without a knowledge of Welsh, writing that 'Mr. Hughes would do well to . . . acquire that minimum of Welsh speech without which he will not make the race yield up the heart of its mystery'.[36] T. Gwynn Jones urged Francis that he 'ought to write a play in [Welsh]',[37] but Francis remained self-conscious about his acquired Welsh, calling it an 'unpliable book-knowledge of the language', a phrase redolent of regret.[38] Interestingly, Emyr Wyn Jenkins points out that the new secondary education was responsible for a 'literary renaissance' in Welsh-language literature and drama. The new writers of this cultural reawakening, including playwrights like D. T. Davies, were 'responsible for attracting the attention and enthusiasm of the new middle class (teachers, ministers, industrialists, and so on) and the working class alike'.[39] It seems thus that education alone cannot be held responsible for Francis's loss of Welsh: his parental home will also have had a decisive influence. But, importantly, the 'literary renaissance' Jenkins mentions created a rich Welsh-language cultural environment to which Francis – however indirectly – wished to contribute.

Like so many Welsh people growing up at the turn of the twentieth century, the young Francis's imagination was kindled less by religion than by politics. He grew up a Baptist but later 'relieved the denomination of the handicap of [his] allegiance'.[40] Politics was a different matter. As Montrose J. Moses wrote in his introduction to the American edition of *Change*:

> during his novitiate years in Wales, Mr. Francis absorbed unconsciously the meaning of what was taking place around him. He saw Socialism slowly gain hold on Wales. In his childhood he heard his elders argue the cause of Liberalism, and during his school years he used to follow the trail of the ever-present political orator.[41]

It appears that Francis, who as a teenager was keenly interested in politics, wanted to become a journalist. At university, his sympathies tended towards the progressive politics of the left and he joined the Fabian Society.[42] Characteristically, though, he did not join the Labour Party. As an older man he seems to have frequented the Liberal Club in London, which may have provided a more congenial political home for him.

Francis studied English Literature at the University College of Wales, Aberystwyth and graduated in 1903 with a First. Throughout his life he retained a sense of indebtedness and deep gratitude towards 'Aber'. He was a personal friend of J. H. Davies, who was Principal of the university between 1919 and 1926. In due course, he contributed a short history of his alma mater to 'aid the setting up of a Student's Union in the Jubilee Year of the College – 1922' when the university was celebrating its fiftieth anniversary.[43] He was a lifelong member of the Old Students' Association, was elected its vice-president in April 1922 and became president of the London Branch of the association in October 1922. And, most importantly for the present volume, he and his friends D. T. Davies, Charles Miles, a fellow lodger at his boarding house in London, and other Old Students formed the Ystwyth Players, later renamed the Welsh Players, an amateur drama company dedicated to performing plays at Old Students' reunions.

At first, the Ystwyth Players performed plays from the traditional 'amdram' repertoire. The student magazine *The Dragon* in 1908/9 describes Francis as a versatile but probably melodramatic actor: as a 'boisterous Charles' in Sheridan's *A School for Scandal*, 'his hearty laughter [gave] a timely reminder that the situation was comic, not tragic'. In *The Sergeant of Hussars*, a one-act play by Cicely Hamilton, Francis was cast as Voisin and 'gave an excellent study of a doddering old man'.[44] After 1912 he and his friends began writing original plays for the Ystwyth Players, among them *The Bakehouse*, *The Poacher* and *Change*.

Like many other graduates of his day, Francis became a teacher. He took up an appointment as an English master in Paris where he remained for two years.[45] After returning to Wales, he worked as an assistant English master in Ebbw Vale County School before moving to London to take up a post at Holborn Estate Grammar School. When the First World War broke out he did not join up at once. He may have been reluctant to become a soldier, but it is also possible that he was busily shaping his writing career. *Change* had been successful beyond the author's wildest imagination and seemed set to launch him into a career as a professional playwright. The play was performed in London, Aberystwyth and then went to New York and Chicago. The reviews were unanimously positive. *'The Stage' Yearbook 1914* singles it out as the best play by a promising young playwright of 1913 in the UK:

> Only one dramatist of special note has made his début this year. I refer to Mr. J. O. Francis, whose 'Change,' produced by the Incorporated Stage Society, came as an absolute surprise. It is a simple little Welsh drama, dealing with the old and new spirit in a small South Wales village, and has scenes of great emotional tension as well as much quiet humour. The denouement, always such a difficult matter to the inexperienced dramatist, has a suspicion of being forced, and is certainly not inevitable; but the play is otherwise one of the most notable achievements of the younger school. Mr. Francis is quite young, and his future will be watched with interest.[46]

Despite the slightly condescending tone of the piece, it mapped out a bright future for Francis. After the war had begun, the actor and producer Lyn Harding approached him with an invitation to write a one-act play about war. Harding was a professional Welsh stage actor who became a star of the silent film, for example featuring as Dr Moriarty in early Sherlock Holmes films. He strongly supported the national theatre movement in Wales and attended the performances of the first National Drama Week at the New Theatre in Cardiff in May 1914.[47] Francis's play *For France* (1915) was duly produced at the London Palladium and starred Lyn Harding himself. A second one-act play, *The Guns of Victory* (1916), followed fast. Both plays display entirely conventional attitudes towards war and avoid political commentary by focusing on the exploits of the common soldier. However, they might have been steps to something greater – Francis might have prefigured Emlyn Williams's professional trajectory by moving to the professional stage in London. The censor's synopsis of the farce *Antony Settles Down*,[48] which was first produced after the war in 1922, but which may well have been written years earlier, suggests a move away from Welsh themes at this time and towards popular West End comedies:

> This is a quietly amusing farce, which seems to have been produced last year by the Repertory Players. Sir Simon, a self-made rich man, insists that his son Antony shall settle down and orders him to propose to three named women within a fortnight. With the clever assistance of Margery, Sir Simon's secretary, who wants him for herself, Antony contrives that two of them reject him and that the third who accepts him shall afterwards throw him over. Then Antony and Margery have a mock engagement to please Sir Simon, but of course it ends in their really marrying. It is all innocent and not bad fun.[49]

The Repertory Company performed the play at the Shaftesbury Theatre on 17 December 1922 and it received at least two other performances in England.

If the farce was, indeed, written shortly after *The Guns of Victory*, Francis's call-up papers came at an inopportune moment and the war may have destroyed a blossoming professional writing career. He had enlisted as a Private with the Royal Welch Fusiliers and was given the Regimental Number 34690 in 1915 – just before conscription began. However, he did not begin active service until 1916, which meant he was entitled only to the British War Medal and the Victory Medal after the war ended. It is unclear which Battalion he joined but it is tempting to think that he and D. T. Davies served in the 15th Battalion (London Welsh), which also had the painter and poet David Jones in its ranks.[50] Disappointingly for the biographer, Francis left no journal or notes giving more details about his war experience, nor did it leave a mark on his work. However his writing career might have developed had the war not intervened, it is certain that he never quite recaptured the momentum of his early years nor did he manage the step from amateur to professional theatre. Instead, he devoted himself fully to writing plays about Wales designed for the amateur stage.

In 1919, Francis opted for the safe option of a career in the Civil Service and rejected an offer of the job of editor of *The Welsh Outlook* from the industrialist, philanthropist and Member of Parliament David Davies – an understandable decision as the post had only a nominal salary attached. He worked for the National Savings Committee until his retirement. He received an MBE in 1945, presumably for his work as Publicity Officer during the Second World War, but he chose not to attend the ceremony. He retired late, at the end of August 1954, when he was already over 70 years old. In a profile published in 1954, he was described an active retiree: 'he is as young as men half his age'.[51] He further developed his writing, continued to work for radio and travelled frequently to Wales, on one occasion addressing the students at the Royal Welsh College for Music and Drama in 1955.[52] He also discovered a new hobby – gliding – and enjoyed himself so much that he began a journal, the only private journal in his papers. It is full of the joy of learning something new at an advanced age. His entries are characterized by the gentle humour that pervades his work. Poignantly, he reflected on his age in his last entry, which was written on 21 September 1956:

> Most of the people I meet at the flying ground are youngish: there are a few grey heads in the club but I've seen only three or four. Most of the members are, I should say, not 35 + the majority under 30. Being myself now 74 years old I catch myself 'putting on an act' that gives me – perhaps – the air of a man of much younger years. I don't, of course, make known that, after 'a day at Dunstable' [where the London Gliding Club was and is located] with all the walking to + from the flying ground and all the pushing and pulling of machines I there take part in, I have my breakfast in bed next day + a lazy lie in, wrapped not only in bed clothes but in a sense of my own virtuous endeavours.[53]

J. O. Francis died on 1 October 1956 in the London house ('Bwthyn') he had shared with his sister Queenie. He received warm obituaries and personal notes of remembrance in the newspapers, including a note by Paul Rosé, evidently another member of the London Gliding Club, who wrote: 'To us fortunate enough to be on intimate terms with him, the world is a far poorer place for his passing. Especially shall we miss his erudite and searching queries on subjects as diverse as sport and politics among a host of others'.[54] G. C. Ager, a former pupil at the Holborn Estate Grammar School, noted that '[h]e was very much liked and admired both in the school and out. One always remembered that his encouraging voice from the touchline came from one who had played Rugby for the London Welsh'.[55]

Obituary notes like this allow a rare glimpse of Francis's personality, interests and temperament. Saunders Lewis offers another assessment of Francis in his review essay 'Dramâu J. O. Francis'. Lewis recalled that he had given a talk on nationalism in London and that Francis had been in the audience. After the talk they met, Francis apparently listening with courtesy and concentration as was his wont,[56] leading him to think that 'Mr. Francis appeared to agree with my ideas'. However, when they met again at lunch the next day, Francis told him: 'Oh, I have thought over our conversation yesterday night, and I do not agree with you. I see the other side now'.[57] Francis's fence-sitting must have been infuriating to Lewis, the political thinker, but to Lewis, the literary critic, it made perfect sense given the character of Francis's work. Gareth Parry, the central character in *Cross-Currents*, can also see the merits in opposing points of view, and this may be the closest we get to Francis's own position. His cautious, polite way of expressing himself did, however, mask a passionate and emotional nature, which emanates from the few surviving personal letters.

Considering that he worked full-time as a civil servant, he was astonishingly prolific as a writer, producing some seventeen published plays as well as unpublished manuscripts, essays, 'radio talks' and radio plays. At least seven of his plays were translated into Welsh by R. Silyn Roberts, John Hughes, Magdalen Morgan and Mary Hughes. Notes indicate that he wrote until his death in 1956, leaving the overall number of his plays at not far off thirty. Yet, despite his prolific output, it is unlikely that he would have been able to make a living from royalties alone. Most of Francis's early plays were published by Lord Howard de Walden's Educational Publishing Co. After it ran into financial difficulties, Samuel French bought the company Ltd in 1928, agreeing to keep the complete Welsh list. The Samuel French stock books survive and provide some insight into sales figures. Compared with print runs for drama today, French's were generous: in 1930 more than 800 copies of *The Poacher* were reprinted and the runs for *The Bakehouse* and *The Dark Little People* were approximately 1,000 each. Plays that were popular with amateur theatre companies sold well: *The Poacher* sold 743 copies between 1930 and 1935, and 834 copies between 1943 and 1948. The most popular play in terms of sales was probably *Birds of a Feather*: 1,000 copies were reprinted in 1946, a further 2,000 copies in 1948, 2,000 copies in 1954 and a final 1,000 copies in 1961. The play seems to have gone out of print in 1984, an impressive achievement for a comedy about rural Wales written fifty-seven years earlier. *The Bakehouse*, which had first been performed as *Mrs. Howells Intervenes* at an Old Students' Reunion in 1913 and which was particularly useful to Womens' Institute amateur companies as it required an all-female cast, was similarly successful. It was reprinted four times between 1933 and 1950 with print runs between 600 and 1,000. In 1950, 2,000 copies were reprinted, followed by 2,000 more in 1954 and a final 1,000 in 1961. Mostly, though, his plays sold steadily in smaller numbers.

The most unsuccessful of Francis's plays according to French's stock books was *Cross-Currents*, a political play that was difficult to stage and which dated quickly. It sold only fifty-six copies between 1927 and 1935. The sales figures for the Welsh translations of Francis's plays compare well with their English originals but they were not reprinted as often. *Y Potsier* sold 619 copies between 1927 and 1935 but was not reprinted. Francis may have been less popular in Welsh-speaking areas of Wales, or, more likely, there simply were more amateur dramatic companies in the populous anglophone areas of Wales. Overall, the figures show that the sales figures for Francis's plays compare favourably with those for other British and Irish playwrights. Serious plays did not sell well in general: the adaptation of John Galsworthy's *In Chancery*, for example, sold only 113 copies between 1927 and 1943. On the other hand, Sean O'Casey's dark comedy *Juno and the Paycock*, which must have appealed to amateur companies, sold over 1,100 copies.

The time when Francis's stature approached that of a national playwright was probably before 1935.[58] The premieres of his plays received extensive notices in the *Western Mail* and other newspapers. In 1924, the MP and millionaire philanthropist David Davies sponsored a £50 for a prize for 'a local amateur dramatic society giving the best performance in Welsh or English or the work of a Welsh playwright' and chose Francis's pageant *The Crowning of Peace* as the play to be performed.[59] In 1933, his historical romance, *Howell of Gwent*, was chosen as the first play of the newly formed Welsh National Theatre Company. As a well-known dramatist, he was often asked to be involved in social and cultural organizations, although he did not tend to hold posts for long. He adjudicated drama competitions, for example one held in Aberystwyth in August 1920 when his co-adjudicators included T. Gwynn Jones and D. C. Thomas (Clydach). He gave public lectures on drama, including 'Wales and the drama' (Charing Cross Chapel, London, 19 January 1923).[60] He was chair of the Honourable Society of Cymmrodorion for a time and he served on the board of the Welsh National Theatre Company during the 1930s. After 1935, his interest seems to have drifted towards other media, particularly the radio, and the plays published between 1935 and 1950 do not break new ground. However, he wrote two more important full-length plays in the 1950s, *The Devouring Fire* and *The Whirligig*, which, unfortunately, were neither produced nor published. Despite the quality of these two plays Francis's time had evidently passed by the 1950s.

Throughout his life Francis retained an essentially Edwardian vision of a culturally unified Wales, which allowed for an organic interrelationship between people, place and language. The main threats to this vision were the forces of capitalism and anglicization. His main literary vehicles were popular in nature – popular plays for the amateur stage, journalism and 'radio talks' – and he remained a populist throughout his life. Intellectual, high-culture Modernism passed him by as did the kind of experimental theatre pioneered in the 1920s by Bertolt Brecht and Erwin Piscator in Germany, Antonin Artaud in France and by Constantin Stanislavski in Russia. He also did not seem to engage with the new post-Second World War developments in the theatre that gave rise to the 'Angry Young Men' (and women) such as John Osborne and Shelagh Delaney, although he professed himself impressed by Arthur Miller and Tennessee Williams. His main innovation lay in helping to create the realistic 'play of Welsh life' that dominated amateur theatre for decades until that theatre was itself largely superseded by other forms of entertainment after the Second World War.

CULTURAL BACKGROUND, THEMES AND IDEAS

J. O. Francis's formative years, namely the 1890s and early decades of the twentieth century, fell into a period in which social, political, religious and cultural change seemed to be accelerating in Wales. Bell describes the fin-de-siècle period as characterized by 'the emergence of contrasting and, to some extent, conflicting features'[61] as the Edwardians – still propelled forward by a Victorian sense of purposeful progress – started to question the assumptions on which that progress was based. There is a curious way in which these late Victorian and early Edwardian years seem to be both forward-looking, keen on social reformation if not, indeed, outright revolution, and at the same time pessimistic, fearful of a degeneration of people and culture, and uncertain about what the future held. For example, the social consensus that characterized the industrial communities in south Wales from around 1850 onwards, which saw working-class leaders 'accept the direction of the middle class' in a spirit of compromise, 'was becoming increasingly fragile' by the 1890s as relations deteriorated.[62]

The workers were faced with the introduction of the Sliding Scale and the loss of Mabon's day, a worker's holiday, and became increasingly militant in turn. Furthermore, as can be seen from the popular periodical press of the time, Wales still considered itself as a nation with one culture, a culture that was expressed through the Welsh language. 'Welsh literature' meant literature in Welsh. And yet, the census of the year 1901 showed that, for the first time, more people spoke English in Wales than Welsh. During the years in which it was published (1914–33), the Liberal monthly periodical *The Welsh Outlook* became increasingly worried about the state of the national culture and began including translations of poetry from Welsh, reviews of books on learning Welsh and 'Whither the language?' jeremiads with increasing frequency, betraying a fear of the disintegration of a distinctive Welsh-language culture. Similarly, the exultation that accompanied the movement for the disestablishment of the Welsh Anglican Church, which culminated in the Welsh Church Act in 1914 but took effect only in 1922, went hand in hand with indications of a decline in religiosity – a decline mirrored in the state of the Nonconformist denominations after the revival of 1904/5. Janus-like, the opinion formers of the period seemed to look forward and backward at the same time. This spirit is encapsulated by Tom Jones, who, in the 'Foreword' to the first issue of *The Welsh Outlook*, conjured up the vision of a small nation, proud of its distinctive inheritance, but simultaneously attacked by the forces of global capitalism. It was a nation with a unity of vision, which was endangered by linguistic, cultural and religious diversity. Looking back to Wales's past, Jones asked how this nation could 'maintain any semblance of its ancient self',[63] invoking an ahistorical, 'timeless' sense of an ancient history that is juxtaposed with the threats of the immediate present. Jones, however, would not have subtitled his periodical 'magazine for national social progress' if he had not believed that Wales's salvation lay in a progressive attitude, so he ends by arguing that 'we can make some contribution, however small, to the common treasury of the nations, if we have the courage to be ourselves'.[64]

J. O. Francis responded to this state of affairs by writing two kinds of plays. One type puts the struggle to carve out an identity and a way of life between the Scylla of progressivism and the Charybdis of conservatism itself at the centre of the play (*Change, Cross-Currents, The Beaten Track, Howell of Gwent, The Devouring Fire*). Another type creates a reality and a place largely untouched by politics. Occasionally conflict threatens disruption, but virtuous behaviour tends to be rewarded and peace quickly restored (*The Poacher, The Bakehouse, Birds of a Feather, The Dark Little*

INTRODUCTION

People, etc.). Francis's creative non-fiction, in turn, revisits many of these themes.

The ethics of the 'play of Welsh life', which Francis helped to invent, is above all concerned with creating an 'authentic' reflection of real Welsh life. Up to 1912, Francis and the Ystwyth Players wrote, directed and performed plays that were part of mainstream English 'amdram' repertoire. But a radical change of purpose occurred in 1912:

> Up to the year 1912 we in our group made items about Wales only part of what we wrote and produced. But by Easter 1912 we'd had a prod that made us completely native-minded. The prod was given us by the players from the Abbey Theatre, Dublin. They were then at their best and came touring at times on our side of the water. We went to see them perform. . . .[65]

It is unclear to which performances Francis refers. The Irish National Theatre Society toured England many times and generally came to the Royal Court Theatre at least once a year, usually in early June to early July. The performances in Francis's recollections may have been those of June/July 1911, including J. M. Synge's *The Playboy of the Western World* (1907), Lady Gregory's *The Workhouse Ward* (1909), St John Ervine's *Mixed Marriage* (1911) and W. B. Yeats's *Deirdre of the Sorrows* (1909). He might also have got his dates mixed up and been thinking instead of the June/July performances in 1912, which included Synge's *Playboy of the Western World* and W. B. Yeats and Lady Gregory's *Cathleen ni Houlihan* (1902).[66] What is important is that he saw plays – both serious plays and comedies – which represented rural 'Irish life' with a degree of realism and authenticity that was refreshing and spurred him and his friends on to create a similar type of play that also 'implaced' characters in a recognizable contemporary Welsh landscape, whether urban or rural.

J. O. FRANCIS AND THE LAND ETHIC

Francis's urban and rural landscapes of Wales have moral attributes. His rural settings, in particular, evoke assumptions about the ethical meaning of place, which go back to the cultural nationalism of O. M. Edwards and the anthropological school around H. J. Fleure, whose views that he may have encountered for the first time when he returned to Aberystwyth after 1908. In the twentieth century there developed two related discourses of Welshness, namely that of the rural, Nonconformist, Welsh-speaking *gwerin* ('folk') and that of the mainly anglophone, urban, industrial Welsh working class,[67] each, according to Pyrs Gruffudd, with its own geographical imagination. From the Romantic period onwards, Welsh patriots saw the rural areas and the gwerin as the bastions of national strength and morality, and this happened at precisely the same time that industrialisation was at its peak.[68]

This geographical imagination located the locus of Welsh culture in the rural heartland of Welsh-speaking Wales. The landscape itself was imbued with moral virtue, which transferred itself to the community residing there and vice versa.[69] The philosopher J. R. Jones was later to call this ideological construct centred on the supposed unity of language, land and people *cydymdreiddiad tir ac iaith*, the interpenetration of land and language.[70]

The roots of this idealized relationship between place and people that so influenced Francis goes back to German Romanticism. Thinkers like Schelling reacted strongly against the purely mechanistic conception of nature put forward by the Enlightenment. They 'saw nature as a constantly creative coming-into-being, which developed organically according to her own internal laws, an independent whole, which was not created for human beings, but, rather, to which human beings belonged, as the same godly powers operated in them, too'.[71] Place and its community were conceptualized as dynamically interdependent: the spirit of landscape helped the spirit of human beings come into being and vice versa. The more human beings were estranged from the land, the less 'human' they were.

The American Transcendentalists adopted this way of thinking. Ralph Waldo Emerson wrote in 1836 that those who have an appreciation of nature have 'retained the spirit of infancy',[72] being still 'whole' and in touch with their human spirit and also with the divine spirit. Less mystically and more practically, Henry Thoreau's *Walden* (1854) argued for a life of simplicity, of living close to nature and only taking from it what is necessary. He set himself against striving for luxuries and property and, indeed, against the capitalist economic system as a whole because, in his view, capitalism turns free human beings into slaves of their possessions and acquisitive habits.[73]

This way of thinking about the relationship between place and people holistically, crucially informed Western thinking about human beings and place in the early twentieth century. Highly influential was the work of the American geographer Carl Sauer, who wrote *The Morphology of Landscape* in 1925. In Sauer's work 'landscapes are seen as both a product of cultures and as reproducing them over time'.[74] Linking his work with that of Vidal la Blanche in France, who ascribed 'personalities' to landscapes, Sauer spoke of 'cultural regions', thus describing landscape not in terms of its physical characteristics 'but from the way of life organised across those features' in a dynamic whole.[75]

At the same time, the ecologist Aldo Leopold developed the first land-based ethics. Writing from what was essentially a conservationist point of view, his 'land ethic' seems to follow directly from Thoreau. Leopold condemns the treatment of land as property and nothing else and thus as subjugated to human beings. Defining ethics as the way in which human beings put aside their differences to co-operate, he simply seeks to add the land to the equation: 'The land ethic simply enlarges the boundary of the community to include soils, waters, plants, and animals, or collectively: the land'.[76] In this way the idea of community includes human beings, nature, non-human animals and the land in one organic whole. This requires a significant change in the way human beings interact with the land: 'a land ethic changes the role of *Homo sapiens* from conqueror of the land-community to plain member and citizen of it. It implies respect for his fellow-members, and also respect for the community as such'.[77]

In Britain, too, 'an exclusively instrumentalist interpretation of nature, in which human progress was underpinned solely by materialist, utilitarian values' was considered inadequate. 'By contrast, an interpretation that placed greater emphasis on humankind as integral to, rather than in opposition to, the rest of the natural world' provided a new vocabulary by which to understand the human condition and, more specifically, notions of citizenship.[78] Taking his cue from Sauer's concept of 'cultural regions' and following his mentor Patrick Geddes, who, in turn, was indebted to Vidal la Blanche, the anthropologist H. J. Fleure mapped ethnic types in Wales between 1905 and 1916:

> Mapping demonstrated that Wales was characterized by marked regional differentiation (. . .), understood as the result of interplay between heredity and environment. . . . What Fleure called the simple folk of Wales represented types of humankind whose distinctions dated from a remote past. . . . This subterranean geography of Welshness was further strengthened by Fleure's humanist insistence that local types be studied in relation to natural regions rather than administrative units. In this way, Welshness was constructed as an organic unity between humans and environment.[79]

In this way, the erstwhile Romantic, somewhat mystical link between people, land and culture (including religion and language) was given a scientific backing. While Fleure rejected the notion of a 'Celtic race' promoted by the agricultural scientist George Stapledon, he, nevertheless, agreed with him that the relationship of people and landscape was moral, thus echoing Leopold and going significantly beyond Sauer's thinking.

'Fleure was convinced that the peasantry cherished universal and abiding values, and that peasant life retained a vital diversity.'[80] The early Plaid Cymru, through Fleure's student Iorwerth Peate, co-opted this idea and developed a 'back to the land' campaign, which was to encourage industrial workers to 'return' to rural Wales and, ultimately, make Wales autonomous by safeguarding, in the modern parlance, food security.

Furthermore, during the time Francis grew up, the Oxford historian, educationalist and journalist O. M. Edwards contributed more than any other to the (re)connection of Welsh people with the history, culture and language of their homeland, thus shaping the image of what that homeland consisted of. In numerous publications that were partly aimed at adults, such as the magazine *Cymru*, and partly aimed at children, such as the children's magazine *Cymru'r Plant*, Edwards created a Wales of villages and organic communities. If Francis should have glanced at *Cymru'r Plant* in his early teens, he would not have recognised it as *his* Wales, living as he did in the centre of Merthyr Tydfil. But he would have been inculcated in the image of the 'real' Wales that was fast becoming a national ideology, to be recreated over and over in the national periodical press, for example in *The Welsh Outlook*. The ideological locus of Welsh culture was located in rural, Welsh-speaking Wales, where the unity of language, religion, culture and land was still preserved and where no large-scale in-migration had diluted historical links between community and place.

The importance of place for conceptions of Welshness, but also more generally as a topic in public discussions in Wales, may be gleaned from articles in the periodical press. *The Welsh Outlook*, for instance, commissioned a series of articles on 'The personality of towns' in 1914, following la Blanche's notion that places have personalities. And, in common with many such movements in Europe at the time, the *Outlook* advocated a healthy, outdoor life as an antidote to modern-day stresses and illnesses, evident in such articles as R. F. Wright's 'Bathing' on the pleasures of sea-bathing. The magazine was also interested in open-air schools as part of the fight against tuberculosis, for instance printing a photograph showing 'Brynaerau open-air school' in the April edition of 1914 as well as Dr T. H. Morris's short piece 'The need for open air schools' in February 1919.[81] Partly this was a response to 'widespread concern over the decline of British society' as mirrored in the health of its citizens after the scale of undernourishment and illness of mainly working-class would-be recruits for the Second Boer War (1899–1902) had become a national scandal.[82] The campaign, however, also illustrates how a reconnection with nature was seen as supplying at least part of the answer to the threat of decline. Another example is the *Outlook*'s campaign for better housing for colliers. Both the January and the February issues of 1914 include photographs, which juxtapose cheap, badly built terraced houses in the south Wales valleys with colliers' houses elsewhere, such as Woodlands, Yorkshire, and Llandegai, near Bangor. These images show houses integrated in a landscape, which thus contributes to the physical as well as mental health of their occupants.[83] In this way public discourse replicated the holistic notion of the interrelatedness of people and place and argued that an ethically virtuous relationship with place broadly based on Leopold's concept of mutual respect led to a virtuous life, or at least the possibility of virtuous life, for communities.

Francis's work shows that he was aware of and engaged with these ideas, particularly the impact of the inescapable equation of 'real Wales' with 'rural Wales'. However much he was attracted by this vision, he could not escape his Merthyr background – and maybe did not want to. Perhaps the fact that he did not write from within Wales but from London allowed him to sit on yet another fence. Certainly, the fact that he grew up speaking English contributed to a writerly position that was slightly outside the assumed centre of this imagined community. While he never questioned the logic of *cydymdreiddiad*, his plays complicate notions of Welshness by showing that a virtuous attachment to place is possible in the largely anglicized, industrialized south (*The Poacher* and other plays featuring Dicky Bach Dwl) and that an unthinking adherence to outmoded forms of tradition does not serve to make for virtuous action (*Change*). It is the quality of one's attachment to tradition and to one's locality that makes for the possibility of a virtuous existence (*The Beaten Track*). Moreover, his series of plays that include the tinkers and poachers Dicky Bach Dwl and Twm Tinker develop Francis's theory of human nature as closely connected to the environment and the virtuous relationship communities should have with that environment. Here, it is not so much the distinction between Welshness and un-Welsh behaviour that is at issue, but that of a virtuous Welshness and a un-virtuous Welshness. Seemingly echoing Thoreau's observation that '[t]o be a philosopher is not merely to have subtle thoughts, nor even to found a school, but so to love wisdom as to live according to its dictates, a life of simplicity, independence, magnanimity, and trust',[84] Francis created characters who live a simple life according to the laws of nature and whose practical wisdom, Aristotle's *phronēsis*, rivals the more theoretical, contemplative wisdom of characters like the Bishop of Mid-Wales in *Birds of a Feather*.[85] In his late play *The Devouring Fire*, Francis showed what can happen if place is not respected – if a rapacious capitalism and human self-interest triumph. His is a deeply romantic and often nostalgic vision, but not an uncritical one.

Indeed, 'fence-sitting' may only be another epithet for the Aristotelian idea of balance: virtuous action is never excessive. One could argue that Aristotle's notion of striving for compromise, for a middle ground is linked with his emphasis on contemplation as the highest form of virtuous activity: excessive action is more likely to result from rash rather than considered action, although what exactly may be considered 'excessive' partly depends on one's point of view. I am not seeking to ascribe an Aristotelian outlook to Francis himself (although it is tempting), but his work clearly reveals an aversion to excess, an emphasis on considered action and on action that is true to a character's nature. Gareth Parry in *Cross-Currents* does not fully commit to the nationalist or to the socialist cause, which are both considered 'excessive' because they demand total commitment and a certain blindness to the merits of other causes. Instead, he chooses the career of the university professor, which allows him to think about a better future.

J. O. Francis, through his writing and his cultural activities, made a considerable contribution to the cultural life of Wales. A study discussing his work within its historical, cultural and political background, taking into account main intellectual currents of the early decades of the twentieth century and detailing the true importance of the world of amateur theatre for Welsh culture between 1914 and 1950, is overdue. The following chapters will attempt to redress the balance. Chapter 1 will set the scene by narrating the story of Welsh drama and theatre up to 1914. Chapter 2 will provide a detailed description of the world of amateur theatre between 1920 and 1940, the theatrical world for which Francis wrote his plays. Chapter 3 will engage with the possibilities of realist theatre and its ethical implications for the Welsh new drama written by Francis and his contemporaries. Chapter 4 will look closely at his comic plays, examining them with particular reference to the interrelationship between community and place, and their possible ethical impact on audiences. Chapter 5 will focus on his non-fiction writing and seek to establish the kind of ideological commitment to Welsh community espoused in his essays, 'radio talks' and journalism. This book will not deal with the entirety of Francis's work. Excluded are the plays not set in Wales and the (fictional) 'radio talks' as they mainly revisit the territory mapped out in the comic plays and in the essays.

Characteristic for Francis's work is a remarkable unity of vision that remains virtually unchanged in the forty years of his writing career.

Notions of the good are described in terms of virtuous attachment to place and kin. This attachment is expressed in a localized Welsh dialect of English. National identity is premised on the local identity of the *bro*, the locality in question. His notion of national identity is thus highly nuanced. The nature of his work for the amateur stage, for the popular periodical press and for radio itself indicates that Francis put his thought about a community-based ethics into practice. Before exploring Francis's ethics of place, the historical context for his work will be presented so that the extent of the theatrical revolution it engendered can be fully realized.

1

A Son of Wales Enters the Stage

In order to appreciate the central role of J. O. Francis in the revolution of amateur drama that swept over Wales in the early decades of the twentieth century, it is essential to discuss the context in which it came about. Wales in the nineteenth century had not been a hospitable place for the development of drama. The chapter will outline the cultural and moral reasons for this Nonconformist society's disapproval, while showing that a certain type of drama, namely amateur drama, was tolerated to an extent. It will also discuss the new realistic drama of Welsh life – which Francis helped develop – in terms of a paradigm shift in Welsh playwriting whose repercussions can still be felt today.

In January 1914 the first issue of a new Welsh monthly magazine appeared. *The Welsh Outlook* was launched with much fanfare as an entirely new magazine devoted to questions of 'national social progress'. It would blow away the cobwebs of tradition and it would fearlessly address the burning questions of the young twentieth century. Although the magazine did not initially plan to devote many pages to cultural topics, the first issue included a programmatic article on Welsh drama. It advanced an argument that was to be rehearsed over and over in the magazines and newspapers of the nation: first, the new Welsh drama, which had so recently appeared, could be and had to be understood in national terms. Secondly, it was a foundational movement because there was a blank page in the great book of Welsh cultural history where the chapter for 'Welsh drama' should have been.[1] Dramatists like J. O. Francis, D. T. Davies and R. G. Berry were celebrated as the figureheads of an entirely new movement, which would finally bring forth the Welsh Shakespeare – or at least the Welsh Ibsen or Shaw. Drama historians and critics like Cecil

Price,[2] O. Llew Owain[3] and Anwen Jones[4] have shown that there was considerable theatrical activity in various guises in Wales from the sixteenth century onwards. And yet, when Edwardian commentators looked, they saw nothing. Why was this so?

The most important reason was that many Edwardians looked back to their Victorian forebears and found a society that seemed to them to have been dominated by a dour Nonconformism, which displayed a 'puritan prejudice' against the theatre and supported the 'tyranny of tradition', which privileged other forms of art, primarily poetry and music, through institutions like the National Eisteddfod.[5] Earnestly progressive and increasingly secular, many Welsh commentators of the early twentieth century impatiently waved aside Victorian moral scruples and attempted to harness the new drama to their socio-political bandwagons. As a result they overlooked the actual history of the theatre in Wales in the process.

In the eighteenth century, the theatre had been fashionable. The Welsh gentry encouraged drama festivals, 'the well-to-do subscribed generously and permanent playhouses were erected at Aberystwyth, Brecon, Cardiff, Carmarthen, Merthyr, Swansea, Tenby, and Wrexham. They were visible proofs of the prestige of town and drama'.[6] By the mid-nineteenth century, however,

> [t]hose who valued their good name [in Wales] would have nothing to do with the theatre. As a consequence, the country actors sank once again to the level of outcasts. Even the performers in the permanent theatres lost the esteem which they had enjoyed thirty years earlier. They would have to learn to play not to the gentry but to the gallery. The working classes in the towns were growing rapidly and they would one day seek relief from their toil in 'pops' and 'penny gaffs,' in farce and melodrama.[7]

Wales was by no means unusual in this reaction to the professional theatre. The ascendancy of the middle classes – often Nonconformist in belief and proponents of a sometimes prudish sense of morality – meant that the Victorian age did not produce many good plays of lasting value in the UK as a whole.

Moreover, the theatrical system itself, which was based on the star system, did not encourage authors. The noted Irish author, dramatist and theatre critic St John Ervine described the impact of realist writers like Ibsen and Shaw in England in terms of a revolution, which swept aside the 'actor's theatre' of the nineteenth century and replaced it with the 'author's theatre'.[8] As long as actors like Edmund Kean, William C. Macready and Henry Irving reigned supreme, they chose theatrical vehicles that best supported their star status. Plays were generally written according to the template provided by Eugène Scribe's 'well-made play', which allowed often badly paid authors to produce plays at great speed. Tom Taylor wrote about 100 popular plays in his lifetime but neither the author nor his plays are remembered today.

What exacerbated the situation in Wales was the fact that large parts of the country were sparsely populated, that many people were poor and that communities could not sustain permanent theatres, especially as Nonconformist disapproval of the theatre decimated potential audiences further. In an essay about the amateur theatre tradition in Wales published in 1926, J. O. Francis wrote that 'until industrialism created the crowd and the mood of the crowd, Wales had not those aggregations of people out of which drama has almost always arisen'.[9] Strolling players and travelling companies visited smaller towns and villages, but 'kept away [after 1850] because they knew that in many of the smaller towns, people felt that the theatre was, at best, the home of frivolity and, at worst, of vice'.[10]

Except for the popular musical theatre, the professional theatre virtually ceased to exist in Wales. Theatrical activity itself, of course, did not end and was, in fact, often supported by individual chapels. As the century progressed, amateur dramatic performances increased. In the 1860s, performances of plays seem still to have been rare. A report on a penny reading in the Library and Reading Room of St George's Hall, Llandudno, in 1865 notes:

> We ought, perhaps, to add that Mr. Williams after thanking the audience for their attendance at this second reading, stated that another was about to be organized, in which the Rev. Mr. Parry had promised to interest himself, and at which if possible, a Welsh drama would be performed. This, from its great rarity, must prove a powerful attraction....[11]

By the 1870s, though, plays were incorporated in local eisteddfodau, an example being 'a Welsh drama founded on events connected with the battle of Crogen, near Shrewsbury', which was submitted to the Porthmadog eisteddfod by Thomas Jones (Taliesin o Eifion), a glazier from Llangollen and which won first prize (£15 15s. and a medal).[12] By the 1880s, amateur performances seem to have been commonplace. The long review of the play *Dy Nerth* by T. E. Roberts which was performed by the Bethesda Amateur Dramatic Company in Bethesda Market Hall fails to show any disapprobation of theatre on the part of the community and reveals that performances were frequent: 'This piece was strongly cast, most of the members of the company being no novices, having "trod the boards" before this occasion'.[13] The veritable explosion of amateur drama in the 1920s and 1930s is prefigured by these local performances.[14]

In his article 'The revival of the drama in Wales', the journalist Owen Morgan, who wrote under the pen name Morien, hinted at the reasons why those who felt responsible for the nation's morals disapproved of the theatre so strongly:

> Plays, under the name of cantatas, appeared from time to time in the Welsh language. "Ceiriog" composed a charming cantata, in which he described, in a most interesting fashion, the incidents relating to the birth of Edward of Caernarvon and his acceptance as Prince of Wales by the Welsh nobility, as the representatives of the nation. This was wedded to delightful music by the late 'Owen Alaw,' and has often been performed, but, mark, not in character. Prejudice against the dramatic art would have been instantly in arms had the Welsh nurse of Edward of Caernarvon appeared on the stage in a Welsh woollen gown and wearing on her head a cockleshell bonnet. That would have been too realistic to please certain people, and the thing consequently was never attempted.[15]

The moral sticking points were, first, the notion that acting (pretending to be someone else) was immoral and, secondly, the way reality was represented on stage. The more true to life the performance, the worse were the consequences considered to be because it was assumed that live performance, more so than any other art form except the realistic novel, had a direct ethical influence upon actors and audiences, which were liable to be utterly taken in, their reason silenced and their passions inflamed.

Abel J. Jones rehearsed the moral argument against the theatre in the pages of *The Welsh Outlook* in 1914. He suggested that live theatre could have potentially uncontrollable effects upon audiences, especially if their emotions were overstimulated. Thus even melodrama, despite its clear-cut distinction between evil villain and virtuous hero, was suspect because it was apt to present villainy in striking and even attractive colours before good was finally allowed to triumph. Worse, however, were realistic plays without a clear moral message; that is, precisely the kind of problem plays written and produced by Bernard Shaw and Harley Granville-Barker in the late nineteenth and early twentieth centuries: 'If our Welsh dramas are going to present totally conflicting moral ideals – what availeth it? The result can only be conflict and uncertainty in regard to moral issues'.[16] Moreover, the consequences of the lifestyle of professional actors, who, unlike amateurs, did not have a solid grounding in their communities, were dire as the professional actor was 'practically compelled to live to a great extent a life of insincerity, of make-believe, of emotional dissipation, of travelling in mixed company away from home'.[17]

Jones's arguments against the theatre have a long pedigree going back to Plato's *Republic*. Plato's rejection of fiction is based on his notion that a fictional reality is a false version of reality and can potentially lead audience astray. Reality is always to be preferred to fiction because the audience can never be sure if she is, in effect, lied to:

> In inviting audiences to take these copies [i.e. fictional characters and plot] for real, theatre not only leads them into a confusion about reality, with all the ethical problems that a failure to distinguish truth from fiction must entail; it also encourages them to prioritise emotion over reason. This is because the moment you start reciting poetry or performing a role in a play, you are, according to Plato, sucked into inhabiting the psychology, emotions and ethical position of the character you are representing. . . . By instilling such false ideas of potential transformation, theatre undermines your capacity to be happy in the life that you are actually living.[18]

Plato disapproved particularly of the dramatic arts because he considered that the emotional effect of performance destabilized the mental and emotional equilibrium of audiences, thus enfeebling their reason.[19] Christian doctrinal opposition to the theatre added that God had created human beings with one stable identity,

> which nature forbids us to alter or diversify. When we alter or diversify for pleasure, when the body is made the instrument for that pleasure, when the pleasure is available to anyone who can pay for it, as with the actor, the activity turns into a form of metaphysical prostitution for which no loathing can be too strong and no repudiation too absolute.[20]

The fear of the apparently corrupting power of theatrical performance – corrupting because it suggested to audiences and actors that identities might be mutable and unstable – was shared by a variety of social groups throughout the UK in the nineteenth century. Added to this was a dislike of spectacle. The middle classes in London were only enticed back to the theatre after the theatre had changed and 'the intimate interior scene began to displace flamboyant spectacle and broad acting, as well-upholstered stalls and circle displaced the pit and gallery'.[21] Semi-realistic plays like Tom Robertson's *Society* (1865) and *Caste* (1867) rung in the changes.

At the turn of the twentieth century reformers discovered the new drama and realized its potential for discussing ideas of social and cultural change in a medium with direct intellectual as well as emotional impact. This new drama emerged from the 'numerous "new" cultural formations' of the fin de siècle: 'the "new realism," the "new drama," the "new science," the "new woman," the "new journalism," and so on'.[22] The new drama was characterized by a new realism: not simply the apotheosis of nineteenth-century verisimilitude in settings, costumes and décor, but a newer, moral realism that prize[d] truthfulness even at the cost of pleasantness of subject or tidiness of dramatic construction. Included in this characteristic is a concomitant sense of earnestness, thoroughly Victorian and yet more discriminating, and more skeptical than Victorian middle-class morality ever was. Also present is a sense of the importance of adducing a definitive social environment for events and human actions. In short, this [was] a realism that view[ed] society simultaneously in social and moral aspects as a matrix of moving and shifting values, rather than as an essentially monolithic conglomeration of persons and classes with fixed attributes. This new realism thus appeare[d] as the product of an insistent, restless drive to see things for what they really are, name them accordingly, and set them into meaningful contexts.[23]

Married to this new realism was a sense of idealism, which regarded the theatre as able to educate and initiate social change. If necessary, audiences addicted to the pleasures of the theatre of spectacle had to be re-educated. Ervine wrote that the new 'author's theatre' was represented by

> Pinero and Henry Arthur Jones, Bernard Shaw and J. M. Barrie, John Galsworthy and Harley Granville-Barker [, who had] rushed through the stage-door of the English theatre and made the actors take the count. Henrik Ibsen, almost forgetting what a poet he had been, became a despondent sociologist, and the dramatic critics, led by William Archer, ceased to be interested in acting and wrote only of the play. . . . Ideas were everywhere, bewildering and even disgusting the general playgoer, who, going to the theatre to see villainy triumphant until the penultimate scene, found himself invited to listen to four acts on main drainage and the housing question or the relationship of sweated industries to prostitution.[24]

Proponents of the new drama of ideas like Bernard Shaw and Harley Granville-Barker shocked audiences with plays about social morality. Shaw's *Major Barbara* (1905), for instance, dealt with the moral issue of accepting charitable handouts from an arms manufacturer. Galsworthy's *The Eldest Son* (1912) is about the double standards in the sexual morality of the upper class when asked to deal with pregnancy out of wedlock among their servants and in their own ranks. Most shockingly of all, Granville-Barker's *Waste* (1907, not licensed until 1936), deals with Henry Trebell, a promising young politician, whose life is cut short when his mistress dies after a botched abortion. It was not that the issues themselves were new: George Eliot had presented the case of a young woman who was seduced by her landlord, became pregnant, delivered the child herself, panicked and left the child to die of exposure in *Adam Bede* (1859).

New was the emotional impact of seeing Amy O'Connell and Henry Trebell's suffering enacted on stage in an environment that had been mainly associated with (more or less refined) entertainment since the Restoration period.

It is easy to see why the new drama was so attractive to Welsh reformers who were keen to continue the work of Cymru Fydd, who established civic national institutions like the federal University of Wales (1893), the National Library of Wales (1916) and the National Museum of Wales (1912/27) and who vigorously campaigned for causes like the fight against tuberculosis, workers' education and garden villages. The Welsh drama movement was to be appropriate to Welsh circumstances, focusing on issues of national importance but carefully avoiding any depiction of Welsh people that could be construed as negative. Lloyd George encouraged the development of a national drama movement at the Bangor National Eisteddfod in 1902, and in 1911 Lord Howard de Walden began sponsoring a prize worth £100 for the best play in English or Welsh, which dealt with 'Welsh life'.[25] The supporters of the theatre responded to objections by making it part of their programme of social reform and thus giving it a role that was far from frivolous: it was to serve as the debating chamber of the nation. Modernity, which had shaken up social structures and ruptured stable identities, was to be discussed and solutions were to be proffered. Contrary to the theatre of spectacle, which sought to make the audience gasp, the new theatre was to make the audience think. Bernard Shaw, the high priest of the new drama, had written programmatically that the theatre was 'as important as the Church was in the Middle Ages. . . . A Theatre to me is a place "where two or three are gathered together"'.[26] It was to be a place where the community gathered and where the truth was told. J. O. Francis's friend, the dramatist and critic D. T. Davies, concurred: 'Wales is to realise itself with a greater completeness and a fuller consciousness as a nation through the medium of the drama than through any previous agency in our history'.[27]

The Edwardian middle-class dramatists and critics may have believed that they were rejecting the attitudes of their fathers and mothers wholesale but that was not quite true. Both shared a distaste for spectacle, which became identified with the 'low' entertainment of music hall and melodrama. What they wanted to see was realistic literary theatre, which was why, to come back to the question posed at the beginning of this chapter, they believed that there had been no theatre in Wales before the twentieth century. To them the medieval morality plays or the bawdy and irreverent Interludes by Twm o'r Nant were the beginnings of theatre, whose progress was then inhibited and whose promise remained unfulfilled because they did not reach the kind of socially aware realism that they themselves saw as the pinnacle of stagecraft. Both Victorians and Edwardians shared a belief in the power of the theatre to affect audiences, but the Edwardians believed that the new drama could be used in the service of progress. In 1920, the dramatist R. G. Berry was quoted as arguing that the 'paramount necessity of Welsh national literature was a pourtrayal [sic] of realism as opposed to the excessive romanticism that had prevailed in the past.'[28]

Indeed, critical voices were quick to point out that the Nonconformist 'puritans' themselves had not been averse to a little theatrical showmanship, arguing that the preaching style of evangelical ministers, the *hwyl*, had a great deal in common with the histrionic acting styles of the actors of old, and that the opposition to the theatre was, therefore, somewhat hypocritical. Emyr Wyn Jenkins notes in his short *Y Ddrama Gymraeg yn Abertawe a'r Cylch* (1985) that the way some preachers acted out their sermons in the pulpit rivalled the acting in the best London theatres.[29] And R. A. Griffith (Elphin), a playwright whose plays *Ifor Bach* and *Yr Archesgob Williams* won prizes at the National Eisteddfodau of 1899 and 1900 respectively, noted slightly tongue-in-cheek:

> I will not stop to discuss the sincerity or intelligence of our religious leaders in treating the drama as a menace to the morals of the people. But to be quite candid, I do not think their opposition is altogether disinterested. The preacher seems to regard the stage as a formidable rival to the pulpit. He is evidently afraid of losing his sway over the people. He thinks that full theatres would mean empty chapels. So he denounces the play as one of the allurements of Satan. ... A moment's reflection ought to convince the heads of the Non-conformist churches that even from the moral standpoint it would be infinitely better to encourage the growth of a healthy home-drama, springing naturally from the genius of our people, than to leave the youth of Wales at the mercy of the dubious things which occasionally cross the borders, the very sweepings of third-rate English theatres.[30]

The response to the Platonic objection to the theatre was thus to stress rationality and authenticity. A realist theatre was to be created which did not 'lie' to audiences because they would see their own lives reflected on stage. Griffith encouraged the growth of home-grown drama that did that job much better than English theatre and which could also be more easily controlled and channelled in the 'proper' directions.

In the absence of professional repertory theatre, the new Welsh drama movement was made up of the mostly small amateur drama companies dotted around Wales, which were often attached to chapels. The MP Llewelyn Williams, who seems to have assisted Howard de Walden and Owen Rhoscomyl in adjudicating the plays sent in for the Howard de Walden Prize competition in 1914, commented that

> [o]ne of the most extraordinary things is that I get letters nearly every week from rural villages all over Wales asking me to suggest what play the dramatic company that has been started in connection with the local chapel should take up. The Welsh drama, though it challenges the old rigid orthodoxy, is yet a movement associated with the chapels.[31]

By the time J. O. Francis and his friends began staging plays, Nonconformist objections to amateur theatre had largely abated. In 'The deacon and the dramatist', Francis noted wryly that

> [w]hen it came to the actual production of our plays, the deacons disappointed the dramatists in a most unexpected way. We had looked for a bitter struggle against their intolerant opposition. . . . Somewhat to our consternation, the deacons not only refused to oppose, but insisted on helping us. The only thing worse than martyrdom is to be cheated out of it.[32]

It seems that a generational shift had occurred: men like Elphin and Francis had felt oppressed by the 'chapel' and, therefore, they blamed the Welsh hostility towards the theatre in the nineteenth century exclusively on chapel culture. However, it was the desire for respectability of particularly the lower-middle and middle classes in Wales in the wake of the scandal of the Blue Books in Wales after 1850[33] that trumped any theologically motivated opposition to the theatre. Once the moral reaction to the scandal had ceased to define standards of behaviour, amateur theatre became more acceptable. Twentieth-century critics of the theatre like Abel J. Jones were so vociferous because they sensed that they were fighting a losing battle. By 1914, the effects of the last Methodist revival of 1904/5 had ebbed away and younger ministers were often influenced by the 'social gospel' of socialism and Marxism and increasingly saw their vocation as having a social mission. Part of that mission was to ensure that worthwhile entertainment was provided, so that their flocks did not stray into the more insalubrious environment of the new mass entertainment like cinema and sports.

Realism became the *sine qua non* of the 'new Welsh drama'. What mattered was authenticity of situations, settings and language. Theatre was to display 'Welsh life' in a simple and straightforward way. Francis and his contemporaries were particularly inspired by the example of the Irish National Theatre Company because, as theatre professionals like William Archer commented, the performances of their 'homespun' plays achieved a sense of freshness (at least at first) and authenticity seldom achieved by professionals.[34] It was the apparent artlessness of their acting and delivery that contrasted so sharply with earlier, more histrionic forms of acting. Their use of Irish dialect and the simple and yet precisely placed settings moved Francis to write similar plays about Wales. He also shared the Abbey Theatre's concern with representative national characters, in other words, not the upper-class and upper middle-class characters that still dominated the London stage and which were only slowly being displaced by the drama emanating from the provincial repertory theatres, such as that of the so-called 'Manchester school' of dramatists including Stanley Houghton, Githa Sowerby and Harold Chapin. The political motivation for realism was progressive: in the absence of formal markers of nationality, a national identity was to be inscribed by authentically representing typical situations of Welsh life on stage. Of course, it is the word 'typical' that makes this undertaking potentially problematic, as only a relatively narrow spectrum of situations was considered to be representative of Welsh life. This problem was exacerbated by the unwillingness of authors to write plays that might potentially upset the audience.

Indeed, this is where the Irish and the Welsh drama differ conspicuously. Irish playwrights seem to have been unafraid to offend the audience:

> By 1910, the idea of the Abbey Theatre play had grown up in the mind of the audience. Such a play took for its subjects the Irish peasant, and presented him really as a modern version of the apelike Paddy who once appeared in the pages of *Punch*. This was a character filthy, drunken, immoral, blasphemous and foul-mouthed, and most typified by Christy Mahon or, worse, his father.[35]

And because, in Yeats's words, the temptation in Ireland was to subordinate 'the artistic vision to the necessities of national propaganda',[36] audiences reacted accordingly. Neither Synge nor the playwrights that followed, notably Padraic Colum, shirked controversy.[37] A critic in the *Evening Telegraph* called Lennox Robinson's 1910 performance of *Harvest* 'repellent, repulsive, abhorrent. The last Act especially is a mere seething pot of vice, filth, meanness, dishonour, dishonesty, depravity and duplicity'.[38] The new Welsh drama was also carefully scrutinized by critics who, without sense of irony, wanted the drama to be realistic but also wanted it only to represent positive aspects of Welsh life. The controversies raging around Caradoc Evans's *Taffy* (1923/5) and Kitchener Davies's *Cwm Glo* (1934) showed that commentators still believed that the theatre could potentially corrupt audiences and give potentially hostile (English) critics of Wales ammunition because Welsh 'misbehaviour' was acted out in front of them. Perhaps because writers were conscious of this scrutiny, the majority of plays written in Wales at the time were unlikely to be controversial.

Also notable is the way in which Francis and his contemporaries preferred the socially engaged realism of Shaw, Galsworthy and Granville-Barker to the mysticism of Yeats. If plays that made use of mythology in the manner of Yeats and Lady Gregory's *Cathleen ni Houlihan* (1902) were written by this first generation of playwrights writing after 1910 they have not survived. Writers of the following generation like Vernon Watkins, who wrote the poetic verse drama *Ballad of the Mari Lwyd* (1941) with reference to the cultural tradition of the Mari Lwyd, did draw on mythology and traditional lore. But Francis's generation, for the most part, was wedded to authenticity and realism of representation and did not attempt plays like that.

Emyr Wyn Jenkins writes that, from around 1910 onwards, 'the drama pushed itself into nearly every region in Wales'.[39] The new Welsh drama was being discussed everywhere and, for a while at least, the column inches devoted to the drama seem to have outstripped actual drama writing. Hywel Teifi Edwards writes that by 1914 '*Y Beirniad*, *Tarian y Gweithiwr*, *Y Brython*, *Y Genedl Gymreig*, *Wales*, *Young Wales*, *Welsh Outlook*, *Western Mail*, *South Wales Daily News* and the *South Wales Daily Post* attested to the growing interest in the possibilities of the drama in Wales'.[40] The journal *Wales* profiled Welshmen who had achieved distinction in their field, in the series 'Sons of Wales'. In the January issue of 1914, J. O. Francis was featured. In the same issue, the editor writes:

> During recent months such plays as *Little Miss Llewellyn* and *The Joneses* have been staged on the London boards, but in spite of their Welsh nomenclature they marked at best but grafts on Welsh scenes and characters. It has been left to Mr. J. O. Francis . . . to give the English public the first real insight into Welsh life through the medium of the drama. . . . It is evident that new forces are being rapidly liberated, and in the near future the drama will be regarded as one of the most potent factors in the development of Welsh nationality.[41]

Critics had high hopes for the drama. Of course, what they were primarily thinking of when they wrote about 'the theatre' was literary repertory theatre – theatre that was of educational value, not merely entertaining. Throughout the period under discussion, critics call for writers to step forward and write the definitive 'play of Welsh life'. Francis's *Change* met this criterion and, as a consequence, its author was lionized. But the interwar period failed to produce another similar play, revealing something of the problems associated with inspiring the nation as a whole to take on the idealistic goals of the literary new drama movement. In

England, too, the literary repertory theatre, whether it was the Royal Court Theatre under the management of J. E. Vedrenne and Harley Granville-Barker (1904–7) or the Gaiety Theatre in Manchester, had problems attracting audiences in sufficient numbers and sooner or later ran into financial difficulties. Amateur companies, too, found that – regardless of their initial motivations – they had to bring in popular plays into their repertory as well as more serious plays.

The plays that won the Howard de Walden Prize exemplify this difficulty. The prize was meant to stimulate new writing, thus creating an atmosphere in which new talent could be fostered. However, not all plays that were awarded the prize were necessarily of high quality. The first winner of the prize was the American academic and writer Jeannette Marks, who won the prize for her one-act plays *The Merry Merry Cuckoo* and *Welsh Honeymoon* in 1911. Marks's Welsh plays, which also include *The Deacon's Hat*, *A Tress of Hair*, *Love Letters*, *Steppin' Westward* and *Look to the End*, have been neglected in Welsh scholarship – astonishingly so as they include familiar themes of the new drama, particularly Welsh cultural and religious traditions and rural ways of life. Marks's short plays are affecting and effective. Her attempts to render Welsh dialect in English are perhaps not always authentic, but it is an affectionate representation comparable to Emlyn Williams's *The Corn is Green* (1938). *The Deacon's Hat* reads like an early version of Francis's *The Poacher*: in this funny, farcical play Deacon Roberts not only manages to steal some eggs and butter from the village shop, but, delivering an impromptu hellfire sermon, gets away with his theft. In this play, the rendering of Welsh dialect is inauthentic but not offensive. *Welsh Honeymoon*, a comedy set in Beddgelert, is a comic reworking of the supernatural theme so prevalent in Edwardian plays: Catherine and Vavasour Jones have been quarrelling and have independently wished each other to the devil. As it is Allhallows Eve, both are in mortal terror that their wishes have been granted. At the end of the play it becomes obvious that nothing is going to happen and they are much relieved. The comedy is similar in feel to some of the Irish comedies written by Lady Gregory. It is also oddly folkloristic as the characters look as if they had just emerged from a St David's Day parade. For all their weaknesses Jeanette Marks's plays mark the beginning of the new drama of 'Welsh life'. Not overly intellectual – and perhaps therefore not interesting to the commentators who filled the columns in the magazines and newspapers – the plays portray everyday people in everyday situations in a realistic way. They fulfil E. E.'s criteria for the new Welsh drama, namely that it had to 'be the work of men and women who are possessed of a close knowledge of the country, and a clear insight into the ways of its people, and who can view the national aspirations and ideals, if not with approval, at any rate with sympathy'.[42] And yet, they remain slight plays that did not obviously help to create a school of drama writing.

When considering the entries for his prize, Howard de Walden had to balance the quality of the writing, its earnestness of purpose and the degree to which the writer attempted to capture 'Welsh life' in a new idiom and form. He awarded the prize to J. O. Francis's *Change* in 1913, but considered the play to be an imitation of English plays (see chapter 3). D. T. Davies shared the prize with R. G. Berry in 1914, the former for *Ble Ma Fa?*, *Y Dieithryn* and *Ephraim Harris* and the latter for *Ar y Groesffordd*. These plays were closer to de Walden's vision of a play of 'Welsh life', and, although his adjudication is not entirely favourable, he seems to have been satisfied with the quality of the plays:

> As the competition and award is more for the purpose of stimulating the authors, than making a definite decision as to merit, I think that it will be well if the prize is divided between these two authors. I am very glad the old tongue has it this year. . . .[43]

Saunders Lewis's review of the winning plays of 1920, Kate Roberts and Betty Eynon Davies's *Y Fam* and Betty Eynon Davies's *Four-Leaved Clover*, praised the playwrights for introducing a 'feminine note' to Welsh drama and carefully noted that it 'would be a poor compliment to these ladies to overpraise their gift. It is a slender talent, a slight but happy grace'. In particular, *The Four-Leaved Clover* is no less slight a play than those by Jeannette Marks and Lewis has nothing to say about the plot. He praises Davies for her dialogue, 'which has a native tang about it and yet avoids on the whole that too easy way of writing in English about Welsh life, which depends entirely on interjections and fluellenese',[44] the kind of 'fluellenese' of which Marks was guilty. Lewis was cautious and polite in his review. It clearly was difficult to provide criticism and not snuff out that small, delicate flame of Welsh drama. Despite Howard de Walden's generosity and good intentions, the plays that won the prize did not develop beyond a certain point. Indeed, the glut of plays written in the interwar period seem to have been of negligible quality and drove D. T. Davies, who assiduously adjudicated at drama competitions, to exclaim that

> it ought to be made a penal offence if anyone attempts to compose a drama without first producing satisfactory evidence that he or she has read carefully at least one play by Ibsen, Shaw, Galsworthy, and, possibly, Barnes, in addition to everything that Synge ever wrote.[45]

This list of playwrights is instructive and opens up an interpretive avenue into Francis's work. He was clearly deeply influenced by Ibsen, Shaw and Galsworthy when it came to his socially engaged 'new Welsh drama', which centred on the national and social issues of the day, such as *Change*. However, in those plays that set out to create a vision of the 'true' Wales, a Wales essentially untouched by social conflict where community and place-based virtues are indebted to an ancient Welsh culture that goes deeper than the version of the national culture created in the mid- to late nineteenth century such as *The Beaten Track*, he is much more obviously indebted to Synge and Lady Gregory. His plays also bear some resemblance to plays by regional English writers, such as Stanley Houghton and Harold Chapin, particularly in his use of language. And yet his drama presents a world that is entirely Welsh. He and his generation of playwrights initiated a tectonic shift in the form, style and subject matter of Welsh drama: instead of writing historical romances as the per-1900 playwrights like Beriah Gwynfe Evans had done, they concentrated on the contemporary lives of everyday people – something that became the prevalent mode of playwriting in Wales throughout the twentieth century.

Such has been the change wrought by a century that it has become difficult for us to imagine the remarkably popular and vibrant theatrical scene of Francis's day. Even though playwrights like Frank Vickery still write popular comedies in a similar style, the context in which the plays are performed has altered radically. Amateur theatre is not dead but the number of companies has shrunk considerably. In an attempt to bridge the chasm, the next chapter will aim to give a sense of what the south Walian amateur drama scene was like in its heyday during the interwar years of the last century and to evaluate the genuine impact of Francis's writing within that context.

2

J. O. Francis and Amateur Theatre in South Wales, 1920–40

Before the advent of a publicly funded literary theatre in the 1960s, Wales's 'repertory theatre' was located in the amateur sphere. In its heyday in the 1920s and 30s, we find a network of hundreds of amateur dramatic companies in Wales. They fulfilled an important social function: they shaped the culture of communities, provided an outlet for creative talent, knitted towns and villages together through amateur dramatic competitions and came to the aid of the needy by means of charitable activities. Francis's work crucially helped to sustain this culture. By using statistical analyses of performances and considering newspaper commentary, this chapter creates a picture of the otherwise largely vanished world of amateur theatre in south and south-west Wales between 1920 and 1940, the years of Francis's greatest impact.

THE ETHICS OF AMATEUR THEATRE

The demands made on the dramatist writing for amateur theatre are notably different from those made on the professional playwright. Francis knew exactly what worked for amateur drama companies and was clear-sighted enough to realize that this imposed limitations upon his art. The primer *Playwriting for Amateurs*, which is directed at the novice playwright who intends to write for amateur companies, highlights some of them: 'the amateur play production market is still what the movies call a family market. . . . If you write a play that contains adult situations and cursing or suggestive language, you will not get it published no matter how good it is';[1] do not 'pick a subject which is overly difficult to treat in dramatic form. . . . The fact is that many very good stories are very, very difficult to handle in the confines of the average theatre';[2] do not include too many scene changes requiring the curtain to come down because '[a]s soon as the curtain comes down . . . and nothing is going on before [her] eyes, the playgoer's minds starts to wander',[3] and so on. All this sounds petty but it is sound advice when it comes to the amateur market. Thus, the suggestion that Francis did not write more experimental plays because he had already plumbed the depths of his talent and was, by the mid-1920s, content to rest on his laurels can be refuted.[4] The late unpublished comedy *The Whirligig: A Comedy of Time's Revenges* is set in three different centuries and comments of theatre managers to whom he had sent the play in 1955, such as Margery Hawtrey at the Embassy Theatre and Stuart Watson at the Haymarket Theatre, suggest that they considered the play to be interesting but 'too complicated' for production at a repertory theatre.[5] Instead, Francis was sympathetic to the needs of amateurs and carefully wrote most of his plays to meet their requirements. One of the main reasons he gave for revising his comedy *Tares in the Wheat* in 1954 was that the required set changes had proved too much for amateur companies. The revised *The Sheep and the Goats* had 'one unchanged setting' and he considered it a 'useful comedy for Welsh amateur companies' although he did not think 'it would have appeal for general audiences that have no knowledge of Welsh life'.[6]

Amateur theatre is not generally expected to measure up to the standards of professional theatre. Anyone who has sat through a village amateur production, has hoped that the actors would remember their lines and has prayed that the delicate-looking scenery would stay upright for the duration of the performance knows this. However, evaluating professional and amateur theatre by the same measure is not quite fair. They have different goals and are equally valid. Professional theatre is meant to develop the art of dramatic writing and performance, and it may well offend audience tastes in the process. The function of amateur theatre may not be to challenge but to affirm values, to create a sense of togetherness, of a shared experience. Depending on context, this may be subversive, for example in some of the agitprop theatre of the late 1960s and 70s, which took performance art to the street to get away from a professional theatre that was experienced as staid and conservative, but it need not be.[7] To apply the same interpretive criteria to all forms of theatre, whether it is the theatre of London's West End, amateur drama in Wales, the performances at the Edinburgh Fringe Festival, theatre in education or youth theatre, seems unhelpful.[8]

Community drama has an ethics of its own. The American playwright Percy MacKaye described it in terms of 'neighborliness' in the early twentieth century.[9] He believed that community theatre could increase co-operation in communities, thinking of it as folk art, which emerges from a community and which enacts and thereby strengthens community cohesion.[10] Yet, this was no mere localism. On the contrary, the spirit of collaboration, once it had suffused a community, could be extended to national and then to international co-operation:

> The difference is between *mine* and ours. *My* country, *my* town, *my* flag, *my* culture – this attitude incarnates the very spirit of egoistic unneighborliness; but *our* country, *our* town, *our* flag, *our* culture – this spirit implies that sharing of one's own which recognizes the world as one community of neighbors.[11]

Community theatre had a social role as well as an artistic role and was thus the opposite of commercial theatre, which was about spectacle and consumption, and which atomized audiences into individual consumers.[12] But this social role was not meant to lead to a neglect of aesthetics: '[w]e must be no more tolerant of bad art than of bad civics [sic], for bad art is bad sociology and bad education'.[13]

On this definition, community drama has the goal of strengthening community ties by means of aesthetically pleasing performances. The best way of achieving it is to write plays without complicated structure and containing characters allowing for different levels of acting ability. An excellent example in recent years was Laurence Allan's play *Angels Don't Need Wings* (2002) written for Odyssey Theatre, an offshoot of Hijinx Theatre, which is an inclusive theatre company working with actors with learning disabilities.[14] It was performed by professional actors and actors with learning disabilities, and the latter were by no means relegated to supporting roles only. Even though the ranges of ability do not vary as much in most amateur drama companies as in this case, directors routinely deal with casts with a range of acting skills. Their interests are best served by characters like Dicky Bach Dwl, which can be interpreted at various levels. A novice can make the audience laugh by exaggerated acting and by virtue of the dialogue alone. An experienced actor is able to bring out the wisdom behind the half-witted facade and allow the age-old jester figure to emerge – a figure that holds up the mirror to the audience and makes them think as well as laugh.

AMATEUR DRAMA IN WALES

The rapid growth of the Welsh amateur theatre movement of the 1920s and the Little Theatre movement of the 1930s took place within a groundswell of amateur dramatic activity in the UK as a whole. Sydney Box's 'The Drama Festival',[15] Lawrence du Garde Peach's 'Village Drama'[16] and the great number of subscribers to the British Drama League, Village Drama Society and Welsh Drama League[17] show the immense popularity of amateur theatre across the UK. To an extent, the amateur movement developed side by side with the professional repertory movement, which sought to establish funded theatres in towns and cities outside London. Annie Horniman purchased the Gaiety Theatre in Manchester in 1907, the Birmingham Rep opened in 1913 and so did many other theatres outside London. Finance was a common problem. In 1917 the Gaiety Theatre was forced to close because of financial difficulties. Issues of finance also delayed the opening of J. B. Fagan's Oxford Playhouse until 1923.[18] It is therefore easy to see why the amateur movement, which operated largely without financial constraints, occupied the place of the professional repertory theatre in Wales. The attempts by some commercial theatres to provide repertory drama, such as the Playhouse in Cardiff in 1932, were invariably short-lived.

Amateur companies wanted to be free from the necessity to put profit above art. Little Theatres like the one in Swansea put on 'plays which the local commercial theatre could not afford to stage: Chekov [sic], Ibsen, Shakespeare, for example'.[19] Once Swansea Little Theatre was set up, 'plays by Capek, Barrie, Galsworthy, Malleson, Housman and Shaw followed in quick succession. Lectures, drama schools, playwriting contests and the presentation of original works helped to make a varied and interesting programme'.[20] Programmes were made up of 'classics' on the one hand and lighter plays on the other hand, but companies avoided overly spectacular fare. Reasons for setting up companies were varied. One motivation was educational: actors and audiences were to be enabled to experience good dramatic writing and to draw moral lessons for their own lives.[21] A further motivation was social: chapel-based amateur dramatic societies in particular were at least partly founded to keep the local youth out of trouble and away from less worthy entertainments such as the 'fleapit' or the boxing ring. Companies varied in size and their theatres, if they had access to permanent performance spaces, were often small. The Aberdare Little Theatre was a refurbished old engine house gifted to the company by Sir D. R. Llewellyn in 1930.[22] The Swansea

Stage Society founded the Swansea Little Theatre in 1929 and took over an Old Church Hall in Southend, Mumbles.[23] Neath Little Theatre did not have its own building but used Gwyn Hall until it was able to move into its own, purpose-built theatre in 1955.[24]

The great majority of amateur theatre companies in the 1920s seem to have been linked to chapel and church groups, which partly explains the number of Welsh-language productions in areas with anglophone majorities. As the movement grew others emerged: societies that were linked to Workingmen's Institutes like the Williamstown Social Centre Players or the East Moor Players in Splott, Cardiff. Unemployed clubs like the Tonypandy Unemployed Club ran drama groups to give their members a meaningful hobby. Women's Institutes also had drama societies and so did large employers such as Seccombe's Dramatic Society, which was made up of employees of a Cardiff draper's shop, or the Cardiff Municipal Officers' Dramatic Society. Schools, colleges and adult education associations frequently supported drama groups, such as the Newport High School Old Girls' Dramatic Society or the Abergavenny W.E.A. Dramatic Society. Other companies were directed by local actor/author managers, such as the GP Naunton Davies's drama company in Llantrisant and the teacher Ken Etheridge's Cymric Players in Ammanford.

The following analysis of amateur theatre activity in Wales between 1920 and 1940 is based on theatre notices for drama competitions, drama festivals (including the National Eisteddfod) and for one-off productions that appeared in the *Western Mail*, Wales's largest newspaper. Also analyzed are 109 opinion pieces and reviews in the *Western Mail*. Table 1 shows the number of articles.

The following section must, however, be introduced with a caveat: the sample is subject to possible errors and should not be taken to be representative of all amateur theatre activity in Wales of the period. First, the systematic sample used for this chapter covers the years 1920, 1924, 1928, 1932 and 1936 and another sampling strategy might have yielded slightly different results. Secondly, the *Western Mail* is not an entirely reliable resource: its coverage of dramatic events in south and south-west Wales

Table 1: Number of performances and opinion pieces in the sample

Year	1920	1924	1928	1932	1936
Number of performances	113	40	107	149	245
Number of opinion pieces	33	21	24	12	19

was outstanding but patchy at best in the rest of the nation. Moreover, the newspaper had no special remit to cover cultural events. Important news items like the death of George V in January 1936 and the abdication crisis in December 1936 are certain to have displaced reports of performances. Also, the *Western Mail* had no regular drama critics and sometimes relied on amateur correspondents. Information was sometimes incomplete. Thirdly, we do not know how many performances took place at semi-private or private functions. It follows that a record based on newspaper cuttings of one newspaper must necessarily remain partial.

Despite these caveats, the *Western Mail* is an astonishingly good source for researching amateur theatre activity between the wars. A large number of performances and competitive festivals were covered, often in great detail. Moreover, important playwrights like D. T. Davies, J. Eddie Parry, James Kitchener Davies and J. O. Francis, and dedicated reviewers like D. R. Davies, contributed to the newspaper. While the record is incomplete, it is nevertheless possible to gain an insight into the world of amateur theatre and the available material allows a certain depth of analysis. It is possible to discern trends and developments that go beyond a merely impressionistic reading of the source material.

To be able to assess J. O. Francis's contribution, a comparison of authors whose plays were performed by amateur companies is beneficial (table 2). The table does not include authors whose full names could not be traced.

In 1920, most plays performed were written by Welsh authors in the Welsh language. Authors include R. G. Berry, D. T. Davies, W. J. Gruffydd and D. J. Davies (*Maesymeillion*, c.1918). Francis was one of a few Welsh authors writing in English. Companies performed contemporary plays

Table 2: Performances and language

Plays	1920	1924	1928	1932	1936
Overall number of authors	25	15	59	62	129
Welsh authors/Welsh language	19	7	14	10	12
Welsh authors/English language	4	5	1	5	12
Non-Welsh authors/English language	2	3	31	39	90
Authors translated into English	0	0	1	2	9
Authors translated into Welsh	0	0	2	2	5
Other	0	0	0	4	1

about Welsh community life, such as D. T. Davies's *Y Pwyllgor* (1920), Ernest George Cove's *Those Who Wait* (1920) or Ada Edwards's *Serch Hudol* (1913). D. T. Davies's critical review of *Serch Hudol* shows how authors of the period tried, and sometimes failed, to create the new 'play of Welsh life'. Davies felt that the play was made up of the elements of

> stock melodrama. ... Over this is superimposed, but not constructively related, a bright and realistic picture of a Welsh countryside, criticisms of chapel life, an occasional temperance lecture, jokes about the chapel organ, the social snobbery of a not too prosperous farmer who regards the village carpenter as socially beneath him ... As it was, it remained as a pretty, but disconnected patchwork which, when removed, revealed the horrible skeleton underneath.[25]

Occasionally audiences saw non-Welsh plays, such as Henry Arthur Jones's *Saints and Sinners* (1884), which was performed by the League of Young Actors (Abercwmboi) at the Workmen's Institute in Cwmaman, or Richard Brinsley Sheridan's *The Rivals* (1775), performed by the Dramatic Society at the University College of South Wales and Monmouthshire in Cardiff. But, overall, in 1920 the amateur drama movement reflected the goals of the national drama movement: it performed and thereby promoted new Welsh writing and the new 'play of Welsh life'. In April 1920, Davies noted with some pride that '[m]ost of our plays are so utterly indigenous; they are folk plays in such a literal sense that no other conclusion is possible'.[26]

The content analysis[27] of long reviews and opinion pieces in the *Western Mail* reveals a general mood of optimism. Upbeat articles promised a bright future for the drama in Wales. At the same time, commentators still felt a need to make a case for the value of the theatre. They stressed the benefits of having a lively amateur drama culture, which was not based on gain and which provided an outlet for the 'naturally histrionic' qualities of the Welsh. At other times, the educational nature of the plays was emphasized, which, in the eyes of commentators, made them more worthwhile than mass entertainment like the cinema. The pieces reflect MacKaye's arguments for community theatre, although they frame the discussion in national terms. Thus, Davies remarked:

> The drama presents, or should present, a group of human actions and inter-actions wherein the individual is seen in his social setting, influencing and being influenced by his fellow-men for good or evil. Thus are the social instincts nourished and developed and national realisation rendered possible.[28]

Despite the celebratory tone, commentators were not uncritical. Familiar with adjudications in eisteddfodau, critics could be severe. Apart from criticizing acting ability, they called for more new plays, for plays of better craftsmanship and for higher production standards. Part of the problem seemed to be the lack of experience of dramatists, who often used stock characters, melodramatic situations and relied on dialogue to disguise a lack of action. Moreover, while Welsh authors accepted realism as the new norm, they hesitated to write realistically about life in all its facets. They did not like to write about things they considered unethical or insalubrious, perhaps because so many companies were attached to chapels or because they considered their audiences to be strait-laced and unused to more 'daring' subject material.[29] Anne Miller noted in *The Independent Theatre in Europe* that this silence on certain subjects amounted to an 'indirect censorship' in Wales, particularly when it came to portraying sexual relationships.[30] J. O. Francis, for instance, dealt with emotions in an entirely innocent way that was unlikely to offend. By contrast, James Kitchener Davies's *Cwm Glo* (1934) caused controversy because of its perceived unhealthy obsession with sex, something the author denied.[31] D. T. Davies argued that this seeming lack of sophistication on the part of audiences was due to a tendency in Wales 'to subordinate artistic considerations to ethical ends' blaming 'our lack of a broad aesthetic training' and the 'almost exclusively ethical exercises of a kind that have occupied the Welsh mind for the last two centuries'.[32] This kind of audience reaction is precisely why the American public intellectual Richard Posner argued that the right evaluative norms for literature should be aesthetic, not ethical.[33] While Davies's conflation of the moral and the ethical is not helpful, he was undoubtedly right that audiences responded to cues in moral terms because they were socially conditioned to do so. Moreover, the public nature of performance led to an additional complication. For some critics, Welsh characters on stage had to be indisputably 'good' because acting out 'bad' behaviour reflected badly on the nation as a whole, particularly when performances took place in London in front of a potentially unsympathetic audience. The reaction of Welsh reviewers to Caradoc Evans's mildly offensive farce *Taffy* in 1923 and 1925[34] was one of disbelief and indignation, partly because Evans was already infamous as the author of *My People* (1915), and partly because of the immediate emotional impact of the medium of live theatre. It is difficult to say, however, whether critics' automatic recourse to moral categories when evaluating Welsh realistic plays was responsible for its relative lack of development in the 1920s and 1930s.

By the end of the 1920s the balance shifted towards non-Welsh authors. Now Welsh authors writing in Welsh and in English made up less than 40 per cent of the total. Interestingly, the decrease in popularity of Welsh-language authors did not entail an increased take-up of Welsh authors writing in English. Instead, amateur companies turned to canonical playwrights (Shakespeare, Bernard Shaw or John Galsworthy) and popular repertory and West End dramatists (St John Ervine, A. A. Milne, Clemence Dane or Sutton Vane). Also on the increase were translations into Welsh of playwrights like Frank Stayton and J. M. Barrie.

The decrease in popularity of native authors meant either that the amateur drama movement had disengaged from the goals of the Welsh national drama movement or, which is more likely, the many and varied companies did not see themselves as one movement with one goal. The national drama movement had been organized and discursively constructed by a few influential commentators and patrons like Howard de Walden, Owen Rhoscomyl, D. T. Davies and J. Eddie Parry. The amateur dramatic companies that now proliferated in the 1920s emerged because amateur drama had become a popular pastime and not necessarily out of a commitment to the development of national drama. Some companies were interested in supporting particular playwrights, such as the Gwaelod-y-garth Dramatic Society, which performed R. G. Berry's work (Berry was minister of a chapel in Gwaelod-y-garth), or Swansea Little Theatre, which had an interest in performing Jack Jones's work in the 1930s. But generally, drama companies compiled programmes to meet their needs – to develop artistically, attract audiences and be successful at competitions – and not necessarily to support a national drama movement.

In the 1930s the trend towards English-language plays of non-Welsh provenance continued. The slight increase in the number of plays written by Welsh authors writing in English in 1936 was not a sign of a return to the goals of the national drama movement: only a few new writers like Diana Morgan, Florence Howell and Ken Etheridge appeared, while older plays by established writers like Francis were performed as well. Writers like Caradoc Evans, Rhys Davies and Emlyn Williams did not write to develop Welsh drama. Plays by Emlyn Williams such as *Night Must Fall* (1935) and *The Late Christopher Bean* (1933), an adaptation of René Fauchois's *Prenez Garde à la Peinture* (1932), included Welsh characters – in the case of *Night Must Fall* probably because Emlyn Williams had written the evil character Dan for himself. However, there is nothing intrinsically Welsh about the plays.

The number of international plays increased, perhaps out of an enjoyment of the exotic: 1936 saw repeat performances of Karel and Josef Čapek's *The Insect Play* (1921, translated into English in 1922), S. I.

Hsiung's *Lady Precious Stream* (1934), Serafín and Joaquín Álvarez Quintero's *A Hundred Years Old* (translated 1929) as well as Leonid Andreyev's *He Who Gets Slapped* (1914, translated into English in 1922). The Insect Play, *Ze zivota hmyzu* in Czech, was translated relatively quickly into English by Paul Selver and adapted for the English stage by Nigel Playfair and Clifford Bax. It received its first performance in the UK in the Regent Theatre in London on 5 May 1923. It was written almost at the same time as the more famous *R.U.R. (Rossum's Universal Robots)*, which introduced the word 'robot' to the English language. *The Insect Play* is a whimsical, imaginative allegory with an anti-capitalist and anti-militaristic message, which presents three groups of insects, the flirty, airheaded butterflies, the down-to-earth, grasping, petty beetles and the soldierly ants, as allegorical representations of different societies – aristocratic, capitalist and socialist. It is a demanding choice for an amateur company because it demands a large cast of actors who have to portray the different insects convincingly. Plays of this kind could not be further removed from the ethos of the 'play of Welsh life'.

Particularly when compared with these plays, the limits of the narrowly realistic 'play of Welsh life' become obvious: it was virtually impossible for Welsh plays to be about a place other than Wales or people who were not Welsh. This was particularly true for Welsh-language drama. James Kitchener Davies believed that the number of possible subjects a writer could tackle had dwindled:

> In spite of our unimaginative critics who howl at the persistent appearance of [rural and familiar] characters in our folk-drama the artist must realise that these alone remain to him of Welsh social life, and that all he can hope to do is to breathe upon their dry bones the breath of his genius that they may live again in his work . . . The Welsh life to be found in the cities (. . .) and in the industrial towns is but a diluted form of rural social life. The artist must perforce use the chapel and the kitchen as his settings and the minister and deacon as his personæ.[35]

That a Welsh playwright could have written on any subject under the sun and located anywhere on earth seems not to have occurred to writers (and audiences). Given the competition from the large number of English and American plays now regularly performed in Wales, commentators throughout the 1930s stressed the need to write better plays, be more ambitious in theme and form, and leave the cottage kitchen setting behind. Already in 1924 R. G. Berry was of the opinion that

> we must get rid of the very prevalent idea that the Welsh drama must be what is termed 'national,' that it must 'deal with Welsh life,' and so forth. This

encourages a narrow and destructive provincialism. . . . The Welsh drama – the novel likewise – should be of such quality as could appeal to humanity everywhere. But it should, beyond everything, possess the Welsh tone; it should bear the distinct and characteristic Welsh stamp.[36]

This sentiment was echoed by M. Morris-Roberts in 1936, who explained the dearth of good Welsh plays by arguing that

[t]he reason for this lack of inspiring drama is that so many playwrights set about their plays by thinking, 'I must portray Welsh character and Welsh life.' Their plays are far too racially conscious and have become parochial and unplayable except before a Welsh audience. . . . If only our playwrights would write about people and not exclusively or predominantly Welsh people![37]

Taking a postcolonial perspective, one is inclined to question why Welsh companies saw no problem in staging English and American plays whose settings and plots were equally 'implaced' in a particular environment. Frank Stayton's *The Joan Danvers* (1926) is located in the upper-middle class environment of Clifton in Bristol and deals with a family of ship-owners. J. B. Priestley's comedy *Laburnum Grove* (1933) is set in the middle-class home of a North London suburb. In their 1936 season, Blackwood Amateur Dramatic Society performed the quintessentially English upper-class comedy *Leave it to Psmith* by Ian Hay and P. G. Wodehouse, apparently without sense of incongruity. The fact that a great number of non-Welsh plays deluged Wales and only a tiny trickle flowed the other way – J. O. Francis's *The Poacher* among them – must be ascribed to the inescapable centrifugal force of the London-based theatre and publishing industry.

This point is connected with the fact that Irish plays – contrary to plays from England – were not much performed by Welsh amateurs. On the political stage, pan-Celtic congresses were held, which stressed the family relationship between the Celtic nations. However, this feeling evidently did not translate into a wider acceptance of each others' drama. The sample contains evidence of only two performances of Synge's *Riders to the Sea* (1904), performed by Neath Little Theatre Company and Blackwood Amateur Dramatic Society in 1936, and one performance of Synge's *Shadow of the Glen* (1903), staged by Brecon Little Theatre Company also in 1936. Playwrights may have incorporated Synge-inspired themes into their work, but his plays themselves were not often performed.

Who were the most popular authors in the interwar years in Wales? Table 3 provides a list of authors ranked by popularity. Counted are authors who received multiple performances by more than one drama company, thus excluding Naunton Davies, for instance, whose work was only

Table 3: Relative popularity of authors, 1920–36

1920	1924	1928	1932	1936
R. G. Berry (W)	D. T. Davies (W)	J. O. Francis (E)	J. Ellis Williams (W)	Bernard Shaw (E)
J. O. Francis (E)	Richard Hughes (E)	St John Ervine (E)	William Shakespeare (E)	J. O. Francis (E)
W. J. Gruffydd (W)	Clemence Dane (E)	Clemence Dane (E)	Bernard Shaw (E)	J. B. Priestley (E)
D. T. Davies (W)	R. G. Berry (W)	Frank Stayton (E & W)	A. A. Milne (E)	Emlyn Williams (E)
R. Rhys Evans (W)		W. J. Gruffydd (W)	Henrik Ibsen (E & W)	S. I. Hsiung (tr. to E)
W. Bryn Davies (W)		Bernard Shaw (E)	R. G. Berry (W)	Ian Hay and P. G. Wodehouse (E)
John Phillips (W)		Idwal Jones (W)	Brinley Jones (W)	J. M. Barrie (E)
Ada Edwards (W)		R. G. Berry (W)	John Galsworthy (E)	Serafin and Joaquín Álvarez Quintero (tr. into E)
Rev. J. Tywi Jones (W)		Brinley Jones (W)	Trevor Morgan and A. G. Prys-Jones (E)	Philip Johnson (E)
		J. M. Barrie (E)	Eden Philpotts (E)	Gertrude Jennings (E)
		Allene Tupper Wilkes (E)	D. T. Davies (W)	Rhys Davies (tr. to W)
		Horace Hodges and T. Wigney Percyval (E.)	Philip Johnson (E)	A. A. Milne (E)
		John Galsworthy (E)	Miles Malleson (E) Stanley Houghton (tr. into W)	Clemence Dane (E) D. T. Davies (W)

Table 4: Plays most often performed

1920	1928	1932	1936
R. G. Berry, *Ar y Groesffordd*	Clemence Dane, *The Way Things Happen*	J. Ellis Williams, *Y Pwyllgoddyn*	St John Evine, *John Ferguson*
J. O. Francis, *Change*	Frank Stayton, *The Joan Danvers*	A. A. Milne, *Mr Pim Passes By*	Sampson Raphaelson, *Accent on Youth*
W. J. Gruffydd, *Beddau'r Proffwydi*	St John Ervine, *The Ship*	Roland Pertwee and Harold Dearden, *Interference*	S. I. Hsiung, *Lady Precious Stream* (tr. from Chinese)
W. Bryn Davies, *Colli ac Ennill*	J. O. Francis, *Change*	Bernard Shaw, *Candida*	James Bridie, *Tobias and the Angel*
D. Gwenydd Morgan, *Cyfrinach y Fasged Frwyn*	Henry Hubert Davies, *The Mollusc*	William Shakespeare, *Twelfth Night*	Ian Hay and P. G. Wodehouse, *Leave it to PSmith*
Wil Ifan, *Onesimus*	Gayer Mackay and Robert Ord, *Paddy the Next Best Thing*	William Shakespeare, *Othello*	Norman MacOwen, *The New Tenant*
R. Rhys Evans, *Aeres Maesfelin*	Sutton Vane, *Outward Bound*	Howard Irving Young, *Hawk Island*	J. M. Barrie, *Dear Brutus*
R. G. Berry, *Noson o Farrug*	Bernard Shaw, *Man and Superman*	Stanley Houghton, *Yr Ymadawedig* (tr. into W of *The Dear Departed*)	W. Somerset Maugham, *For Services Rendered*
Naunton Davies, *A Monologue for One*	Horace Hodges and T. Wigney Percyval, *Grumpy*	Percy Robinson, *To What Red Hell*	William Shakespeare, *King Lear*
Naunton Davies, *The Epidemic*	J. O. Francis, *Y Bobl Fach Ddu* (tr. into W of *The Dark Little People*)	W. Somerset Maugham, *The Sacred Flame*	Serafin and Joaquín Álvarez Quintero, *A Hundred Years Old* (tr. from the Spanish)

Naunton Davies, *The Village Wizard*

D. J. Davies, *Maesymeillion*

John Phillips, *Wiliam*

R. G. Berry, *Dwywaith yn Blentyn*

John Galsworthy, *The Skin Game*

Israel Zangwill, *The Melting Pot*

Lechmere Worrall and J. E. Harold Terry, *The Man who Stayed at Home*

Allene Tupper Wilkes, *The Creaking Chair*

D. T. Davies, *Pelenni Pitar*

St John Ervine, *John Ferguson*

Brinley Jones, *John a Jams*

Reginald Berkeley, *French Leave*

R. G. Berry, *Dwywaith yn Blentyn*

R. G. Berry, *Ar y Groesffordd*

Eden Philpotts, tr. D. Matthew Williams, *The Farmer's Wife* (in Welsh)

T. C. Murray, *Tân y Hydref* (tr. of *Autumn Fire*)

J. Eddie Parry, *Points*

J. Ellis Williams, *Pen y Daith*

Trevor Morgan and A. G. Prys-Jones, *No Damage Done*

William Shakespeare, *The Merchant of Venice*

R. C. Sherriff, *Journey's End*

Henrik Ibsen, *John Gabriel Borkman*

Roi Cooper Megrue and Walter Hackett, *It Pays to Advertise*

John Galsworthy, *Escape*

Karel and Josef Čapek, *The Insect Play* (tr. from the Czech)

Jean Bart, *The Squall*

J. B. Priestley, *Laburnum Grove*

Emlyn Williams, *The Late Christopher Bean* (tr. and adapted from the French)

Bernard Shaw, *The Devil's Disciple*

Winifred Carter, *Moloch*

W. W. Jacobs, *The Monkey's Paw*

J. O. Francis, *Birds of a Feather*

J. O. Francis, *The Poacher*

Stanley Houghton, *Dewis Anorfod* (tr. of *Hobson's Choice*) performed by his own company. The letters indicate the primary language of performances ('W' for Welsh and 'E' for English).

Such a 'league table' of authors can only give a general indication of popularity. J. Ellis Williams (1932) will be excluded from further considerations because his play *Y Pwyllgorddyn* was the main test piece of the National Eisteddfod that year where it was performed by fourteen companies. However, the play was not performed elsewhere.

Considering that the number of different authors performed throughout the period increases steadily, the enduring popularity of J. O. Francis's plays is striking. Among Welsh playwrights only R. G. Berry was equally popular. Indeed, the longevity of the first generation of Welsh playwrights – Francis, Berry, D. T. Davies and, to a lesser extent, W. J. Gruffydd[38] – is astonishing. With the exception of J. Eddie Parry, newer Welsh writers were only popular for a short time. The table also shows the increasing number of translations, of canonical authors and of authors of escapist comedies. By 1936, the variety of writers had increased considerably and Welsh writers had become the minority.

Table 4 reproduces the plays that were most often performed. This time multiple performances by one company are included because the number of plays proliferated to such a degree in the 1930s that not many were performed several times by different companies. Thus the table gives a general flavour of the kind of plays that were produced rather than providing a faithful ranking. The year 1924 was excluded because too few multiple performances were recorded that year.

In 1920 a mixture of pre- and post-war Welsh plays were performed. *Beddau'r Proffwydi* was written in 1913, *Ar y Groesffordd* was first performed in 1914, *Noson o Farrug* in 1915. Plays like *Colli ac Ennill, Cyfrinach y Fasged Frwyn* or *Maesymeillion* were more recent, as were Naunton Davies's plays. If the First World War was experienced as a dividing line that radically altered authors' *Weltanschauung*, it was not apparent in the kinds of plays performed. Only a few critics thought that the old plays had served their purpose and should be replaced. Commenting on a performance of W. J. Gruffydd's *Beddau'r Proffwydi* on 28 April 1924, J. Eddie Parry commented somewhat sourly:

> It appears that this play was repeated at the request of numerous patrons. Maybe it describes Welsh life towards the end of the last century, linking us with the near past and with that old type of Welsh play with which we associate preachers and deacons and poached rabbits.[39]

In 1928 the 'old favourites' were still performed, but the majority of plays were London successes. Some of them had received premieres in provincial repertory theatres, like *Paddy The Next Best Thing*, which was adapted from the novel of the same title by Gertrude Page (1908). It was first performed at the Queen's Theatre in Manchester in February 1920, and quickly transferred to the Savoy Theatre in London and afterwards to the Strand Theatre for 886 performances between 1920 and 1922. The play, a comedy about a loveable young Irish woman and her adventures, was made into a successful film starring Janet Gaynor and Warner Baxter in 1933. It was undoubtedly one of the major plays of 1920 and provided the right sort of escapism from grim reality in 1920s south Wales. St John Ervine's *The Ship* deals with a shipbuilding family and their conflicts as the son, who has imbibed socialist ideals abroad, returns home. It was first performed at the Liverpool Playhouse on 24 November 1922 and then transferred to the Everyman Theatre in London for a modest run of twenty-four performances in 1929. The fact that the Pontlottyn Dramatic Society and the Swansea Stage Society picked up *The Ship* before it went to London speaks for the importance of St John Ervine as a playwright and may also mean that news of the play came from the Liverpool Welsh community. Typical repertory plays of this kind were thus performed side by side with Welsh plays.

In the more experienced companies, for instance Trecynon Amateur Dramatic Company, Mardy Amateur Dramatic Company, Port Talbot YMCA Amateur Dramatic Company and Barry Amateur Dramatic Company, moved towards including 'difficult' plays in their repertory. *Candida* and *Ghosts* were performed by Barry Dramatic Company, *King Lear* and *Othello* by the Port Talbot YMCA Dramatic Company and St John Ervine's *John Ferguson* by the equally experienced Blaengarw Dramatic Company. However, a few 'young' companies also opted for canonical plays, such as the East Moor Players (Splott, Cardiff), which performed Galsworthy's *Escape* in the East Moor Institute, Cardiff, on 9 March 1932. Most companies opted for light comedy, however. Patrick Carleton described amateur theatre as the antidote to mass-produced Hollywood films and an expression of a living local culture but also noted a preference for 'easy' plays, saying that

> the *average* A[mateur] D[ramatic] S[ociety] does not, and does not wish to, concern itself with either old wine or new bottles: . . . most people who produce plays for fun in their spare time are more than content with the comedies of J. B. Priestley and the melodramas of Edgar Wallace.[40]

The same can be said for amateur dramatic companies in Wales.

By the mid-1930s, thus, the programmes of amateur theatre companies in Wales were diverse and included few Welsh plays. Critics complained about this, such as a reviewer of a competition held in Trecynon's Public Hall in November 1936, who noted that: '[n]ot one Welsh[-language] play or a play about Welsh life is included in the competition'.[41] If any attempts were made to remedy the situation it was through the involvement of Little Theatres and educational bodies. In 1932 Swansea Little Theatre in Mumbles, Aberdare Little Theatre and 'the society for promoting educational facilities in the mining valleys of South Wales' organized a one-act playwriting competition, which offered prizes as well as the chance of being performed by Swansea Little Theatre (plays in Welsh) and Aberdare Little Theatre (plays in English).[42] The committees received fifty plays in English and fourteen plays in Welsh. Unfortunately, the competition did not succeed in stimulating new writing more generally and the plays of the prizewinners were not performed elsewhere. Just like the companies, Welsh dramatists were mostly amateurs and found that they could not compete with non-Welsh professional playwrights. By 1936, Lord Howard de Walden was forced to conclude that the movement had stalled.[43] Even a playwright as successful as J. O. Francis found it necessary to caution his publisher in the 1950s that *The Sheep and the Goats*, the revised version of *Tares in the Wheat*, might not be suitable for publishing. In February 1952, he wrote to French's representative Cyril Hogg: 'The more experience I get of the amateur world the more necessary does it seem that one should wait for some good evidence that a play is going to be fairly popular before seeking to have it printed by anybody'.[44] Francis was not being modest: a new edition of *The Sheep and the Goats* would have required considerable financial outlay on his part. Perhaps he was acknowledging in this letter that he was no longer as popular as he used to be. Equally likely is that the 'play of Welsh life' had reached its nadir.[45]

AMATEUR DRAMA COMPETITIONS

The amateur dramatic movement acquired an extraordinary momentum in the 1930s and its engine was undoubtedly the competitive 'drama week'. Although controversially discussed by critics, competitions allowed companies to meet, exchange information and occasionally lend each other props. Regular adjudications helped them to develop a more professional attitude towards acting. Arguably, competitions also led to the take-up of plays by non-Welsh authors as companies tried to impress the adjudicators.

In 'The drama festival' (1939), Sydney Box distinguished four kinds of amateur drama competition: drama festivals, which were run on national lines like the Welsh National Eisteddfod and the British Drama League Festival, independent festivals, particularly those sponsored for the purposes of advertising, competitions organized for charitable purposes, and those run to generate income. Most Welsh drama competitions raised revenue for charitable purposes to benefit a particular cause or to aid the needy in areas of pervasive unemployment.

The typical drama festival in Wales was organized much like a competitive event at the National Eisteddfod except that there were no test pieces. Instead, companies performed the plays they had chosen for their current season. Competitions were a good way of practising performances in front of different audiences. Some companies went to great lengths to attend as many competitions as possible: expenses were usually covered, so no company lost money and there was always a prize to be won. Table 5 shows which amateur theatre companies were most active in attending competitions and how many different plays they performed. Companies are usually identified by the name of their village or town, or that of their chapel or church. The year 1924 has been removed because there is too little evidence to form reliable conclusions.

Some companies were astonishingly long-lived. Mardy Dramatic Society, Garrick Dramatic Society and Trecynon Dramatic Society were active across decades and developed high production standards. Moreover, the more experienced companies, notably Mardy, retained an ability to perform in Welsh even though they were located in an increasingly monoglot anglophone cultural environment. Also, companies' level of activity increased over time. In 1920, Pontardawe attended six competitions and performed two plays. By contrast, Barry attended ten competitions and performed three plays in 1932 and, in 1936, Blackwood attended a staggering thirteen competitions in 1936 performing no fewer than six different plays in a season of roughly six months. Competitions clearly became a main focus for amateur theatre activity in south Wales. They also became regular fixtures in the social calendar of towns and villages. On average, the most active companies travelled around 420 kilometres/260 miles per season purely to attend drama competitions, which is remarkable given their amateur status. When contemplating this figure, one has to remember that this was a time without motorways and dual carriageways when journeys would have been slow and not many people privately owned vehicles. Organizing journeys for the actors, the production team and the set several times during the season was no mean feat.

Table 5: Drama companies and attendance at competitions

Company	Place	Number of competitions attended	Language
1920			
Pontardawe	Pontardawe	6	W & E
Mardy	Maerdy	5	W & E
Soar	Pontygwaith	5	W & E
Horeb Welsh Dramatic Society	Treherbert	5	W
Cynon	Aberdare	3	W
1928			
Garrick	Mid-Rhondda	6	E
Mardy	Maerdy	6	E
Trecynon	Trecynon/Aberdare	6	W & E
Blaengarw	Blaengarw	5	E
Ebbw Vale	Ebbw Vale	4	E
Swansea Stage Society	Swansea	3	E
1932			
Barry	Barry	10	E
Trecynon	Trecynon	6	E
Blackwood	Blackwood	6	E
Port Talbot YMCA	Port Talbot	5	E
Garrick	Mid-Rhondda	3	E
Mardy	Maerdy	3	W & E
Port Talbot Rep	Port Talbot	3	E
1936			
Blackwood	Blackwood	13	E
Blaengarw	Blaengarw	7	E
Garrick	Mid-Rhondda	6	E
Swansea YMCA	Swansea	6	E
Treharris and District	Treharris	6	E
Barry	Barry	6	E
Cardiff Little Theatre	Cardiff	5	E
Mardy	Maerdy	4	W & E
Grovian	Cardiff	3	E
Penarth	Penarth	3	E

What is more difficult to assess is the impact of competitions on audiences. Sometimes drama weeks took place in out of the way locations and audiences could not have been large. The correspondent who attended the Cwmaman Drama Week held in March 1920 noted: 'While the patronage might have been larger throughout the week, it was not disappointing when the fact is realised that the event took place at a village two miles from Aberdare and mainly accessible only by foot'.[46] Usually, though, drama weeks seem to have been well attended, which meant they generated valuable income for charitable causes. Thus, the report for the Dowlais Drama Week held in April 1936 reads:

> A drama week opened at Dowlais on Monday was organised by clergy. Its purpose is to raise money for the churches of the parish, where, owing to the closing of Dowlais's steel works and collieries, 80 per cent of the parishioners are unemployed. Church work has been severely handicapped through lack of means.[47]

Bearing MacKaye's discussion about the role of community drama in mind, competitions were clearly immensely successful when it came to their community development role. But were they equally successful at developing the drama as an art form? In 1939 Sydney Box raised the question whether festivals had 'any real purpose other than that of satisfying emotions similar to those experienced by a man who pays his shilling to see his favourite football team beat its rivals. . . . Has the festival movement achieved anything for drama?'[48] Having attended many performances, he admitted that

> the time for [more experimental work] has not yet arrived. For the fact is that the overwhelming majority of amateur groups which enter festivals are barely equipped technically, as yet, to handle with precision the simplest of one-act comedies and farces.[49]

It appears that in Wales the number of companies kept pace with the increasing number of competitions, but the quality of the performances did not rise accordingly. Nor did competitions fulfil their initial promise of developing a distinctively Welsh drama or performance style. The *Western Mail*'s drama critic observed in 1932:

> We have almost ceased to wonder at the success of the Welsh Drama Movement with its week's festivals, for it has settled down on competitive lines. Perhaps the impelling rivalry between the competing societies explained the measure of success attained, but the competitions are not developing a distinctive Welsh drama or style of acting, which seemed to be the desired object at its commencement.[50]

One response to the criticism that competitions encouraged companies to perform with one eye on the adjudicator and the other on the prize money was to hold a non-competitive festival. The Monmouthshire Drama League, an 'off-shoot of the Rural Community Council', held a county-wide non-competitive festival in 1932, reasoning that

> [t]he Drama League do not encourage the competitive spirit, and the idea of bringing the teams together to produce plays of their own selection is that they may learn from one another and receive valuable advice from the adjudicator in regard to the finer points of stage craft. The selection of teams from the groups to appear in the final is not made on competitive lines. It does not necessarily follow that the best plays are selected, but the finalists are mainly chosen for their representative character.[51]

While subsequent articles celebrate the success of this venture, the competitive drama festival held sway. It is perhaps fair to say that competitions helped good companies improve because they provided plenty of opportunity to perform and see others perform. But they also encouraged companies to study the judging criteria and 'play to the adjudicator', which means they selected their plays mainly with a view to winning competitions, not to support a national movement.

J. O. Francis's main interest lay in helping to develop Welsh drama and the amateur movement was the vehicle that allowed him to do so. In his radio talk *National Drama in Wales*, which was recorded on 19 November 1952 and presumably broadcast by the BBC shortly afterwards, he assessed the impact and the future of amateur drama in Wales. Even though he wrote that 'the drama movement in Wales [was] an amateur movement', he was not convinced it would always remain one. In his talk he acknowledged the efforts of Howard de Walden and the arts council in funding theatre activity in Wales. Noting that 'the difference between professional achievement and amateur achievement is a big difference', he argued that a professionalization of the theatre ought to be attempted by selectively employing professional actors who would join amateur companies:

> Between our present amateur phase and the professional flowering that may come later on there seems to be room for developing an intermediate arrangement that has already had some success. A few of the professional Welsh players who work on the English stage have returned to Wales for certain occasions and combined with amateurs in special performances. One notable case was Mr. Clifford Evans's appearance some years ago at the National Eisteddfod as the 'lead' in 'Pobun'. And there are now plenty of professional Welsh players who could be called on. It begins to look as if the export trade

in Welsh actors will soon catch up with the export trade in Welsh preachers – and that's saying a lot. ... For some years to come the combining of professionals and amateurs maybe our way of advance in the acting and stage presentation.[52]

The amateur theatre movement in Wales had done a great deal to develop the drama in Wales but its two purposes of providing inclusive forms of entertainment and strengthening community ties on the one hand and developing craftsmanship and standards in dramatic writing and performance on the other hand proved difficult to reconcile. Without the amateur theatre movement, there would have been very little development of the dramatic arts in Wales. Activity would have concentrated on the large towns and cities, and it would certainly not have commanded such large-scale support. Indeed, the 'export trade in Welsh actors' Francis mentions would have been impossible without amateur theatre. Nevertheless, the limitations of amateur theatre and its emphasis on popularity meant that the goals of the Welsh national drama movement of 1914 were not achieved.

In the last minute of his talk, Francis calls on new writers to break out of the realistic mould, develop 'a more flexible technique in the construction of plays' and to 'give their elders', including himself, 'a shake-up'.[53] The kind of 'shake-up' he and his generation of playwrights had delivered decades earlier when they had developed the realistic 'play of Welsh life' will be the subject of the following chapter.

3

Place, Politics and the Possibilities of Realism

Martha Nussbaum has argued that a central claim underpins an ethical criticism of literature, particularly novels, namely 'the claim that there is, with respect to any text carefully written and fully imagined, an organic connection between its form and its content'.[1] An ethical reading of fiction thus goes beyond potentially reductive readings of the 'morality' of the characters and attentively looks at the connection between form and content and then moves on to situate the work in particular context. J. O. Francis's work is underpinned by an understanding of the relationship between localities, traditions, history and identity as organic. Similarly organic is the way this relationship is expressed, namely by means of realism – although it tends to be a realism that includes elements of tragedy, symbolism and so on. This chapter focuses on the way in which the aesthetics of Francis's use of realism conveys ethical meaning in his serious full-length plays.

The postmodern critique of realism has been that realism presents one kind of reality as *the* reality. It appears to be 'natural' and 'privileges and reinforces the status quo. Because realism presupposes an agreed-upon world view that can be considered authentic and understandable, it creates a hegemonic model of reality that is seen as natural and hence beyond change'.[2] This conception of realism is inadequate because it disregards the use to which it is put as well as the specificity of the sociocultural and political context in which realistic texts are read. Nussbaum argues that an ethical reading is alive to the complexity of realistic representation: 'Life is never simply *presented* as text; it is always *represented as* something'.[3]

Furthermore, the kind of Aristotelian ethical criticism proposed by her does not detach form (and content) of a text from the context of its production. Nussbaum calls this 'perception' – 'the ability to discern, acutely and responsively, the salient features of one's particular situation . . . to show the ethical crudeness of moralities based exclusively on general rules, and to demand for ethics a much finer responsiveness to the concrete'.[4] Francis's use of realism needs thus to be read and understood 'acutely and responsively' as part of a cultural analysis of place.

The premise for this chapter is the argument that realism has been used in the context of the new drama to forward a socially and politically progressive agenda, particularly in nations like Wales and Ireland, which had experienced various degrees of colonialism. On the Welsh stage realism of representation was in itself political, whereas in England it was the medium by which progressive agendas and ideologies were transmitted. Around the time of the Welsh National Drama Week in May 1914, audiences were able to see ordinary Welsh people in everyday situations on stage for the first time, thus supporting notions of a meaningful and distinct local and national identity. Today, realism is the default form from which dramatists with literary aspirations try to distance themselves. As shown in chapter 1, J. O. Francis served his theatrical apprenticeship at a time when Wales had just emerged from decades-long moral disapproval of the theatre. For that generation of writers, the realist form was revolutionary. One of these revolutionary plays that excited actors, audiences and critics alike was *Change*.

CHANGE (1912)

Change is a play in which the social upheavals of the time are presented as a conflict between father and sons. The play is set in Aberpandy, a south Wales valleys town, probably a fictional conflation of Aberdare and Tonypandy. The father, John Price, is the embodiment of an old-style, Victorian Nonconformist Welsh Liberalism. To his horror, his elder sons Lewis and John Henry come to reject his way of life: Lewis is a socialist and John Henry, whom the combined financial sacrifice of his family had enabled to study for a Bachelor of Divinity at the University College of South Wales and Monmouthshire in Cardiff, loses his faith and abandoned his vocation. Tension builds up as Lewis and John Henry – more or less impatiently – try to make their father understand their position, while the third son, Gwilym, whose tubercular illness and poet's sensibility place outside the conflict zone between father and sons, pleads for mutual understanding and compromise. In the tragic climax of the play, Gwilym is killed during the violent clash between protesting strikers, police and army. The family disintegrates and the last affecting image is that of Gwen crying inconsolably 'Not one, after all! O Dduw, not even one – Dim un! Dim un!'[5]

Change is a twentieth-century version of Gotthold Ephraim Lessing's *bürgerlichen Trauerspiels*, the 'bourgeois tragedy'. Lessing had argued that 'the names of princes and heroes can lend a play pomp and majesty; but they don't affect us. The misfortune of those whose circumstances are most similar to ours, must naturally penetrate our soul the most'.[6] Francis brought the conflict 'home' by writing a play about the effects of economic and social change on an ordinary family in the industrial valleys of south Wales. *Change* has a hybrid form – it is both realistic and tragic: the action is stylized, scenes of high tension are carefully counterbalanced with scenes of comic relief and the denouement has a tragic inevitability, but is not necessarily the inevitable outcome of events in a realistic sense. Much like Lessing's *Miss Sara Sampson* (1755), *Change* 'ennobles' its working-class characters by making them the subject of tragedy and simultaneously makes tragedy more 'realistic'.

Realistic action had to be embedded in a realistic setting according to the advice of the Scottish actor and theatre critic William Archer: 'Whether we like it or no . . ., scenery has ceased to be a merely suggestive backdrop against which the figures stand out in high relief. The stage now aims at a complete picture'.[7] Francis's stage directions for *Change* serve to locate the characters socially, and in a specific community and place before they have even entered the stage:

> *The walls are covered with paper, bold in design, but now rather faded. . . . On the mantelpiece above are brass candlesticks, clock, flat-irons, tin tea-canisters, etc. . . . The furniture is humbly serviceable, and has seen long usage. At the back, in a central position, stands an old dresser hung with jugs and set with plates. A simple vase filled with sweat peas is on the second shelf. On the lowest shelf stand a row of well-worn books, and two small book-shelves, well stocked, hang one on each side of the dresser. . . . At the back, one on each side of the dresser, are pictures of Gladstone and C. H. Spurgeon. In other places are pictures of Henry Richard and some of the well-known Welsh preachers.* (p. 8)

Today it is difficult to gauge just how radical this kind of setting was for a Welsh audience. Simply by looking at the stage, audiences knew that John and Gwen Price are respectable working-class late-Victorians, who experience Welsh culture primarily through religion and whose politics are Liberal. This background has faded – a signal that John and Gwen Price's way of life might no longer be appropriate for their sons. This type of realistic, almost fussy set in which each prop refers to real-life objects[8] had been available to the professional European stage from about 1870 onwards.[9] Francis's play was among the first to employ this stage design in Wales, an ambitious decision given the lack of professional theatre provision. A set like the one for *Rhys Lewis*, a Welsh-language play performed by Cwmni Trefriw in 1886, which had a painted backcloth showing a generic scene, was far more common and also more affordable for amateur companies.[10]

Francis's set is closer to the typical cottage interior of the Irish National Theatre than to contemporary plays on the London stage, which tended to focus on signifiers of class but were vague when it came to signifiers of culture and place. A comparison with the set for *Little Miss Llewelyn*, the English translation of a play by the Belgian playwrights Frantz (Jean-François) Fonson and Fernand Wicheler entitled *Le marriage de Mademoiselle Beulemans*, first performed on 31 August 1912 at the Vaudeville Theatre in London, is instructive because of the play's Welsh plot and setting. As the play was originally set in Belgium, a small country with different linguistic communities, the translation is not inappropriately transposed to Wales. The producers employed Welsh actors, such as Ernest George Cove, R. A. Hopkins and Tom Owen, who were members of de Walden's Incorporated Stage Society and would later appear in *Change*. The principal actors Hilda Trevelyan (Hilda Marie Antoinette Anna Tucker) and Edmund Gwenn (Edmund John Kellaway) were English, though, having been born in Hackney and Wandsworth respectively. More importantly, the play had no Welsh cultural significance and the set, while successfully indicating the family's aspirational, lower middle-class status, fails to signify place and culture because generic stage furniture was used.[11] While London audiences enjoyed the play – it had a successful run of 186 performances compared with *Change*'s three[12] – Welsh critics were incensed. E. E. fumed: 'I doubt if it can fairly be described as drama; I am certain it is not Welsh'.[13]

By contrast, the naturalistic set designs employed by the Irish National Theatre defined what became a typical stage set for Irish plays with a national theme: 'The humble cottage featuring tenant farmers, industrious women, resilient fishermen, or traveling musicians came to represent Irish rural life. Whitewashed walls, thatched roof, and turf fire became iconic of the Irish landscape'.[14] Responding to the plays they saw performed by the

Irish Players, J. O. Francis, D. T. Davies and the other playwrights of the first national drama movement created authentic sets as background for realistic stage action. Later, the setting of the Welsh house established by the pre-First World War writers – a house experienced as alternately supportive and stifling – would become the backdrop to many Welsh plays of the twentieth century, notably Gwyn Thomas's *The Keep* (1961), Alan Osborne's *In Sunshine and in Shadow* (1985), Ed Thomas's *House of America* (1989) and *Gas Station Angel* (1998).[15]

Rather than focusing on one specific incident, *Change* provides a 'composite study'.[16] The characters were examples of a larger conflict gripping the nation, at once realistic and emblematic. Identifiable incidents that influenced Francis include the strike and the riots in Tonypandy in 1910, which were crushed by Winston Churchill's ill-judged deployment of troops,[17] and the national railwaymen's strike in Llanelli in 1911, when soldiers had been called in to break up the strike and two men where killed.[18] Rather than pit the mine owners and managers against the workers as Galsworthy had done in *Strife* (1909), Francis locates the conflict within the mining community itself: it is a conflict of people who should be on the same side. The play thus escapes ideological pigeonholing.

Gwilym describes John Price as a representative of 'the old valley. At heart he's of the agricultural class – slow, stolid, and conservative' (p. 50). He and Gwen are personifications of the ideal of the *gwerin* transposed into an industrial, urban setting: they are Liberal-voting, chapel-going pillars of the community. John Price is a proud workman who believes in compromise and considers strikes to be ultimately destructive. The conflict with Lewis arises because, a generation later, any remaining room for compromise had vanished. Conditions of work were steadily deteriorating and levels of pay did not rise with levels of expenditure. The only hope for socialists like Lewis seemed to lie in collective action: 'As long as Labour and Capital exist as they do now, you must stir up strife – all over the place' (p. 33).

Change thus deals with competing notions of the good and with the conflict that ensues when one tradition – the one adhered to by John and Gwen Price – is no longer meaningful for the next generation. Underlying this discussion is the question of what a 'living tradition' is made of. MacIntyre has argued that a 'living tradition . . . is an historically extended, socially embodied argument, and an argument precisely in part about the goods which constitute that tradition'.[19] In *Change* the struggle becomes destructive as neither side can see value in the other's position. The play suggests that if no compromise can be reached, Welsh society itself may be in danger.

In setting a play about such different political opinions in the heart of the industrial valleys in south Wales, Francis achieved two aims: first, he claimed a *gwerin* identity for his Aberpandy characters. John and Gwen Price are more at home using Welsh than English and, presumably having been educated at Sunday school, find writing a letter in English a laborious task. The sons converse in English, but pepper their speech with Welsh expressions and are unaccountably drawn to traditional Welsh hymns. Secondly, Francis complicates the easy equation of 'south Wales' with 'industrial unrest' that lies behind Galsworthy's decision to locate *Strife* in the borderland of Wales. In *Strife*, the political views of the Welsh characters range from apathetic to fanatical, but their disagreements represent variations on a theme.[20] Francis does not deny the reality of industrial unrest and neither does he support its concomitant violence. But his play shows a much greater variety of political positions in one community, from Price's small-c conservatism, Gwen and John Henry's largely non-political stance, the lodger Sam Thatcher's 'everybody-is-out-for-himself' egotism, to Lewis's socialism.

I doubt that Francis's political motivation was very different from that of Galsworthy, whose plays often addressed social ills with a view to effecting change, such as *Justice* (1910), whose argument against solitary confinement led to a revision of penal laws. However, Francis was more successful at presenting the issues around socio-political change because he did not personalize the issue. *Strife* suggests that the unofficial workers' leader David Roberts and the Chairman of the Board of the Trenartha Tin Plate Works, John Anthony, are personally responsible for the industrial dispute and its consequences. It argues that the conflict is best resolved 'through compromise, good will, and family feeling', thus confirming the paternalistic role of the owners and managers and the subordinate role of the workers, 'rather than the violence of the law', which would drag the conflict from the semi-private to the public sphere.[21] Instead, *Change* suggests that the way political and social movements develop is beyond the control of individuals despite instances of personal culpability.

Not all Welsh drama in English of the period tried to see the merits in both of the main opposing political views. Naunton Davies, a GP in Llantrisant who was also a novelist and playwright, saw socialism as an alien creed, which disrupted the traditional paternalistic social structures in south Wales. In *The Human Factor* (1920),[22] the Englishman James Walford is a socialist agitator who challenges the hard-working and benign Welsh colliery manager John Williams: 'It's a fight between you and me. And there's no room for the two of us in the valley' (p. 40). His lust for power is contrasted with the idealism of the Rector's son Rhys Morgan, who believes that 'Socialism is the highest form of organised liberty, and only evil minds can turn it to evil account' (p. 12) without realizing that he is being manipulated by the unscrupulous Walford. In the end even Walford crumples, though, when he realizes that his actions have led to the death of Mrs Williams (p. 140). For Galsworthy and Davies the political conflict is essentially a struggle between personalities that is best resolved in private. *Change*, on the other hand, situates the struggle in the public sphere and presents its impact on the private sphere of the family. Closure does not mean resolution: the ethical thrust of the play is that audiences are to engage with the problem posed after the curtain has gone down.

The second major topic of the play, namely the creeping secularization of Welsh society in the early twentieth century, is portrayed as the conflict between John Price, for whom belief, culture and way of life are indivisible, and John Henry, whose emotional but shallow response to the religious revival led by the charismatic Evan Roberts in 1904/5 did not withstand the onslaught of intellectual argument and the new experience of living outside his community. John Henry's step of giving up studying for the ministry can be considered moral as he prefers risking his family's displeasure to living a life of hypocrisy. For John Price, whose pleasure in his son's educational career had not been untouched by vanity, it is a personal insult: 'Haven't we been slaving and sacrificing all these years? Haven't we given you education when you might have had to go into the pit?' (p. 66). John Henry's choice is also utterly incomprehensible to him and thus constitutes a wilful, total rejection of all he stands for. He is unable to grasp what Gwilym is trying to say when he begs him, 'But, nhad, does he despise your coat because it doesn't happen to fit him?' (p. 66).

The theme of the progressive loss of the hold of religious belief over the younger generations in Wales 'implaces' the play and expresses an ethical dilemma peculiar to Wales. It was an inescapable topic for playwrights like Francis and D. T. Davies, as was the related question of where one's moral knowledge and codes of behaviour came from if not from religion. In Davies's *Ble Ma Fa?*, for instance, the widow of a collier anxiously ponders whether her atheist husband has gone to heaven as he had been a good man.[23] Not many of the English new dramatists address the subject of religion. Granville-Barker's *Waste* deals with the disestablishment of the Church of England, but only because it is a suitably radical political topic for Henry Trebell: it is not important as a question in its own right.

Both John Henry's loss of faith and Lewis's turn to socialism represent a change in meaning-making systems but also illustrate how traditional ethical value systems sometimes have to change. Paraphrasing Aristotle, Nussbaum argues that

> [t]o hold tradition fixed is . . . to prevent ethical progress. What human beings want and seek is not conformity with the past, it is the good. So our systems of law should make it possible for them to progress beyond the past, when they have agreed that the change is good.[24]

What goes for systems of law also goes for political and religious systems: change is sometimes inevitable if systems are no longer just. John Price's tragic flaw is that he does not recognize that conformity with the past is no longer appropriate. But are rupture and revolution the right responses? Gwilym, who represents Aristotle's virtuous path of the 'golden mean' between extremes, is killed, but arguably his death only serves to heighten the play's ethical effect: it is now up to the audience to engage with the conflict in real life.

What makes Francis's realism so compelling is that he refused to create villains for his plays, characters like Galsworthy's John Anthony and David Roberts, who are prepared to sacrifice lives to gain their ends, or the thoroughly unlikable owner of the fustian works and his equally unattractive employees Pfeifer and Neumann in Hauptmann's *The Weavers*. It is through his failings and in the tenderness he shows to his wife that the hard, unbending John Price is humanized. Gwilym is not entirely unsuccessful when he reminds his brothers (and the audience) that their father needs their sympathy, not their scorn:

> GWILYM: You've only got to wait, and you'll win. But the old brigade can only see that they're losing, and they're bewildered, pressed on all sides by things that they don't understand. If they argue with you, they get beaten. Why? Because they've been careful to give you the education they never had themselves – (p. 49)

Members of the audience are not meant to simply side with any of the characters but to gain an understanding by watching the action unfold and determine their own positions accordingly.

A further innovation is the way language is used to denote place and not just class. The dialogue follows natural speech patterns and is tinged with the local dialect, including interspersed Welsh words and phrases, sentence structures based on Welsh grammar ('There was her father had been a deacon all those years', p. 14) and interjections ('Aay'). This use of language underscores the play's realism and it elevates the local variety of English, which had seemed 'ugly both in sound and in the written form' to the editor of *The Welsh Outlook*,[25] to the status of a literary language. In this Francis resembles writers like Ibsen, Frank Wedekind, Gerhart Hauptmann and Githa Sowerby. Their aim was to create a literary version of actual speech in order to make their plays both authentic and literary. In Ibsen's case, the representation of spoken Norwegian served to support the national project shortly after Norwegian independence.[26] Githa Sowerby reproduced a literary version of a north-east English accent, which locates the action and serves to differentiate the characters into those who have stayed at home and whose dialect is more pronounced, and those who have lived elsewhere and have received an education, whose accent is milder. A highly naturalist version of a local dialect is represented in Hauptmann's *The Weavers*, which is almost unintelligible today as it was written in the now extinct German dialect of Silesia, an area now largely situated in Poland, its erstwhile German population dispersed. Dialect here signifies location, (lack of) education and class: the poverty-stricken weavers speak in a thick dialect and the middle-class characters use a strongly accented High German. Compared with the use of language in *The Weavers*, *Change* represents the English dialect of the Rhondda in a less naturalistic way and uses dialect to distinguish generations rather than social classes. The older generation's speech echoes the Welsh that underlies it whereas the language used by the younger generation is more standardized regardless of their levels of education. Lewis's friend, the teacher Dai Matthews, and the collier Twm Powell are of one generation and therefore sound alike even though one has received a university education and the other has not.

Most importantly, the local dialect is presented as dignified, not as a stigma or for comic effect, as in Tom Robertson's *Caste* (1867) or Bernard Shaw's *John Bull's Other Island*, a play about Ireland (1904).[27] This becomes clear when the English of the Welsh characters is compared with that of the Cockney lodger Sam Thatcher. Sam is a character who provides comic relief and whose overdrawn dialect is obviously meant to be funny, as is his '*general air of suffering superiority to Aberpandy and all its works* [which] *indicates a haughty metropolitan outlook*' (p. 19). Sam lost his arm in an industrial accident and is thus dependent on the goodwill of the Aberpandy community. Despite this, he is an unrepentant strike-breaker and makes no attempt to fit in. His overconfident use of badly mangled Welsh ('Skooliki da, as yer say dahn 'ere, missis, Skooliki da', which is an attempt to say 'Os gwelwch chi'n dda' and which means 'Yes, please' in this context, p. 21) only serves to underline his unmerited feeling of superiority. Francis's humour often works by means of reversal and thus of unexpected incongruity, and a postcolonial reading suggests that Sam was created as a response to the comic stage Welshman. Francis created the first comic Londoner for the Welsh stage.

Given Francis's indebtedness to some of the English new drama, the question whether Francis invented a new form for Welsh drama needs to be asked. On the one hand, as John D. Lewis wrote in 1921, *Change* was perceived to be 'altogether in a new type, marking a distinct and refreshing advance in our drama'.[28] On the other hand, Howard de Walden commented in his adjudication for his prize in 1913:

> I feel a certain grudge against the author of 'Change' in that his work might well have been submitted to the horde of hungry managers in London with a good chance of success. . . . Henceforward any contribution founded too obviously upon an English model will be viewed with a baleful eye. Steal from the English but don't copy them.[29]

The problem with this assessment is that no playwright exists in isolation, no matter how determinedly he seeks to give expression to a particular local or national spirit. D. T. Davies seems implicitly to have responded to de Walden when he wrote in 1920:

> 'Change' raises an issue which is of paramount importance to the present movement. When the play first appeared Francis was hailed as a disciple of Galsworthy, a shallow comment based on a resemblance between his theme and that in 'Strife.' As a craftsman, Francis derives from Ibsen, directly and indirectly, but largely the former. Technique apart, the remainder of 'Change' is accounted for by the simple fact that its author was bred and born in industrial South Wales. In other words, 'Change' is a Welsh play to the core, an integral part of, and as yet the most considerable contribution to, the present outburst.
>
> It is necessary to emphasise this. We who are endeavouring to write plays are urged frequently to avoid imitating the products of the English and, for that matter, other theatres, otherwise our efforts can never be inherently and peculiarly Welsh, a sound, but unnecessary piece of advice. This is construed narrowly by some to mean that we are to acquire our technique in some mysterious manner within the aesthetic borders of Wales, an absurd and ruinous conclusion. The craft must be learned from other craftsmen whatever be their nationality, and as long as we are true to our national instincts, sympathetically responsive to the stimuli of our surroundings, we need not fear that the source of our craftsmanship will ever affect adversely either the individual or the national character of what we produce.[30]

The difficulty lies in writing drama that is an expression of a specific national or perhaps local spirit while not being insular, parochial and badly crafted, for, as Davies argues, one can only acquire craftsmanship if one reads widely and assimilates other styles. Francis's solution was to create a place-based ethics. Using an established format, the feel of the play is, despite de Walden's comments, wholly Welsh, particularly when performed in Wales. Whether a play of ideas like *Change* is able to convey its particular national identification as well when there is no congruence between audience and characters, for instance when the play is translated and performed in a different cultural environment, is more difficult to say.

The play was first performed at a reunion of the Old Students' Association in Aberystwyth in 1913. After it had received the Howard de Walden Prize, the Incorporated Stage Society performed the play at the Haymarket Theatre in London on 7 December (evening), and 8 and 9 December (matinees). The Incorporated Stage Society then took the play to Broadway where it was performed at the Booth Theatre on 27 January 1914. It ran for eleven performances. It was also performed to great acclaim in Chicago and other American cities. Given this triumph of a completely unknown playwright, *Change* became essential to the success of the Welsh National Drama Week (11–16 May 1914), which kick-started the first Welsh national drama movement. *Change* was performed twice, on 11 May and on 13 May 1914. At first the audience response was disappointing. But when Lloyd George announced that he was going to attend and travelled to Cardiff with his entourage, including Tom Jones and the department store owner John Lewis, audience numbers picked up. Indeed, the event became important enough to warrant a disturbance by the Suffragettes. Lloyd George's support for the drama movement boosted the standing of the national drama movement considerably.[31] Reviews praise *Change* fulsomely, drawing particular attention to its realistic detail and authentic feel:

> It is impossible to convey an idea of the wealth of incident, the side issues, the play of mental forces and moral passion, the righteous indignation, the mortification and despair which are intermingled in this drama. . . . The author's plan is taken direct from the life of the people of the colliery valleys of South Wales. His incidents are the incidents with which we are familiar, and the result which he depicts is faithfully and convincingly attained.[32]

Change was truly foundational – so much so that, in the eyes of John D. Lewis, the template it established proved too powerful to resist for the dramatists who followed: 'To the majority of people Welsh drama began with "Change" in 1913, and to them, also, it seemed to express all Wales had to express in drama'.[33] The most recent performance of the play was by Neath Little Theatre (14–19 May 2012). Even though the subject matter of the play was no longer current, all performances were virtually sold out, thus attesting to the power of the play after such a long time.

CROSS-CURRENTS (1922)

Cross-Currents was meant to continue where *Change* left off. It is set in Bronawel, a prosperous farm near Dinas in north Wales. It had been the home of Gwilym Parry, a noted nationalist politician and supporter of Cymru Fydd. His widow keeps the house as a shrine to her dead husband and her most fervent wish is that her son Gareth, a lecturer in economics at the University College in Cardiff, might step into his father's shoes. The chance comes when the local MP dies. Mrs Parry, Gareth's Uncle Evan Parry, and the Reverent Trefnant Jones try to persuade Gareth to contest the seat as an independent nationalist. Gareth is tempted but cannot decide. On the one hand, nationalism powerfully appeals to his emotions. On the other hand, in Cardiff he grew interested in the socialist cause and became friendly with his cousin Gomer Davies, the son of a farm labourer. Gomer is now standing as a Labour candidate for the same seat and tries to induce Gareth to support him. Gareth is torn between two positions he believes in equally strongly – one with his heart, the other with his mind. At the end of the play Gareth takes neither path, deciding to accept a post as Professor for Political Economy at the new University College of Wales Swansea:

> I've made up my mind. Gomer, Trefnant, I'm not the man for either of you. You've brought me right up against great issues, and I feel that some people must stand out of the hubbub. Some people must keep clear of all your programmes and your practical politics. And it may be that, in the end, they'll do what is most needful, if all that humanity has built is not to perish. . . . Think—think—think![34]

This ending encapsulates Francis's own view and is a prime example of his refusal to support any political side fully. In his foreword, he writes that the play 'is not meant to be propaganda for or against any political creed. It is an attempt to render, with the greater concentration and clarity which drama adds to the data of experience, a conflict of forces in our Welsh life'.[35] The answer does not lie in political argument: it lies in stepping back from the fray and developing the intellectual tools to think the issue through from first principles. According to Aristotle's *Nicomachean Ethics* there are various ways to wisdom, but true 'flourishing' (*eudaimonia*) can only be achieved through a life of contemplation.[36] Contemplation allows one to make virtuous decisions and to reinforce the self-discipline required to habitually act virtuously. Gareth is thus not dithering: disengaging from active politics allows him to contemplate the situation and potentially determine where the path of virtue lies. Moreover, as in *Change*, the author refuses simply to tell the audience what resolution he prefers. The ethical effect of not proffering a solution means that audiences will need to contemplate the problem and come to a decision themselves.

The nationalist side is represented by the Rev. Trefnant Jones. Trefnant had been a close friend of Gareth's father and of the other politicians of the Cymru Fydd movement, the nationalist movement that had been launched in 1892 by men like Tom Ellis and D. A. Thomas. It had argued for increasing national self-determination of Wales culminating in Home Rule but soon petered out, particularly when Lloyd George lost interest in the movement after the disastrous reception he received at a rally in Newport in 1896.[37] The Liberal Party responded to the nationalist challenge by forming the 'Welsh Parliamentary Party', which was supposed to represent Welsh interests in Westminster, but which never quite managed to stand its ground when faced with party discipline and determined whips.[38] In the 1920s, the Welsh media, particularly magazines like *The Welsh Outlook*, became frustrated with what they saw as inaction on the part of the Welsh Party and a renewed interest in Home Rule emerged, supported by the MPs E. T. John and David Davies. *Cross-Currents* thematizes this brief return to nationalist politics in the 1920s. However, the nationalists in the play have no concrete political aims. They stand for an entirely spiritual, romantic nationalism.

Socialism, on the other hand, speaks to reason and is based on the kind of understanding of equality and justice described by John Rawls in *A Theory of Justice* (1971).[39] Rawls posited that decisions should be made behind what he called a 'veil of ignorance', meaning a state of ignorance of one's own position and standing in the world. This precondition would, he argued, ensure that decisions are truly fair because they are arrived at without preferential treatment. Similarly, *Cross-Currents* presents socialism as a system that seeks fair distribution of resources. It comes from the largely anglicized working-class context of Glamorgan (pp. 32, 40), but it is not an alien force in north Wales. Gomer Davies, the son of Mrs Parry's sister, who had married a labourer, is living proof that a class-based politics is not, as the Parrys will have it, a south-Walian phenomenon and, as such, somehow un-Welsh. And to people like Gomer, socialism is a creed, which goes just as deep as Mrs Parry's nationalism:

PLACE, POLITICS AND THE POSSIBILITIES OF REALISM

MRS. PARRY: Oh! Won't you try to understand? I am an old woman, guarding a great memory.

GOMER: I've got memories, too, black, bitter memories. You ask me to try to understand. Are you trying to understand me? Do you realize that I'm fighting for a cause, *my* cause, and that it means as much to me as ever your husband's did to him?

MRS. PARRY: They say you're gaining ground in the South. Isn't that enough? Can't you let us alone up here?

GOMER: No, it is not enough. And I can't let you alone. I was once a ragged, ill-fed boy in this County, the son of a farm-labourer with five children and an ailing wife. You don't know what that means. How can you know, you that never lacked a single comfort? (pp. 47–8)

Gomer's politics are just as much 'in the blood' as nationalism is for the Parry family, but the spiritual link to place is replaced by the link between members of the same class. In Gomer's words: 'I remember all those who died before their time, worn out and broken. I think of those yet to be born. And I've sworn, by any God that is, to give my life to altering things for my own class' (p. 48).

Contrary to Rawls's theory of justice that is based on true equality, Gomer's thinking has a blind spot: his sense of sympathy is limited to people he recognizes as his own. It is unclear what Gareth and Gomer's friendship is based on, as Gomer signally fails to empathize with him. When they look out on the same land they see something entirely different:

GARETH: D'you think it's true, Gomer, that Owain Glyndŵr once lay hidden with his army in that wood?

GOMER (*indifferently*): I don't know.

GARETH: I love that dark belt of pine-trees above the corn (. . .) D'you find, Gomer, that, as soon as you come back home, you begin to recall all the Welsh poetry you've ever learnt? . . .

GOMER: You're thinking, Gareth, of your happy childhood here in Bronawel.

GARETH: Yes, I daresay it's that.

GOMER: I know it's all beautiful enough on the surface. But, Gareth, what about the lives of the poor here? You know the death-rate. Don't forget—I'm a farm-labourer's son. (p. 51)

Gareth feels an instinctive, warm connection to the land and its history that momentarily distracts him from noticing the lives of those who make a meagre living as farm labourers. Gomer is blind to the beauty of the land

and indifferent to its history, perhaps because the history of his people is largely erased and because to him it is a waste of time to look at the land and muse upon the past when there is injustice in the here and now. However, in his ardour he is blind to the needs of the actual poor. He shows little sympathy with the conservative views of Old Thomas, a servant to the Parrys, for whom loyalty to the family, identity and rootedness to place are one and the same, calling him the 'last of the slaves' (p. 55).

The high point of the play is Trefnant's impassioned speech in favour of nationalism at the public meeting organized to manipulate Gareth into announcing that he is willing to contest the seat. It is a master class in oratory. Beginning *'in a quiet, conversational tone'* Trefnant soon *'show[s] himself a master of that emotional and dramatic delivery for which the older generation of Welsh preachers was famous'* (p. 64), the *hwyl*. Trefnant warns against too close a relationship with the Liberal Party because '[i]t has no special concerns for us'. He sees 'the danger from England' not as oppression: 'The danger is that we may be absorbed' (p. 67). Calling on his audience to remember Owain Glyndŵr and evoking him vividly in his audience's minds, he calls 'There is a sound in the valley, an echo that cannot die. Listen! Oh! Can you not hear it? It is the bugle of Glyndŵr' (p. 70). It is a bravura performance and it receives a passionate response from the audience. Gareth is almost won over, but some doubts remain: 'My father was a fine man, a really great man. . . . But I live in a different time. There's been a great war. It's torn away the pretty wrappings. Things that my father took for granted have become suspect' (p. 78), for instance nationalism itself after a terrible war that had been fought as a result of the clash of competing national ideologies. The implication is that nationalism does nothing for social equality. An intellectual like Gareth is not swayed by emotional appeal alone regardless how powerful it is. But Gomer's socialism lacks the emotional pull of nationalism. Unsurprisingly, Gareth – and, by implication, the author – makes up his mind to opt for the life of contemplation, which seems a more virtuous way of life than making imperfect political choices.

The central weakness of *Cross-Currents* is that the conflict, although presented with much passion, remains at the level of discourse. It is a singularly untheatrical play, whose argument is presented by essentially stationary characters and not translated into action. It is telling that the good reviews the play received came from people who had read the play and a bad one from somebody who had seen it. The play was hailed a success by people who shared Francis's experience, notably T. Gwynn Jones, who wrote in a letter to him:

> I . . . must write to you at once, to convey my thanks for the copy [of the play], + my most cordial congratulations on the very fine play you have produced. It reaches down to the very roots. I was, naturally, brought up a Nationalist, but became a convinced Socialist before I was twenty. My father, who is 80, has become sympathetic to Socialism in his old age, having been a Radical from his youth. I was discussing the subject with him last summer, + he told me that, intellectually, there is nothing for it but Socialism, of an international character, + yet, he admitted the pull of the old sentiment. I find that my son, who is not twenty, is distracted in the same way. My own nationalism has been internationalism for over 20 years, but I confess I want to Think—Think—Think! like Gareth.[40]

R. G. Berry's review is equally positive. He applauds the play's 'artistic sincerity', its realism, and its intellectual questioning: 'Mr. Francis touches a deeper chord in all thinking Welshmen, North and South'.[41] Berry even calls Gareth 'a modern Welsh Hamlet', because he is an intellectual, who is torn between conflicting loyalties.[42]

J. Eddie Parry, who saw the play in its Welsh translation (*Deufor Gyfarfod*) on 30 April 1924 at the Grand Theatre in Swansea, was much less inspired:

> Mr. Francis, rightly or wrongly, has been given the foremost place as a Welsh dramatist. Last evening's performance did not enhance his reputation. This is a 'political' play, but it is not drama. There are no dramatic situations, no humour. It is nothing like 'Change' in its dramatic value. In his preface to the play the author observes that political plays have an essential drawback, but he adds that they claim quite as good a chance of a place on the bookshelf of immortality as do the 'modern' plays of the West End. Maybe he is correct, but these latter plays do not bore us quite so much as 'Cross Currents' did last night.[43]

It seems that the production was hampered by the illness of one of the principal actors, Professor Henry Lewis (Gomer Davies), and, having learnt of 'the stupendous difficulties under which "Cross Currents" was produced"', Parry relented somewhat in his review on the following day.[44] However, it is clear that, despite the fluidity of the dialogue, it is a play that is difficult to stage.

The realism of *Change* and *Cross-Currents* served the purpose of understanding the truth of the social forces at work in the nation in the years leading up to and immediately following the First World War. Yet writing about the less savoury aspects of life was problematic. Commenting on Caradoc Evans's work, T. Huws Davies expresses the opinion that 'the realist fails both as an artist and as a social recorder if he finds nothing in human life but ugliness and depravity'.[45] A brief comparison between Evans's and Francis's work is instructive because of the different ways they handle realism. Caradoc Evans purported to give an unsparingly realistic picture of rural Wales, which was deeply offensive to his readers and theatre audiences, and which is, arguably, a cleverly fabricated pseudo-reality. He placed the body centre stage rather than the mind, focusing particularly on the visceral, ugly aspects of life.[46] Francis's realism, by contrast, is more cerebral and concentrates on ideas – at least in the serious plays.

Evans's *Taffy* (1923, revised 1925) is a three-act comedy, which has all the familiar ingredients of Evans's prose, although, written by an inexperienced dramatist, it lacks the sharp characterization and the tight structure of the short stories. The play is set in rural Cardiganshire in a by now conventional rural Welsh cottage. The plot itself is unimportant: the play consists of a series of loosely connected comic scenes. Two preachers, Ben Watkin and Spurgeon Evans, whose name recalls the famous preacher C. H. Spurgeon, whose picture hangs on the wall in the Price's cottage in *Change*, are called to a 'preaching match' in Capel Sion so that the deacons, the 'Big Heads' of the village, can decide on the most suitable minister for their congregation.[47] The self-important preening of the preachers, particularly that of the older Ben Watkins whose penchant for *hwyl* is here caricatured as mere sentimentalism ('You should hear the sermon about the boy bach who came home from Australia to find his mother dead. "Where is mam?" he cried at the cottage door – at the cottage door. "Your mam is in the grave – in the grave is your mam." What a sermon. Am I not called Tearful Ben?', p. 23), is made fun of, as is the hypocrisy of the deacons and the desire of Ester, the daughter of 'Big Head' Josi, to make a romantic match at all cost. By the end of the play, Ben Watkins has become the minister, Ester is married, and Spurgeon has rejected the ministry to ask Marged, the daughter of one of the deacons, to marry him.

The dialogue is written in a milder version of the 'see-through English', which Evans had used in his short stories and which was 'designed to give the illusion of direct access to the underlying Welsh actually being spoken by his characters'.[48] The language is caricatured, but, overall, the effect is more benignly comical than in the short stories, where characters are often malicious and even outright evil. In *Taffy* they are merely oafish, hypocritical and selfish.

The fact that Spurgeon and Marged are virtuous characters, who can see through the veil of stupidity and hypocrisy that blinds the other characters, is made obvious by the way their speech grows less comical and more grammatical as the play progresses. During the course of the play it also emerges that belief as such was not the target of Evans's satire. Spurgeon says:

> I abhor the righteousness of the capel, whose tears are less a sign of godliness than a donkey's braying is of bravery. Our works have cornered even God, and He has put us apart in a room for our strange misbehaviours. And the room is Wales.... The pulpit is a sorry lamp. It keeps us from the Church. It guides us to the polling booth. It turns our joy into sorrow. (p. 82)

Evans thus accuses Welsh Nonconformist culture of having the nation in a stranglehold. He also suggested that Nonconformist culture was responsible for Wales's present lack of importance as the nation's opinion-formers squabbled impotently among themselves while real power was being wielded elsewhere.

As a comedy, the play is, of course, less realistic than Francis's serious plays. It is discussed here because reviewers and Evans himself discussed the play in terms of realism. John D. Lewis found it unforgivable that the play gave ammunition to a potentially hostile audience who saw the play in London:

> It is like a dirty broth which, dished out to English people, is swallowed with avidity.... The cream of England might be said to have been in the theatre, and they were all 'taken in,' all impressed by the 'wonderful genius' of the author in so 'faithfully' pourtraying [sic] life.[49]

Crucially, it is the apparent realism of the play that offended. Read as farce, the play is much less offensive, but neither Lewis nor Evans read it that way. Commenting on the revised version of the play in 1925, which was performed in the Q Theatre in London on 8 September 1925, a theatre devoted to new and experimental plays, Evans wrote:

> [The play] embodies from first to last my observations in and about Wales. Everything I know of the Welsh people, good and bad – mostly bad – is in this play.... I feel that if [Welsh people] are annoyed and attack the play they will only do so because of the truthfulness of the pourtrayals [sic] of the rascals and of the lovers. I poke no fun at the Welsh because I like the Welsh too much. I want them to be tolerant. I want them to show a London audience that they can at least listen to what I believe to be the truth.[50]

Caradoc Evans's complicated relationship with literary realism – he presented his grotesques as realistic portrayals, thus implicitly encouraging the kind of outraged response he then affected to scorn – was probably largely responsible for the media reception of Evans in the 1920s, which was thus partly a reaction to a confusion about the play's ethics.

Evans had deliberately violated the ethics of the 'play of Welsh life' in which characters are 'implaced' in a Welsh environment and where virtuous action is identified with 'good' Welshness. In *Taffy*, the virtuous characters are less obviously marked as 'Welsh' than the less virtuous characters. Francis, by contrast, seems to have wholeheartedly subscribed to the notion that virtuous action in his plays went hand in hand with a 'good' Welshness, although the terms by which the 'good' was measured were not always uncritical of ideological images.

THE BEATEN TRACK (1924)

Whether he was disappointed by the lack of success of a play he must have considered a worthy successor to *Change* or whether he tired of political topics is difficult to say. In any case, Francis's next full-length serious play was to sound an entirely different note. *The Beaten Track* is a sombre play despite the themes of homecoming, family reunion and the continued survival of a small rural community. The play is set in Tŷ Mawr, an old house in the village of Trefeglwys in Cwm y Môr in what may be north-west Wales. Shân Powell, a woman described as looking '*very old, broken by work and sickness*',[51] has lost all her family to tuberculosis – all except Tom, who had fled to America. Her greatest fear is that the family line will die out. And thus she experiences a pleasurable shock when her grandson Owen, Tom's son, comes for a visit – a visit that is gradually extended as he falls in love with the young teacher Myfanwy Rees. Owen had come to Wales with his American friend Vaughan Morgan and was meant to go to Peru with him to devote himself to a career of public service. However, after a brief struggle with his conscience, he decides to stay in Wales and marry Myfanwy. The play closes with the birth of Shân's great-grandchild in Tŷ Mawr and Shân's peaceful death. At the heart of the play, though, is the symbolic struggle between Dafydd Evans y Beddau, the local gravedigger, a sinister figure who embodies the inevitability of death, and the sometimes joyful, sometimes painful force of life, emblematically personified by Shân and her family.

The Beaten Track diverges from Francis's previous serious plays, which had followed the model of the play of ideas of the 'new dramatists'. Its form and content are both realistic and symbolic. The *Western Mail*'s critic described the play thus: 'In "The Beaten Track" Mr. Francis has not been concerned with rendering the immediate environment of Welsh life in detail, the play being an attempt to use a Welsh medium for the treatment of certain fundamental human issues common to all peoples'.[52] D. T. Davies concurred:

> 'The Beaten Track' is the way of all flesh – the much trodden and tortuous highway that runs from birth to death. It is impossible to conceive a theme so saturated with universality, with that common appeal and general interest to mankind under all conditions and in all ages.[53]

While avoiding issues of an obviously political nature, the play is one of Francis's most avowedly nationalist plays, giving voice to Francis's mature notions of what he considered to be the constitutive elements of a nation and why it is worth defending. *The Beaten Track* continues an engagement with the importance of roots and tradition for the continued survival of the nation, which he had begun in his essays. 'Tradition' has no precise definition and cannot be grasped intellectually, being made up of more or less formalized customs. Politics is of the moment but tradition is timeless. Tradition knits communities together and connects people to place and thus forms the basis from which culture can grow.

Francis's conception of tradition and of people living by their traditions is similar to Yeats's idealized portrait of the Irish peasant who views the world without political blinkers and for whom the speed of modern life has no meaning, thus implicitly rejecting the Modernist preoccupation with time and speed and placing his faith in the seemingly ancient, ever-present place:

> His thoughts are not organised. He is not a reformer. All the collective opinions created by young Ireland and those that came after have left him untouched. He sees to-day as he saw centuries ago, and he preserves to-day the old legends, the old songs, and above all he has his beautiful dialect of English. . . .[54]

This character is recalled in R. S. Thomas's Iago Prydderch some forty years later, although Prydderch is flawed and the reader's invited response to him is more complex than an audience's response to Francis's characters Shân Powell and Dafydd Evans y Beddau. They embody age-old principles: the mother and death. Their exchanges have a ritualized air about them:

> DAFYDD EVANS: You have had your troubles.
>
> SHÂN: Full of the cup.
>
> DAFYDD EVANS: You say I have taken much.
>
> SHÂN: You have not even left me tears.
>
> DAFYDD EVANS: Sometimes I give, Shân Powell.

SHÂN: Give? What is there for you to give?

DAFYDD EVANS: Rest. (p. 21)

His voice is alternately seductive and patient and all characters except Shân are terrified of him. There is a sense that none will escape him. In D. T. Davies's words he is

> one of the most unique creations that have yet appeared in Welsh drama. He is a symbol rather than a being of flesh and blood, utterly impersonal, incapable of love, hate, sorrow, or pity. He merely waits for those who come along the beaten track, the embodiment of an unvarying, inflexible, natural law. Dafydd is the sombre, even sinister background against which the author has grouped his characters; they derive all values of tone and perspective from him.[55]

Indeed, without the sinister presence of Dafydd, the main plot would have been merely sentimental. With Dafydd in the background, Owen's homecoming acquires profundity and transcends the immediate concerns of the characters in important ways: first, it is a realistic representation of the struggle of rural communities to remain viable despite depopulation and the threat of unsympathetic new settlers who do not understand the village's moods and traditions. Secondly, the play enacts a conception of family that goes beyond the nuclear family. It is about the link between family, community and land. It is a play about the importance of rootedness, about the emotional and sustaining impact of being part of a living, active community, which must lie at the heart of a love of one's nation if it is to be more than rhetoric. Simone Weil has noted:

> To be rooted is perhaps the most important and least recognised need of the human soul. It is one of the hardest to define. A human being has roots by virtue of his real, active and natural participation in the life of a community which preserves in living shape certain particular treasures of the past and certain particular expectations for the future. This participation is a natural one, in the sense that it is automatically brought about by place, conditions of birth, profession and social surroundings. Every human being needs to have multiple roots. It is necessary for him to draw wellnigh the whole of his moral, intellectual and spiritual life by way of the environment of which he forms a natural part.[56]

Owen is immediately integrated into the community in Cwm y Môr. He is valued for himself and for the concrete things he can do to help the community survive: very soon after his arrival he finds himself attending eisteddfodau and judging sheepdog trials as if he had always been part of the community. Against this, his vague career plans in far-away Peru pale into insignificance, partly because they never were particularly concrete in his mind and partly because he could not be a part of the community in the same way there.

Homecoming also means accepting a role as defender of the community. The multi-generational family and the family house form the backbone of the rural community without which it threatens to disintegrate completely. Injecting life into the house by moving in and starting a family is a victory of life over death. It is thus that patriotism becomes a concrete rather than an abstract notion as it had been in *Cross-Currents*. As Owen falls in love with Myfanwy, he also falls in love with Cwm y Môr:

SHÂN (hesitating): Is it – like home? (. . .)

OWEN: I've been happy here, Mamgu – very happy.

SHÂN: Why, Owen?

OWEN (*his glance straying towards MYFANWY*): For many reasons (. . .) I like these old hills and the valleys running down to the sea. I like the white cottages. I like the singing. I like it all. And, though it may sound queer to you, I'm strangely drawn by those graves of ours behind Caersalem. (p. 45)

Owen's references to the graves indicate a deeper sense of rootedness. He includes the dead members of the family in his vision, which symbolizes a victory of life over death and over Dafydd, the patient Stygian ferryman, in whose gift lies 'rest', meaning forgetfulness, and under whose watch things come to an inevitable end.

The play is powerful in a way that is difficult to capture in a summary. But there are weaknesses. For example, as D. T. Davies had pointed out in his review, it is at no time really in doubt that Owen will stay in Cwm y Môr. Vaughan Morgan marshals some powerful arguments, accusing him of wasting his talent that could have been devoted to 'a career of true service', crying: 'As if there's no higher purpose for humanity than to go on breeding like so many rabbits' (p. 62). However, 'the dice are loaded in Shân's favour' and Vaughan quickly fades into the background.[57] The potentially very interesting Vaughan Morgan remains a pale character and the extent and motivation of his friendship with Owen is unclear – a friendship that may be of a homoerotic or perhaps homosocial nature. Vaughan is described as being stern except when he looks at Owen, when '*his attitude softens, as if at the prompting of an affection, as profound as it is restrained*' (p. 28). Seemingly one-sided, Vaughan's friendship, which we may recall is an Aristotelian virtue in itself, is also soon dispensed with in the play, Francis seemingly preferring a heterosexual romance plot – perhaps because the play was written for amateur dramatic companies.

In its emphasis on bloodlines and the emotional pull that the land exerts over the members of the family, even though one of them has never before set foot in Wales, the play displays an essentialism that deservedly became suspect after the atrocities committed in the Third Reich in Germany and during the Second World War. It is not entirely clear whether the 'new settlers' in the play are uncommitted to the village or whether they are excluded. Characters have remarkably little choice when it comes to the issue of belonging and more elective affinities, including friendship, are painted as markedly less important than kinship ties and 'tradition'. The way Owen's previous life, career, and friendships are simply switched off and cease to count once he arrives in Wales, and the manner of his apparently completely unproblematic reconnection with the homeland of his father must be regarded as flaws of the play.

The Beaten Track had an inauspicious beginning but then developed into one of Francis's most popular full-length plays. Its premiere at the Theatre Royal, Pontypool, on 7 August 1924, and the two matinee performances that followed were timed to coincide with that year's National Eisteddfod in Pontypool. Francis himself was producer and director and it was performed by a London-Welsh amateur theatre company, including Jano Clement-Davies, who had acted in the original productions of D. T. Davies's *Ble Ma Fa?*, and John Edwards, who had been in the original casts of Francis's *The Poacher* and D. T. Davies's *Y Pwyllgor*. Unfortunately, audiences were 'absurdly small as the organisers of the Eisteddfod seem to have been unwilling to consider the play as part of the Eisteddfod performances'.[58] This meant that audience members were not allowed free readmission to the Eisteddfod grounds if they had left in order to see the play. The venture, which was part-financed by the author, seems to have been a financial disaster. Given Francis's standing as a playwright in the 1920s, the attitude of the Eisteddfod authorities make little sense unless they are seen as proof of the increasing separation of the English-language and Welsh-language cultures of Wales. Francis wrote a long, appreciative article about the Eisteddfod apparently without rancour[59] but the editor of *The Welsh Outlook* was angry on his behalf and accused the Eisteddfod authorities of pettiness: 'It is perfectly obvious from all the reports that we have received, that officially, the Eisteddfod authorities did nothing to assist in [the play's] success, being mainly concerned with the financial fortunes of the big show which they were running'.[60]

After this difficult beginning, *The Beaten Track* became a popular choice for amateur theatre companies. Apart from *Change* it was Francis's only play to have been performed on New York's Broadway. It opened on 8 February 1926 at the Frolic Theatre and had a respectable run of seventeen performances. The BBC Home Service gave a Broadcast Performance of the play on 12 February 1931. A stock-taking note at Samuel French shows that the play averaged about five performances a year between 1944 and 1948 before the play went out of print.[61] It must still have been produced in the 1950s: Francis renewed the copyright of the play in 1953, protecting the rights to his work until 1982.[62]

Francis's trajectory seems to have taken him away from the realism of *Change* and towards a more symbolic mode. His mid-career work was no longer wedded to the near-naturalistic realism of the 'play of Welsh life', although it remained largely realistic. The type of drama he had helped to pioneer was established in the late 1920s. Indeed, a play whose only merit was that it depicted a 'slice of Welsh life' in the manner of Jeannette Marks, for example, would now have been roundly condemned by critics, whereas it would have been cautiously praised ten years earlier. Francis's serious mid- to late-career plays took a Welsh setting and used it as a springboard for the presentation of universal themes, which emerged from their Welsh setting in an organic way. *The Beaten Track* was a play about the importance of roots, of tradition and of community. *Howell of Gwent* deals with the choice between duty and love and *The Devouring Fire* is about ambition and loyalty.

Francis's move towards a more symbolic drama places him closer to younger writers like A. O. Roberts and Richard Hughes. The setting for A. O. Roberts's powerful one-act play *Cloudbreak* (1924) is a cottage interior very similar to those in Synge's plays. The plot revolves around a very poor couple, which tries to find a little money to put in the chapel collection on Christmas Eve. The woman is desperate enough to invoke Satan and ask him for the money. When some money suddenly appears she takes fright and begs her husband to get rid of it. A mysterious stranger arrives and we infer that he is Judas who is in search of the thirty pieces of silver that he must gather together so that he may be forgiven. The woman gives him her evil coin. The beggar vanishes and the woman concludes gratefully: 'It was a messenger from God. God sent him here to save me'.[63] Form and the theme of the play recall late Victorian plays like the influential *The Intruder* (*L'Intruse*, 1890) by the Belgian writer Maurice Maeterlink as well as those of the Irish National Theatre Company. Ifan Kyrle Fletcher thought that Roberts's play 'rank[ed] with the plays of the great Irish movement' and asked whether Wales had 'a producer . . . of sufficient daring to put aside the drawing-room or back-kitchen style of acting, and to stage "Cloudbreak" worthily, as a complete expression of the mind of the woman'.[64]

Richard Hughes located a tale about the morality of mercy-killing in a Welsh setting – a setting that is, however, much less specific than that of *Cloudbreak*. *The Sisters' Tragedy* was first performed privately at the house of the English poet and later Poet Laureate John Masefield on 24 January 1922. It received its first public performance at the London Little Theatre on 31 May 1922 where it ran for twenty-nine performances until 24 June 1922. Its action is strongly reminiscent of the claustrophobic decadence of Chekhov's *The Cherry Orchard* (1904), although this short one-act play moves much more quickly. The three sisters, the adult Philippa and Charlotte, the teenager Lowrie and their deaf and mute brother Owen live in a run-down Victorian mansion in 'the Welsh hills'.[65] The characters are described as 'slovenly in appearance, suggesting a family possibly of county origin but for at least a generation impoverished and isolated and uneducated'.[66] The fifth character is John, Charlotte's fiancé, 'who is quite obviously of a lower social class than the sisters, though they do not appear to see it; which completes the general air of running to seed'.[67]

The play poses the question whether it can ever be right to kill someone if that person's life is not worth living. Having watched her sister Charlotte kill a rabbit that had been mauled by a cat, Lowrie asks herself whether she ought to kill her brother Owen, as he stops her sisters from living independent lives and, in Charlotte's case, getting married because he requires constant care. Her first attempt to smother him fails because Owen unexpectedly fights for his life. She then leads him to the mill pond outside the house where he drowns. Her world falls to pieces when her sisters do not rejoice but grieve, and, after she has confessed, regard her with utter horror. John walks out, vowing never to return. The moral point is, of course, that all human lives are worth living, a pointed criticism of the eugenics movement of the time. Lowrie cannot bear the burden of her guilt and goes mad at the end of the play.

The three plays share a symbolic mode in a realistic setting. The fact that critics regarded Francis as a national playwright but did not apply that epithet to Roberts or to Hughes was perhaps influenced by Francis's record as a playwright but also by the organic link between landscape and characters in *The Beaten Track*. By contrast, *The Sisters' Tragedy* and, to a lesser extent, *Cloudbreak* could have employed a different setting without loss of meaning. By the late 1920s and early 1930s, Francis was considered an established writer, a safe choice, whereas Hughes was more modern, more daring, which was probably why the Welsh National Theatre Company used Hughes's *A Comedy of Good and Evil* (1924) for their first production in London and Francis's *Howell of Gwent* and Saunders Lewis's translation of the Molière comedy *Le Medécin malgré lui* (1666), *Doctor er ei Waethaf*, for their second production at the proclamation for the National Eisteddfod at Gnoll Hall in Neath.

The year 1933 is usually remembered as the year that saw the memorable performance of *Pobun*, the Welsh translation of the English morality play *Everyman* under the direction of the Austrian director Dr Stefan Hock at the National Eisteddfod at Wrexham. But 1933 was also the year in which the new Welsh National Theatre Company staged its first performances. The 1914 movement had failed when war broke out and in 1932 another attempt at establishing a national theatre company was made. It was to be a professional touring company, which would perform plays throughout Wales and in London. Lord Howard de Walden was once again happy to provide financial backing, but the driving force of the new company was the actor Evelyn Bowen, the organizing secretary, and Meriel Williams, another actor. De Walden eventually gave the national theatre a home at Plas Newydd in Llangollen but the new company saw the light of day in London, which caused a few eyebrows to be raised. D. R. Davies wrote:

> Whether this latest and more definite attempt to make of the movement a symbol of the national significance of the theatre will meet with the success it so richly deserves is perhaps a matter of speculation for, even though perfectly feasible, explanations have been made by Miss Evelyn Bowen and others, some sections of the community in Wales do not feel enamoured of a national project which had its genesis on the other side of Offa's Dyke.[68]

One of the raised eyebrows belonged to Francis, who was happy to support the Welsh National Drama Company by serving on its board of advisors, but who was uneasy about the fact that it was not located in Wales. He wrote in a letter to D. R. Davies in 1932:

> The organising Secretary, Miss Evelyn Bowen, is a friend of mine, keenly anxious to do something towards getting Welsh drama onto a more solid foundation. Between ourselves, I, as you do, see certain weaknesses in the scheme in its present form. Miss Bowen is, however, a very sensible person + realises that where necessary, she will have to adjust her plans to the facts – since the facts won't adjust themselves to people's plans. I have been giving Miss Bowen some advice out of what is now, I suppose, a pretty extensive experience of the Welsh Drama Movement. I have specially stressed – + she has readily seen – the basic need for linking anything she does with the existing amateur companies. . . . My own feeling is (+ this is for you as an individual

– not as a journalist) that it would have been better to begin the scheme down in Wales rather than here in London.[69]

The new Welsh National Theatre Company was placed in a context that was totally different from that of the first national drama company in 1914. Its aim could no longer simply be to provide an opportunity to see realistic Welsh plays and to encourage the first, tentative production of drama. By 1930 hundreds of amateur theatre companies had established themselves and whole shelves had been filled with more or less successful Welsh plays. The nature of the plays performed was changing. Evelyn Bowen was right when she proclaimed that amateur dramatic companies were 'bored by the narrowness of the life depicted in the Welsh plays' and 'were now producing West End successes instead'.[70] There seems to have been an established career trajectory from Welsh amateur theatre to the professional stage in London, which opened up the possibility to recruit professional actors for the new national theatre company. The choice to have the first production in the Arts Theatre Club on 26 January 1933 in London and the second one on 7 July 1933 in Wales was made for reasons of convenience. As Evelyn Bowen explained, most professional actors had engagements in London during the theatrical season and were unable to commit to several performances in Wales.[71] In this context the choice of the plays for the two first performances of the new company is remarkable. Evelyn Bowen suggested that, when it came to the theatre, Wales had 'no cultural centre' and was, therefore, inclined to look towards London for direction.[72] And so the more innovative play was staged in London and the more traditional play by an established writer was performed in Neath.

Richard Hughes's *A Comedy of Good and Evil* was first performed at the Royal Court Theatre on 6 July 1924 for the Three Hundred Club, a society dedicated to the performance of plays of literary merit that merged with the Stage Society in 1926, and a second time at the Ambassador's Theatre, Oxford, on 30 March 1925. It concerns a poor couple, the Reverend John Williams and his wife Minnie. They are visited by a fairy-child, Gladys, a theme borrowed from Yeats's *The Land of Heart's Desire* (1894), in which the arrival of a fairy-child causes havoc in a rural Irish household. Here, the couple receives the child into their house, but no evil befalls them. At the End of Act II, the fishmonger Owen Flatfish arrives to exorcise the evil spirit and Gladys flees for a while, but eventually returns. John Williams dies and Act III is preoccupied with the question whether he will go to heaven as he invited evil into his house of his own free will. However, it is clear that it was not the exorcism but the Williams's true Christian charity that made Gladys unable to commit any evil act.

The setting is realistic: '[a] rather poky little Welsh kitchen: ugly and spotless; full of furniture – varnished deal with a mixture of a little good old oak. . . . Books, photographs, and illuminated certificates (Welsh) in incredible numbers'.[73] The characters are drawn realistically, too, and Hughes makes an attempt at a language appropriate to this location. He is fastidious in his stage directions, consciously differentiating himself from Caradoc Evans:

> The accent is that of the South Snowdon district. The dialect is not intended for a translation of Welsh idiom, but for the English spoken, when occasion demands, by Welsh-speaking country people. Thus it varies considerably according to the speaker's education, and at its most fluent naturally approximates to written rather than spoken English.[74]

That he was not quite successful can be gleaned from Francis's review referred to in chapter 1, in which he suggests that Hughes would achieve a more realistic representation of Welsh English speech if he learnt the basics of spoken Welsh.

What is fascinating is the use of English received pronunciation by the changeling child Gladys, which serves to underline her alien strangeness. However, it seems significant that an intrusive, malignant and yet ultimately unsuccessful spirit should speak the King's English. The play may thus argue for a charitable reception of English intruders in the heartland of Welsh culture, which might render their potentially negative influence null and void, rather than a response that seeds to 'exorcise' any foreign elements.

Predictably, the more conservative members of the audience were disappointed when they saw *A Comedy of Good and Evil*. The play did not refer to the nation directly, it was symbolic rather than realistic, and it addressed abstract ethical issues rather than social, political or historical ones. The Special Correspondent for the *Western Mail* wrote:

> The organisers of the Welsh National Theatre cannot be commended for their choice of Mr. Richard Hughes's play, 'Comedy of Good and Evil'. It is not Welsh in spirit or design and does not give opportunities for the display of emotional acting as one would expect from a company of Welsh players. . . . [T]he general impression among the Welsh section of the audience was that if the Welsh national theatre movement is to succeed, there must be something more essentially Welsh, both in the players and in the play.[75]

It seems that this reviewer had hoped to see another *Change* and got something entirely different. But this view was not universally shared. In a letter to the editor of the *Western Mail*, John Glyn Roberts vigorously disagreed that the audience had been disappointed.[76] However, J. Eddie Parry noted that *A Comedy of Good and Evil*, whatever its literary merits, 'would decidedly "flop" in Wales' being 'alien to every acceptable canon of dramatic art in Wales'.[77] *Howell of Gwent*, sub-titled *A Romantic Drama*, on the other hand, conformed to expectations. And yet it also represented a decided departure from the realism of *Change* and *Cross-Currents*.

HOWELL OF GWENT (1932)

Howell of Gwent was Francis's first attempt to write a historical romance and thus provide a national setting for a play in which emotions, not ideas, are at the centre of the action. It was also openly nationalistic, arguing that the fight for national self-determination is an honourable one regardless of whether it is ultimately successful. Moreover, the struggle is located in Gwent, a county not usually identified with a particularly strong sense of Welsh identity.

The play is set in the early Middle Ages. The Normans are controlling parts of Wales and have driven the Welsh into the hills. The play opens when the lesser lords of Gwent have just decided to bury their differences in order to be able to marshal their forces against the Normans. Their union is reinforced through strategic marital alliances: Lord Cadvan's two daughters have married the lords Griffith ap Ivor and Red Morgan to guarantee the peace. Cadvan has also called back the exiled Howell ap Meredith so that he may begin a revolt to overthrow Norman rule. Howell arrives and seems keen to begin his task but faces two obstacles: one is Cadvan's son Idwal, who has turned traitor out of thwarted ambition. When his treachery emerges, Cadvan kills him. The second obstacle is more difficult to overcome: Howell and Cadvan's daughter Gwyneth fall in love – an impossible situation as Gwyneth is married to Griffith ap Ivor. Howell almost gives up the struggle in order to flee with Gwyneth. However, in an emotional scene, Cadvan persuades Gwyneth to put her duty to her country above her feelings and she drowns herself in Ceridwen Pool. The play closes as a distraught Howell dedicates his struggle to her memory and is about to begin the fight for freedom.

Howell of Gwent explicitly addresses the fate of a conquered nation. Colonial oppression by the Normans leads to divisiveness and needless infighting among the lesser lords of Gwent, who pathetically cling to their grievances and do not present a united front. Moreover, the pillage and rape of the country is symbolized by Norman de Granville's desire to abduct Cadvan's daughter Gwyneth – something forestalled by Howell's intervention. The justice of the revolt is never in question and this makes Gwyneth's self-sacrifice all the more moving.

The way the themes of love and death are explored render the play unrealistic. The fact that Cadvan kills his only son and stands back when his favourite daughter is about to commit suicide does not mean he is a moral monster but that we are to interpret his actions as symbolizing the magnitude of the sacrifices required by the nationalist cause. Romantic love had never figured centrally in any of Francis's plays before and was not to do so again.[78] Love is understood as a powerful, irresistible but also excessive force, which is at odds with the characters' public duty. Howell's principal virtue in the play is courage, but he is propelled off the path of virtue by love. Turning his back on love is presented as the only way for him to be virtuous again.

Like many of Francis's plays, *Howell of Gwent* includes strong female characters who actively decide their fate and that of other characters. Gwyneth is not forced to commit suicide – it is her decision. Her decision compels Howell to act and thus indirectly determines the future of the nation. The play also contains a character Francis was to develop in *The Devouring Fire*, namely the prophetic mother, whose knowledge of the land and of history – of tradition, in other words – gives her a deeper insight into human nature and lends her speech a portentous tone ('Your future is yet for weaving. You have this beauty. It was your gift once. Now it is your burden. I am of Mona, Gwyneth. Men say the old wisdom lingers there. As I look at you I am troubled. Take care, my daughter').[79] In moments like these the break with realism is most obvious. Francis invokes a timeless character: the mother as wise woman and seer, as Cassandra, who foresees disaster but can do nothing to avert it.

A familiar theme is that of homecoming, which is dealt with in a rather more believable way than in *The Beaten Track*. Howell ap Meredith finds homecoming problematic at first and says: 'I've not set foot in this Princedom for thirty years. So what is Gwent to me more than any other stretch of good country?' (p. 29). At the beginning, he is merely interested in increasing his power ('Now – it is princedom for myself. I hunger for it and must have it; and I care nothing whether it comes by the right hand or by the left.' p. 30). Like Owen Morgan, though, Howell comes to love Gwent through loving one of its daughters. And, like Owen, the connection to the land allows him to be aware of his link to its history:

> GWYNETH: No more exile! Now – bright summer – you make a happy return. Gwent wears all her beauty now.

HOWELL: I find more than beauty.

GWYNETH: More?

HOWELL: This voice of yesterdays.

GWYNETH: It moves you?

HOWELL: Strangely. It tells me I have been homeless. Something in me is taking root here. (p. 45)

When Gwyneth dies, her spirit seems to merge with the land, allowing Howell to fulfil his mission.

For all its dramatic scenes, the play is strangely static and inconsistent in its use of realistic and non-realistic elements. Characters use an everyday register, but there are no traces of dialect or local accent and some of the dialogue has a stilted, declamatory air and may have accompanied a histrionic acting style. The only other play in which Francis used language in a similar way was *The Crowning of Peace* (1922), a pageant, and thus an entirely different type of play. The set design and the medieval costumes of the actors were entirely unrealistic. It was this mixture of realism and non-realism that 'A Welsh M.A.' found irritating. Writing that the subject of the play would have lent itself to a more highly stylized diction and acting, he notes that the play

> kept on dissipating the dramatic effect. . . . The homeliness of the speech, the irritating clichés, the melodramatic imprecations, persistently 'let us down,' assorting so ill with the very unrealistic background and the remote, barbaric sumptuousness of the costumes and the general décor.[80]

He continued, perhaps to be controversial: 'Oh, for a nationalist brave enough to declare that, for all its weaknesses, there are more genuinely literary qualities in Caradoc Evans's "Wasps" than, for all its virtues and admirable intentions, in "Howell of Gwent"'.[81]

His protest, however, was drowned out in a general outburst of critical acclaim. J. Eddie Parry considered the performance in Neath a 'decided success' and suggested that the 'play has power and a certain dignity which categorises great drama and to me it suggests itself as a theme for a grand opera libretto'.[82] The *Western Mail*'s drama critic wrote fulsomely about the performance in Cardiff:

> If he has not written plays in the Welsh language he has dealt with Welsh characters, life, and history in a masterly manner, and his latest is his greatest. . . . [T]here is not a false note or doubtful situation in the tragedy, which moves as relentlessly as fate to its final solution.[83]

Reviews like this affirmed Francis's status as a national playwright. The play's demands on an elaborate wardrobe and setting put it outside the range of most amateur companies and it was rarely performed. An exception was its premiere: it was staged by the University College of Wales, Aberystwyth's Drama Club at the university on 15 December 1932. It is clearly a play that is more appropriate for the professional stage, particularly as the roles require considerable acting skill so as not to render them false or ridiculous.

THE DEVOURING FIRE (1953?)

Howell of Gwent remained Francis's only historical full-length play. Indeed, he did not write any serious plays for some time. It is likely that he was fully occupied by the political events in the later 1930s, which would have required his full attention as Publicity Officer for the National Savings Committee. Whatever the reason, Francis wrote few plays during this time and those he wrote were comedies, often one-act plays, aimed at the numerous amateur theatre companies that had sprung up throughout Wales. However, he did write more substantial plays in the 1950s, none of which, sadly, seem to have been published or produced. Among them is a play that is one of his best: *The Devouring Fire*, a tragedy set in the south Wales valleys.

The play was probably finished by the middle of 1953. Francis sent it to Aneirin Talfan Davies, who played a key role as a supporter of Welsh writing in English in the BBC in Wales and – ever the assiduous self-promoter – assured him that the actor

> Hugh Griffith [had] read the play at [an] earlier stage and seemed to like it very much. (He's since mentioned it to me more than once.) Clifford Evans, too, read it at that stage but not till after he'd finished producing at Swansea for the Arts Council. He told me that, had the play come to him while he was in charger there, he'd have put it in.[84]

Remembering the difficulties surrounding *Cross-Currents* and *Howell of Gwent*, he added a disclaimer: 'I'm afraid that the play is anyhow a very tough proposition for Welsh amateur players: that's the immediate point on which I shall be glad to have your opinion'.[85] Unfortunately, Davies's response is not preserved, but Francis was right in his assessment of the play's requirements. Its theme is universal: *The Devouring Fire* is about the political ambitions of a trade union leader and the claims of his community, and it is a play committed to a land ethic much like Aldo Leopold's discussed in the introduction. Contrary to *Cross-Currents*, however, this is not a play in which different political opinions are merely discussed. It is a profoundly theatrical play with thoroughly modern stage craft, including sound effects like the pit hooter, whose 'sound comes crashing into the room' in Act II, and shocks the characters into silence.[86] The play shows evidence of mature craftsmanship and unites the strengths of Francis's previous stage works to create an emotionally and intellectually powerful play.

The main character is Caleb Morgan, the secretary of the Miners' Lodge in the Penymaes Pit in Upper Calog. He has ambitions to outgrow the confines of valley politics and to become an MP, thus following the career trajectory of real-life politicians like Aneurin Bevan, who had left his native Tredegar for London in 1929. His political concerns make him blind to his brother Griffith's grim warnings that 'there's danger in our pit' (p. I. 5). He constantly speaks of escaping the 'backwater' of his village (p. I. 7), of escaping all familial and local ties. His feelings towards the people he represents as secretary of the Miners' Lodge and afterwards as Miners' Agent is affection mixed with impatient contempt. When the carrot of a parliamentary seat is dangled in front of his nose by the MP Evan Powell, he senses a possible escape only to be confronted with a serious pit accident. Thinking with some justification that the neglected issue of security in the pit is his fault, he throws himself into the recovery effort and truly becomes the leader he set out to be. Feeling personally responsible for every man buried alive, he overtaxes his strength. Finally the news comes that seventy men have died an agonizingly slow death, among them Caleb's father Daniel and his brother Ezra. Caleb's spirit breaks and, unable to cope with his guilt, he commits suicide. The play is given an ending reminiscent of *Change* as Caleb's mother Sara is given the last words. Looking at the mountains surrounding the valley she says: 'Bryn Arthur, Bryn yr Hebog, Mynydd Mawr – they're still the masters here. They make us pay them their price in the end – pay the full price!' (III. 40).

The set is a realistic rendering of a miner's house in the south Wales valleys. The furnishings are simple but not poor, and amenities of the 1950s, such as electric light and a telephone make this a modern-looking setting. The language used is less representative of a south Wales valleys dialect than that used in his earlier plays. With the exception of a few interspersed Welsh words such as *bach* or *modryb*, whose meaning is explained in the dialogue ('I like to call Aunt Sara modryb in the Welsh way', p. I. 8), the characters speak a perhaps accented RP. The lack of local dialect seems to be a step backwards compared with the phonetic realism of the earlier plays. Francis may have chosen to create less localized speech because he had not lived in Wales for over forty years by the time he wrote *The Devouring Fire* and did not want to presume that the memory of his boyhood speech still reflected a contemporary 1950s valleys idiom. However, he might also have decided not to make his speech dialectal for commercial reasons: he evidently wanted to write a play that was not targeted at amateur dramatic companies – a weighty and serious play on the universal themes of ambition and moral responsibility – while setting it in a recognizably Welsh locality. The play was not necessarily meant for production in south Wales – otherwise Francis would not have thought it necessary to explain terminology like *firedamp* by means of lengthy exposition.

The community described was recognizable from the earlier plays but suitably updated to reflect a 1950s reality. Caleb's father Daniel is a lay preacher and Sunday school teacher as well as a collier. His brother Ezra is 'a studious looking fellow in his early thirties' (p. I. 9), who has signed up for university extension lectures and, at the beginning of the play, has just returned from the Miners' Library with an armful of books including *New Aspects of Industrial Organisations* for Caleb and a book on astronomy for himself, thus effectively characterizing the two dissimilar brothers. Ezra also confirms the well-known stereotype of the Welsh working-class respect for education. Indeed, Francis is careful to portray his working-class characters in as positive a light as he can without becoming unrealistic: Rachel, who becomes engaged to Caleb during the second Act, and Sara, Caleb's mother, are typical hard-working Welsh women waging war on the ever-present dirt from the pit – Welsh mam and Welsh mam-in-training. Only Uncle Timothy is less than well behaved: he likes spending his time in the pub, particularly on 'Saturday evening – the collier's paradise'. His transgressions are harmless, though, and provide humour through pithy one-liners ('I've never had much patience with the half pint men. They're just trifling with a serious subject', p. II. 4).

Where *Cross-Currents* had displayed a lack of confidence in politics because of the demands of party loyalty, the London-focus of the main political parties and the petty corruption in local politics, *The Devouring Fire* goes further and reveals a deep dissatisfaction with politicians and the hypocrisy they display in order to retain old and win over new voters. As a Miners' Lodge official on the make, Caleb is careful to attend chapel and arranges his meetings at a time that does not interfere with chapel services – not out of piety, however, but to attract and reassure voters. Equally distasteful is the way politics makes decent men so hungry for power that they forget everything around them. Rachel takes her future husband to task in the following terms: 'You've got one great driving force in you, one only – it's your ambition' (p. II. 27).

The significant shift between *Change*, *Cross-Currents* and *The Devouring Fire* is that characters in the early plays are powerless in the face of the forces that shape society. The most dignified position they can occupy is that of the academic, the thinker, who considers these social forces from a safe distance. *The Devouring Fire* is about the struggles of a character who finds himself in a situation that he seems to be master of but that he suddenly can no longer control. His hubris and his blind ambition constitute his tragic flaws. Caleb Morgan is the most striking tragic hero in Francis's oeuvre.

The female characters in *The Devouring Fire* show spirit and determination even if the life goals of a girl like Jessie Morgan do not go beyond being a good collier's wife, thus reflecting the social mores of the 1950s. Yet, the women in the play are anything but passive. It is Sara Morgan who warns in prophetic tones of the revenge of nature on the presumptions of man. The women will not be relegated to a position of ignorance. Jessie argues that 'the more you men try to hide the facts from us the more we will talk. We're not just a lot of dumb rabbits, Caleb' (p. II. 7). Even in matters of love, they prove to be more active than the male characters think. Rachel reassures her future husband Caleb, who worries about having spent the night with her before they were married, by saying

> [s]ome of you men don't quite know how to behave towards women. You're either too bold or not as bold as we'd like you to be – we've got to take the lead.... I'm the real sinner, Caleb. I drew you on.... I felt it would bring you that much nearer to being my husband – and it has. (pp. II. 27–8)

The play shifts to the female sphere when seeking to express a whole community's terror of pit accidents. Locating the action off-stage is an ancient method of avoiding overly complex action on stage but it also effectively heightens tension as the audience is just as excluded from the action as the characters are. Significantly, the women's fear is perfectly reasonable, while the importance that Caleb and Griffith attach to votes, posts and committees is ultimately shown to be delusional and self-defeating. As Rachel points out to Caleb: 'Yes, coal industry, mass meetings, people in a mass – you understand all about that. But when it comes to ordinary living, to downright flesh and blood day by day, you've got a lot to learn yet' (p. II. 28). The women may be in thrall to the stereotype of the 1950s homemaker but they make their presence felt.

The pit explosion is seen as nature's revenge on the greed of capitalist men who seek to exploit both the earth and each other for quick gain. The community is dominated by the three mountains that surround it: Bryn Arthur, Bryn yr Hebog and Mynydd Mawr. They are imagined as literally surrounding the stage with Bryn Arthur stage-right, Bryn yr Hebog on the other side of the valley and Mynydd Mawr ominously facing the stage and situated, as it were, behind the audience. This landscape is an active element in the play. Even though Francis always defended the mining profession as an honourable one, the mining industry is here presented as unnatural and certain to lead to nature revenging itself. Sara Morgan feels the strength of the hills most acutely:

> SARA: As I came down the path I stood for a moment on that wooden bridge over Nant Bach. And as I listened – listened there in that silence I used to know so well – it was as if I could hear the hills breathing around me. These streets, these pitheads, noise piled on noise – it's wrong, I tell you! It's all wrong!
>
> CALEB (A little uneasy): This is your mountain mood again.
>
> SARA: It was my mother's mood. She couldn't bear to see pits being sunk here. I remember that day she stood looking down at the valley. I was only a slip of a girl but I've never forgotten the words she spoke then. 'The strangers have come in,' she said. 'They've come to grab for wealth here, grab for power. They've come to tear at these living hills.' . . . 'The strangers,' she said, 'had better take care. I know these old hills. They give pain for pain.' (pp. I. 12–13)

The disaster becomes a symbolic act of cleansing revenge, which potentially also exonerates Caleb of his guilt, since the sin lies less in his negligence than in sinking the pit in the first place, although he compounds this initial error. The play is probably a less obviously environmental, anti-capitalist play than Ed Thomas's *Gas Station Angel* (1998), in which nature is shown to take spectacular revenge on the house of Wales. But it is suffused with the communalist vision based on an ethical relationship between place and people that characterizes most of Francis's work.

In the third programme of his series of radio talks entitled *National Drama in Wales*, Francis expressed much admiration for the plays of Tennessee Williams and Arthur Miller.[87] He also noted appreciatively how Arthur Miller, in *Death of a Salesman*, was prepared to break the realistic illusion by his use of flexible stage space:

> And what Mr. Miller does with the apron stage is most interesting. He makes characters come on to it, carrying any furniture they need. They act scenes without any scenery. In the course of the play the apron stage is an office,

another office, a restaurant, a room in an hotel and a cemetery. By means of this apron stage the author has given himself a command of place and time that would be quite beyond him if he'd followed the standard practice in play building. Mr. Miller in fact puts the Elizabethan method of stage-presentation cheek by jowl with our modern realistic method.[88]

Even though he acknowledged that his plays are cast in an older mould, an argument can be made that, influenced by modern plays like those of Williams and Miller, Francis developed his stagecraft to use the stage imaginatively by depicting the imagined mountains as looming and threatening presences to which the characters respond in different ways.

To conclude, Francis's use of realism never simply re-inscribes a given reality in a politically neutral, apathetic or conservative way. I agree with Rachel Bowlby who has argued that 'realism can never be simply codeless in its claimed replication of reality (. . .). It is always presenting a particular theory of what will count as a picture of reality'.[89] *Change* was written at a time when an authentically realistic depiction of 'Welsh life' was in and of itself radical and thus, perforce, a political statement. The play created a dignified, noble reality for south-Walian working-class people that was far removed from prevalent stereotypes informed by images of strikes and industrial unrest. *Cross-Currents* was a discussion play about Welsh politics in the early 1920s, which took the discussion into north Wales, which had been considered by some to be immune from the social and political struggles of the south. And, once again, it did so by confidently treating the Welsh political scene as an example of the forces at work elsewhere in the UK. *The Beaten Track* and *Howell of Gwent* turned away from a too-literal realism, although they both kept a realistic idiom. But the reality that was now created was that of an independent, indomitable and unconquerable Welsh tradition, which had survived despite the odds and which would survive if people were prepared to struggle on. *The Devouring Fire*, finally, painted a realistic portrait of a south Wales family – both dignified and tortured like the family in *Change* – and created a powerful tragic hero in Caleb Morgan. Here Francis's use of realism mirrored the change from the naturalism of the new drama to the more symbolic realism of writers like Terence Rattigan, which would, in turn, be challenged by John Osborne's *Look Back in Anger* (1956). Taken as a whole, the plays express a distinctive ethics of place in which the relationship of characters and their environment is seen as central to the development of tradition and thus of identity. And the same ethical concerns are central to Francis's comedies, which are mostly set in pastoral locations. The next chapter will be concerned with an examination of these texts.

4

Poachers in Little Villages

When writing the 'Preface' to his collection of *Great Modern British Plays* (1929), J. W. Marriott noted the 'prevalence of comedy in this collection', commenting that 'comedy is, in fact, the characteristic type of modern drama'.[1] Marriott ascribes this to the nature of the 'Englishman', who 'has a laughing mind and is an amateur of humour'.[2] While this interpretation is obviously inadequate, the fact certainly stands that comic plays were (and still are) immensely popular throughout the British Isles. The amateur drama companies active in south Wales in the first decades of the twentieth century also preferred comic plays to serious plays.[3] There was, thus, a large market for comic playwriting and Francis's output – his comic plays outnumber his serious plays by a factor of 2:1 – reflects that. He wrote some thirteen comic plays in all, of which at least eight were one-act plays. Seven out of the thirteen plays feature the loveable rogue characters Dicky Bach Dwl and Twm Tinker and there is something about the way the same themes are reworked in the later plays, notably *His Shining Majesty* and *Hunting the Hare*, which suggests that Francis might have written them to please an audience. All his comedies, however, are original and particularly the plays involving Dicky Bach Dwl create a coherent world based on the close interrelationship between locality, culture and tradition. Moreover, some of them question stereotypical notions of national identity by interrogating prevailing assumptions about an ethics of place. In the following chapter a selection will be considered with a particular focus on the world created in *The Poacher*, Francis's most enduringly popular play. Before discussing the work, a brief look at the importance of the one-act play for the theatre landscape of the time will provide necessary contextual information.

THE ONE-ACT 'PLAY OF WELSH LIFE'

It is difficult today to get a sense of just how popular the one-act play was in the first half of the twentieth century. Hundreds were written every year and mainly performed on the amateur stage, a fact that, in J. W. Marriott's opinion, underlined the independence of the amateur stage outside London from the professional London stage.[4] The time of the one-act play's greatest popularity coincides with that of the short story, and, indeed, it can be described as bearing 'the same relation to the full-length play as the short-story shows to the novel. ... It aims to produce a single dramatic effect with the greatest economy of means that is consistent with the utmost emphasis'.[5] Like short stories, the best one-act plays are tightly structured. There tends to be little plot development and they are best described as 'dramatized anecdotes'. Although the one-act play has little scope for development, it can give a vivid and subtle portrayal of characters and the environment in which the play is set.[6] A typical example of the genre is Harold Chapin's Glasgow play *The Philosopher of Butterbiggins* (1915),[7] which focuses on an argument between John Bell and his daughter-in-law. The old man wants to tell his grandson a bedtime story but his daughter in law fears that this will spoil the boy. The argument goes back and forth until he outwits her in the end. The focus on local identity – shown by the setting and by the characters' dialectal speech – makes this a typical example of the 'Manchester school' of playwrights. The one-act 'play of Welsh life' closely resembles works like this, thus showing that ideas for dramatic writing crossed national borders easily, especially if, like Francis, playwrights lived outside Wales.

Welsh one-act plays published until 1940 are, as a rule, realistic in style and language, and portray everyday scenes of Welsh life. This meant that the choice of themes and subjects was curtailed: flights of fancy like Lord Dunsany's *The Flight of the Queen* (1920), whose 'theme [was] taken from the nuptial flight of the queen bee' and 'translated it into human terms'[8] and which is set in an unspecified exotic Far Eastern location, were impossible. The focus on contemporary Welsh life meant that there were few one-act plays about Welsh history or Welsh mythology. Nonconformist religion is inescapable: plays like D. T. Davies's *Ble Ma Fa?* (1914) and Jeannette Marks's *The Merry Merry Cuckoo* (1911) deal with morality and religion. However, religious themes are limited to religious practice in Wales and so plays like F. Sladen-Smith's *St Simeon Stylites* (1923),[9] a whimsical piece about a hermit, were not written or produced. Much more typical is the play of the Liverpool Welshman Rev. W. F. Phillips, *The Lost*

Legacy: A Play of Welsh Domestic Life (1918),[10] which was performed at the Liverpool Playhouse in 1918 and which deals with a familiar topic: the blindness and hypocrisy of chapel elders who are prepared to dismiss a solid member of their community, the treasurer of the chapel, because he has failed in business and lost all his money. In the end, poetic justice is served as the family fortuitously find the money of their deceased grandmother. It is a competent play, although its didactic moralizing may be too obtrusive for an audience today. It received a very positive review in *The Welsh Outlook* and it is worth looking at this review more closely to understand what made the one-act 'play of Welsh life' appealing to audiences and critics:

> The characters are simple Welsh village people of sturdy breed, the dialogue is the simple language they talk. The plot in skeleton too, is simplicity[11] itself, the story of difficulties and of the opportune discovery of the lost legacy. Yet the action is brisk and kaleidoscopic and not a moment is wasted; indeed the author seems to have denied himself all luxury of side-plays, and to have devoted all his dramatic power to the natural development of the simple action. Yet problems big and widespread are hinted at . . . This play is not pretentious – it is a simple drama of Welsh domestic life, but as such it is a rare achievement, and worthy of the best traditions of Welsh drama.[12]

The word 'simple' is repeated five times in this short review, showing what reviewers like W. D. P. valued: they wanted realistic drama focusing on 'Welsh domestic life', plays that conveyed a simple idea in a straightforward way. Simplicity meant authenticity: the illusion of direct access to the lives and cultural frames of reference of the characters. Complicated action, exotic settings and fantastic actions would have appeared alien and untrue.

The ethics of the 'play of Welsh life' can be described in terms of a presumed congruence of experience between action on stage and the everyday life of members of the audience. This is particularly true for the one-act plays, a great number of which were comedies. Authors were clearly influenced by the plays produced by the Irish Abbey Theatre, particularly by Lady Augusta Gregory's one-act plays.[13] Contemporary critics found in them 'depicted in charming fashion the life and manners of the simple Irish folk. Simple situations, "out-of-the-way episodes," single ideas, and few characters make up the effectiveness of each'.[14] Again, it is the 'simplicity' of the plays that was applauded. Similarly, J. M. Synge's *Riders to the Sea* was admired because it

> is, on the whole, simply an impression, but a powerful impression. In fact there is little to forget, because there is so little action. The illumination is

great just because there is no thesis, there is simply a transcendent picture of life. In even so short a compass the reader's experience is permanently enriched; he learns for the first time to know the commonplace of death in a community of fishermen; and he is purged by vicarious suffering.[15]

Schafer discusses the ethics of Synge's play in Aristotelian terms: ethical learning occurs through what Gregory Currie has described as an imaginative involvement with imagined action: readers (and, in this case, audiences) identify with and vicariously live through fictional characters.[16] Audiences learn by thus 'experiencing' new situations. Of course, ethical effect is not merely a matter of gaining new conceptual knowledge. It is also, as Carroll has argued, about deepening one's moral knowledge and one's sympathy by witnessing familiar situations in a different way. Additionally, gaining emotional knowledge is, according to Nussbaum, a necessary element of practical wisdom.[17] Empathizing with characters, identifying with them on an emotional level so that humour is shared, and recognizing the way plot and characters are 'implaced', helps audiences to develop emotional knowledge. In this way, the slight and simple one-act comedies of Lady Gregory and those of J. O. Francis in particular help to build community by strengthening a sense of 'us', which is sometimes pitted against 'them', official figures of authority, such as the police and the magistrate in Gregory's *Spreading the News*. Community drama affirms its own central tenets and reminds the audience about its own values, while, at times, gently criticizing them.

THE POACHER (1912)

The Poacher was one of the perennial favourites of amateur theatre in Wales. Samuel French's records show that the last time it was reprinted was 1972, sixty years after it was written.[18] The most recent performance of the play took place at Neath Little Theatre on 24 February 2011. The performance revealed that the play is exceedingly well structured, that the timing is perfect and that the humour of the play is universal. It offers plenty of opportunities for comic acting for actors of varying skill levels, and it allows audiences to identify and/or empathize with characters even after 100 years.

The central characters are Twmas Shôn, a man who has vowed to reform his character, and the tinker's apprentice Dicky Bach Dwl. Much to Dicky's disgust, Twmas has decided to give up poaching. At first his wife Marged is pleased but she soon realizes that not only did she prefer the old 'unreformed' Twmas as a husband but that her larder is now empty. The stage directions describe Dicky as '*young man in ragged clothes*', who '*is weak of wit*'. But, in '*the keenness of his senses and the quickness of his movements when excited*' shows '*a suggestion of the animal*'.[19] He is in his element when poaching and tries to persuade Twmas to go back to his old ways. The twist in the tale is that the deacon Dafydd Hughes, who presents a holier-than-thou facade to Twmas, is revealed to be a poacher himself. Twmas, who had given away the secret of how to catch the elusive rabbit 'Old Soldier' to Hughes, cannot bear the thought of Hughes catching it and the play finishes with Marged telling her daughter that she need not go to the butcher in the morning after all.

The most interesting character in *The Poacher* is undoubtedly Dicky Bach Dwl. Given the degree of influence he has over Twmas, the fluency with which he is able to conjure up the delights of poaching and his curious place half inside and half outside the community, an important question needs to be raised: how 'weak of wit' is Dicky exactly? And might 'weakness of wit' be a metaphor for the character's subversiveness?

Contemporary critics could not praise him enough. J. Eddie Parry thought he was 'a masterful creation',[20] and John D. Lewis described him likewise:

> 'Dicky' is a masterly creation, and although I have seen him played on the 'boards' on several occasions. I have never yet been satisfied with the wan, anæmic presentations of him that have been given. Too often actors are content to perform the part as if 'Dicky' were a country lout and nothing more. I have seen so-called 'polished,' but illiterate townspeople sniggering with joy at his apparent idiocy, and preening themselves like peacocks on their superior 'intelligence.' But what if they understood 'Dicky'? What if they perceived in him the elemental! . . . 'Dicky' is an interpreter of the fields, of the woods, and of the river.[21]

The other characters in the play belong to a typical Welsh village community, but Dicky is a true child of nature. The company of people is sometimes burdensome to him. '*He frequently falls into vacancy, and, sometimes, in his effort to follow what others are saying, there are signs of mental strain*' (p. 14). However, all signs of 'mental strain' vanish when he describes the joys of poaching with a surprising degree of eloquence and vividness: 'There's the pheasants going up with a whir-r-r! – like that. And the rabbits – tap! tap! – and off to go with their little white tails in the air. And there's the salmon as well, coming up the river fat from the sea –' (p. 21). He is not a simple character. M. Wynn Thomas has called him a folk hero and compared him to Twm Siôn Catti and Charlie Chaplin, and argued that the plays celebrated 'the innocent little man's victory over such petty forms of authority as policemen, mine owners, justices of the peace, landowners – and chapels'.[22] Poaching is a metaphor for an implicit, almost inborn, resistance to an externally imposed authority, a theme running through much Welsh writing in English. In Geraint Goodwin's *Heyday in the Blood* (1936), for instance, this same resistance is exemplified by characters like Twm, the landlord of a rural pub, and Dici Weasel. Both play a practical joke on a policeman at the beginning of the novel:

> For the routing of a policeman had some hidden, far reaching significance. It was as though an invader had been beaten off and discomfited; something from the outside that had been set going. The battle, fought often and often, was between staid and unalterable authority and the native cunning. It was, in its way, a game and a delight. The old man would continue to serve drinks out of hours as long as he could stand upright – simply because he could not help himself. He would risk his licence for a complete stranger and for a trifling farthing profit, rather than conform. Twmi's instinct – the Welsh blood in him – ran to poaching as a duck to water: it was innate.[23]

Needless to say, the policeman is also Welsh but he personifies an alien, intrusive authority. Similarly, in Menna Gallie's *Strike for a Kingdom* (1959), a novel set during the General Strike of 1926, a crime is committed. Rather than co-operating with the police, the community closes ranks against the anglicized Inspector Evans and solves the crime itself.[24]

In Francis's play, the central characters are pitted against two different but interrelated kinds of authority, namely that of the landowner Venerby-Jones who has forbidden poaching on his land and that of the chapel personified by the deacon Dafydd Hughes. The play does not have any revolutionary goals: there is no call to take away Venerby-Jones's land nor is the chapel itself really criticized. Instead, the play promotes, first, a land ethic that is characterized by respect for all living beings, and, secondly, a community characterized by friendly, ethical relationships rather than mistrustful hypocrisy.

The setting of the play is pastoral despite the action being set, as later plays make clear, in the 'Four Valleys region', meaning somewhere to the north of the Heads of the Valleys in south Wales. In a sense this may be surprising, as the stereotype of the industrial south Wales valleys is one of pollution, dirt and ecological degradation. Images of the valleys tend to focus on the areas immediately surrounding the pits and the houses of the local population. It is sometimes forgotten that the kind of wild natural environment that is described in the plays could be encountered immediately outside the area of industrial activity, such as the top of the mountains that enclose the valleys. George Ewart Evans invokes a similar landscape in his short story 'Let Dogs Delight'.[25] The story is set in Pontygwaith (Rhondda Fach) and the area between the village and Gilfach Goch. Apart from a few farmsteads and a quarry it is set in moorland. Signally absent from the story are signifiers for the heavy industry that dominated the area: instead it focuses on the 'in-between' space of unspoilt environment and on characters' leisure time. This is not to suggest that the landscape in *The Poacher* is a true representation of a reality other writers ignore. Along with the other plays in the series it shows, however, that even the 'Four Valleys region' does not consist solely of heavy industry.

In *The Poacher*, the natural environment is imagined as almost paradisaically bountiful. The ethical argument that underlies the play is that everyone should be allowed to take what he or she needs but not more. It is a stance of respect towards nature and non-human animals. M. Wynn Thomas writes that 'Dicky seems to be in part a character out of ancient folklore, a lawless relic of Wales's pre-Nonconformist past, a Welsh Puck, a mischievous sprite in league with the forces of nature'.[26] Indeed, he is part of the natural environment in a way that excludes him from the village community. In *Birds of a Feather* he vividly evokes the 'eyes in the dark' of all the animals watching them out on the road at night, imagining himself as part of their habitat.[27] Of the village community, only Twmas has a similar sense of respect for the animals he hunts. When Dicky informs Twmas that others have set a trap for 'Old Soldier', the latter is dismayed: 'He's given us good sport has that rabbit, and he's got to have fair play' (p. 18). Poaching is a game of skill and animals are not just objects to be hunted but opponents, who ought to have a fair chance of escaping. By implication, the landowner Venerby-Jones upsets the equilibrium because he lays claim to large tracts of land for which he has little use, although his 'rights' are rigorously defended by Jenkins the Keeper (in *Birds of a Feather*) and Sergeant Rosser (in *King of the River*).

While Jenkins polices Venerby-Jones's land, Dafydd Hughes polices the ethics of the community in *The Poacher*. This community is organic in nature and it supports those in need in what might be described as a truly Christian spirit. Dafydd Hughes, however, is only interested in the outward signs of religious behaviour, which are here described as chapel attendance and submission to the will of the powerful. Hypocrisy runs through this community and, just like Caradoc Evans, Francis criticizes it, although he employs comic means to do so. However, when a man's character depends on his being lawful rather than morally good, when a deacon threatens to send those who are weakest in the community to the workhouse[28] and when that same deacon then turns out to be a lawbreaker himself, communal ethics are clearly deficient. Francis does not criticize religion itself: the ridiculous Dafydd Hughes is only the holder of secondary power – he is a deacon rather than a minister. The aim of Francis's satire is the hypocritical rule of those who undeservedly think they are better than others.

How is Dicky meant to affect the audience? Because the audience is part of the society that Dicky cannot adjust to, we simultaneously laugh at him and at ourselves because his off-centre perspective reveals what is funny or odd about social customs. He is a jester figure like the late medieval Till Eulenspiegel ('Till Owlglass'), a prankster who by means of practical jokes holds the mirror of wisdom – the owlglass – up to respectable burghers. The anarchic trickster figure is available in many cultures, whether as Till Eulenspiegel, as Punch fighting the Constable, as Reynard the fox, as the coyote or as the raven in North American first nations mythologies, among others. Given the influence of the plays of the Irish National Theatre on Francis, it is likely that Dicky Bach Dwl and Twm Tinker derive from the tinkers, tramps and vagabonds that people plays by Synge, for example *In the Shadow of the Glen* (1903) or *The Tinker's Wedding* (1909), and Lady Gregory's *The Rising of the Moon* (1907).

The Poacher was such a success that Francis wrote a whole series of plays featuring him and Twm Tinker, who replaced Twmas Shôn as the object of Dicky's hero-worship. They are the one-act comedies *Birds of a Feather* (1923), *King of the River* (1942), *His Shining Majesty* (1943?), and *Hunting the Hare* (1943). Full-length plays featuring Dicky and Twm are *The Dark Little People* (1924) and *Tares in the Wheat* (1942), which was later substantially revised as *The Sheep and the Goats* and appears to have first been performed by the Swansea Little Theatre at the Swansea Empire Theatre in 1954.[29] Two of the greatest successes of Welsh amateur dramatic companies at the British Drama League of Community Drama Festival were celebrated by Trecynon Dramatic Society and Mardy Dramatic Society with *The Poacher* and *Birds of a Feather*. Trecynon Dramatic Society performed *The Poacher* at the semi-finals of the Midlands region of the British Drama Festival of Community Drama in Birmingham in December 1927, the first year that Welsh amateurs were allowed to take part. They won and went through to the final in London in February 1928 where they came second. In 1932, Mardy Dramatic Society repeated the success of the Trecynon Dramatic Society, again with *The Poacher*. They won the contest in front of an audience that included the author. Trecynon Dramatic Society won the Festival in 1948, when they entered with *Birds of a Feather*. On that occasion, the play was also performed at Alexandra Palace where a highly gratified Francis watched the play as it was televised. Glyndwr Griffiths wrote an account of the occasion for the *Aberdare Leader*:

> A surprise visitor to Alexandra Palace that evening was Mr. J. O. Francis, author of 'Birds of a Feather,' who, although residing in London, did not know anything about the B. D. L. [British Drama League] final at the Scala [Theatre] until a relative in South Wales wrote a few days later to congratulate him on the fact that his play had been presented by the winning Aberdare Players. However, although in considerable ill-health, J. O. made sure of being at Alexandra Palace for what, incidentally, was the first television show he had ever seen. When he came round to the dressing room after the show, he was emotionally upset, and, sitting down to write some autographs, he commented that he had never realised when he was writing it that 'Birds of a Feather' would have brought him so many honours. It had been played by professionals, had been adjudged the winning play in a B. D. L. community final, had been broadcast, and now televised![30]

A radio version of *The Poacher* and *Birds of a Feather* was recorded in September 1951 as *Nightbirds* and broadcast in October 1951 with a star-studded cast including Richard Burton as Dicky Bach Dwl, Hugh Griffiths as Twmas Shôn, Rachel Roberts as Marged Shôn, William Squire as Jenkins, the Keeper, Michael Gwynn as the Bishop of Mid-Wales and Peter Halliday as the Policeman.[31] It appears that, from the 1930s onwards, Francis may have been regarded as the author of Dicky Bach Dwl rather than of the critically acclaimed *Change*, something that is reflected in the kind of 'story talks' he was asked to write for BBC Radio.

The next play written about the exploits of Dicky and Twm Tinker, *Birds of a Feather*, develops the notion that Dicky's off-centre perspective might be different from, but is just as valuable as, that of other people. He only feels truly alive when he is out poaching, when he can pit his wit against that of the animals (and Keeper Jenkins). In doing so, he displays considerable *phronēsis*, or practical wisdom. According to Aristotle, however, the highest good is *eudaimonia*, 'flourishing' or 'happiness'. In turn, the highest form of virtuous action that leads to happiness is contemplation. Without engaging in the highly technical discussion of the degree to which human beings can reach perfect *eudaimonia* and how realistic, therefore, striving for perfect 'happiness' is for ordinary people,[32] it is clear that, for Aristotelians, contemplation is a more virtuous activity than those leading to *phronēsis*, although practical wisdom is necessary to live a complete life. This is replicated in the way *Birds of a Feather* juxtaposes the kind of practical wisdom displayed by Dicky with the more contemplative wisdom of the Bishop of Mid-Wales.

The Bishop rather incongruously arrives just as Twm Tinker and Dicky are about to set off on a poaching expedition in the middle of a summer night. Having wanted to walk to the vicarage of Lewis Pugh, he has lost his way in every sense: nature, which is Dicky's natural habitat, is a closed book to the Bishop. To Twm's horrified fascination, Dicky's eloquence very nearly persuades the Bishop to join in the poaching, until the latter's conscience is stirred and he reluctantly declines. In the end, the Bishop saves Dicky and Twm from Jenkins the Keeper and Powell the Policeman by hiding the evidence, a freshly caught salmon, in his bag, arguing, 'If you have sinned with your hands, I have sinned also in my heart'.[33] He thus displays the virtues of forgiveness and charity but also, crucially, he arrives at his decision through contemplation. It is obvious that the Bishop is the better man by virtue of his position, because he sees through Venerby-Jones ('I don't like him – a man of wrath'),[34] and because he has the magnanimity to sit down with 'a couple of sinners' and share their food.[35] However, Dicky's practical wisdom saves him, shows him humility and ensures that he will arrive at Lewis Pugh's vicarage safely.

In *King of the River*, the forces of authority finally catch up with Dicky and throw him into the county jail. However, he finds a surprising ally in the wife of Police Constable Parry. Bessie Jane Parry is unhappy in the 'Four Valleys region'. She and her husband are from Tonypandy and she is homesick for urban Glamorgan because 'in Tonypandy we could always be sure of a bit of riot now and then – just to keep things from getting dull'.[36] She is also frustrated that the authorities will not give them a decent cottage to live in, forcing them to use one of their ground-floor rooms as the prison. With the help of her and her father-in-law, Dicky can escape and she, having proved that the jail room is unsafe, will indeed get her new cottage.

Bessie Jane is an interesting character when analyzed from the point of view of an ethics of place. Her ready wit, practical no-nonsense attitude, readiness to challenge those in authority and steadfast sense of justice make her a virtuous character. The fact that she is from Tonypandy, a place considered almost synonymous with rioting at the time – something that Bessie Jane does not deny but makes light of ('I'm from Tonypandy. Fighting the police was one of the popular amusements in Tonypandy. My father was in hospital for a month.')[37] – serves to challenge that perception while, at the same time, producing laughter of recognition. One may wonder whether Bessie Jane was created in response to the fact that the majority of productions of Francis's plays in English took place in the industrialized south in the 1930s and 40s: Francis wanted, perhaps, to create a good character with whom both actors and audiences could readily identify.

THE DARK LITTLE PEOPLE (1922)

The Dark Little People also features Dicky Bach Dwl. It is a full-length comedy that takes place in the prosperous farm Derwenfa close to the village of Pontewyn. The setting appears to be mid-Wales – far enough away from Glamorgan for the character Dai Williams to try to escape his background but not far enough away that he cannot easily return. As the convention of romantic comedy demands, there is a marriage plot: after many ups and downs, Dai Williams persuades Teleri Thomas, a beautiful, dark-haired, 'wild' girl who is very similar to the romantic depiction of Catrin Rees in Allen Raine's *A Welsh Witch*,[38] to marry him and not Seth Pritchard, the prosperous farmer's son. However, the marriage plot is less important than the story of how Dai Williams, the boy who was brought up in a Glamorgan workhouse, finds his 'character' by finding his roots.

The play contrasts the settled, comfortable and prosperous Pritchard family, whose farmhouse *'suggests a long, unbroken domestic tradition'*,[39] with the unsettled life of Dai Williams, who never stays anywhere for long because his workhouse past keeps catching up with him. At the beginning of the play, Dai appears to be broken in spirit, and this is the reason Teleri gives him for not wanting to marry him: 'You let people trample on you – even the biggest fools in the valley. I've seen it. I loathe it. You can't stand up for yourself, Dai' (p. 26). All he can do is repeat mantra-like the good references he has received from previous employers – his 'characters'. But this is precisely the problem: he does not know who he is, so he tries to internalize what others say about him, much to Teleri's exasperation: 'Bother the characters! Man alive, aren't you ever going to stand on your own two feet?' (p. 41).

Why is Dai so timid? It is not only his workhouse past. More important to him is that he does not belong anywhere:

> Can you imagine what it's like to feel that you're alone – absolutely alone on the face of the earth? Suppose there wasn't a stick or a stone that you could turn to and say, 'Here's something that I belong to!' What if you looked to the four corners or the world, and, out of all the centuries and all the men and women who've lived and died – you had nothing to cling to – nothing at all! ... There are lamps in all the windows of the valley – Melindwr, Blaenpant,

Hafod, here in Derwenfa, and in those cottages by Plas Gwyn. There's one deep red up there, half hidden by the trees. And I can't help thinking, Teleri, of all the generations that have come and gone in these homes and the names they've got of the grandfathers and grandmothers, handed down. ... If a man's to live his life as it was meant, he's got to have roots that go down and grip him fast to the earth. And I'm no more than a leaf blown anywhere on the wind. (pp. 42–3)

The need to belong is a thread running through most of Francis's work – the serious plays as well as the comedies – although rarely does he express it so eloquently than in *The Dark Little People*. As discussed with reference to *The Beaten Track*, Francis's conception of the family takes in many generations and true tradition is created cumulatively through the centuries. The same idea is invoked here. Indeed, it is given scientific backing, for the cast of characters includes Professor Hughes-Lewis from the university at Aberystwyth, a thinly disguised portrait of H. J. Fleure, who is engaged in excavating prehistoric settlements as well as 'going round measuring people's heads' (p. 45). Hughes-Lewis is able to give Dai what he has been seeking: a family – one that goes back thousands of years. In this way, 'Francis's drama is ... an important attempt to establish the native Welsh identity of the supposed "newcomers", the suspect working class of the south Wales coalfield with their reputedly un-Welsh activities'.[40]

How does Hughes-Lewis restore Dai's self-esteem? First, he identifies Dicky, Teleri and Dai as Iberian types – and it is interesting that these three characters, who all appear less connected to the community than the wealthy Pritchards, are thus chosen. Hughes-Lewis considers Dai to be 'the pure type' and asks for his photograph, so that it may be displayed in his book. According to the professor, the Iberians permeated Wales because, as the real Fleure wrote, 'its early waves were coming into an almost empty land'. According to him, this type came from the Mediterranean and very likely 'did not speak a Celtic language'. References to the 'little dark people' 'may well provide the substratum for a number of Welsh folk tales, and one cannot but recall the frequent mention of the dark and rather wizened changeling baby'.[41] Speaking about his excavations, the fictional Hughes-Lewis proceeds to conjure up the past of Dai's people: 'There was a time, of course, when the Iberians possessed the land. They ruled in this valley. ... Before William the Conqueror, before King Arthur, before ever a Roman trod our soil, you Iberians made that camp as a place of refuge' (pp. 52–3). Hughes-Lewis then recounts how the old Iberians 'went under' beaten by a 'new race ...

a different people altogether – tall and fair' (p. 54). Dai's sense of self is strengthened by the discovery that he does belong to the valley after all, that his roots go deeper than everyone else's, particularly those of the tall, fair Seth, whom he now regards not only as a rival in love for Teleri but also as an ancient enemy. Dicky speaks the truth when he says 'Well, after this, . . . people will know who they're talking to. 'Tisn't everybody's got the right to boast that his relations were here in the time of the wild pigs' (p. 58). By the end of the play not only has Dai discovered his real character, but Teleri accepts his proposal of marriage and he can give his rival Seth a good beating.

The Dark Little People was first performed by 'past and present students' at the Parish Hall in Aberystwyth on 21 April 1922 and was 'well received by a crowded audience'.[42] In 1924 the Repertory Players performed the play on 23 April at the Aldwych Theatre in London. A preview note published on 11 January 1924 drew attention to the 'considerable interest' this event was to attract, especially since 'Mr. Lloyd George himself [took] a keen interest in the author's progress' and it was rumoured that he might attend,[43] although it is not recorded whether he did so. The performance was reviewed very favourably:

> In his latest play he displays in a conspicuous manner a rapidly developing craftsmanship, and it will not be surprising if in the near future London managers, always with a keen eye on the commercial possibilities, will pay special attention to him. . . . It is one of the great merits of Mr. Francis's play that his championship of the 'dark little people' never becomes an obsession with him. He extenuates nothing, nor sets down aught in malice, and you feel that the denouement of his story is perfectly natural, and, in fact, as inevitable as destiny itself.
> In this play the author tells with great charm and truthfulness a story of Welsh rural life. He shows in this, as in other stories, a refreshing freedom from cant. With the crabbed and arid conventionalism which has imparted so much that is unlovely to Welsh life he shows no manner of sympathy. . . . He evinces unfailing sympathy with the weak and defenceless.[44]

The underlying ethical point is that wealth and status on their own are – as in the case of the Pritchards – a poor indication of the justice of their claim to their position and power. It turns out that the lost soul from Glamorgan has a much better claim based on heritage rather than mere force of personality. The play has a very clear moral lesson but delivers it unobtrusively.

TARES IN THE WHEAT (1942)/THE SHEEP AND THE GOATS (1951?)

The full-length comedy *Tares in the Wheat*[45] was first performed by the Trecynon Amateur Dramatic Society at the Coliseum in Trecynon on 18 June 1942. It is set in rural mid-Wales in the fictional village of Trefelyn and the action takes place in London House, a comfortable home and General Store, whose business has slowed down. The owner, Rebecca Morgan, only slowly realizes that her dead father had mismanaged his affairs and that she is now in financially dire straits. Her way out – as usual in comedy – is marriage. She should, and eventually does, make the wise decision to marry Watkin Peters, the slightly dull but respectable owner of Cambrian Stores, instead of the flamboyant and decidedly dangerous Twm Roderick (Twm Tinker), who does not realize that the shop is in trouble and thinks of it as a place to settle down. At the end of the play, however, Twm and Dicky have been caught poaching again. The community allows them to escape back to Glamorgan and washes their hands of them.

A subplot concerns Dicky and two pleasant but rather weak men: Johnnie Ben, whom everyone calls 'bookworm' because he enjoys reading weighty tomes, and Rebecca's uncle Micah Morgan, an insurance salesman and poet. Johnnie is dominated by Hannah Lloyd, a paid help, and hopelessly wishes to do something that makes him appear strong. Thus he allows Dicky to persuade him to come on a poaching expedition with him. Micah seeks inspiration for his eisteddfod 'Ode on Rural Life' and joins them despite moral misgivings. Finding himself the leader of two apprentice poachers, Dicky is, for once in his life, out of his depth while engaged in his favourite activity: 'Pity Twm isn't with us. Now I'm here I don't think I've got brains enough to be leader. I feel out of place now; quite out of place' (p. 68). Once Twm has joined them, he is jubilant: 'H'sh! The trees; the grass – don't you feel there's whispers? . . . And the stars: those watching stars – *they've* got the whisper now. The whole night is whispering. News, mighty news. Twm Tinker's out' (p. 69). Having been momentarily unsure of his social place, he is now comfortably implaced both as follower to Twm Tinker and in his environment.

Of course, the ill-assembled group run into the police and can barely escape. When the once respectable Micah Morgan returns home in torn clothes and with muddy hands and face, he is distraught:

> I'll never forgive myself, Rebecca – not if I live a thousand years. But that Dicky is to blame. . . . I wanted the mood of it for my competition-poem. No poaching. Nothing illegal. Only the mood. . . . If I had dreamt I could even

feel tempted to do more, I'd never have left the house. But that fellow *lured* me on. . . . And there's something worse I owe that fellow. . . . I've learnt the real truth about myself. . . . I've been jealous all this time of Bevan of Carmel [a fellow eisteddfod competitor]. A silly, jealous old fool – that's what I am. (pp. 84–5)

Micah, like Rebecca, is a Calvinist Methodist. Indeed, the Morgan household is not unlike that of the Price family in *Change*: here, too, the set includes a dresser, a row of books on a shelf and the '*pictures on display as decoration are of the kind usually found in a household which has long been a fortress for the Welsh Nonconformist tradition*' (p. 8). As Micah is a true believer, his horror at having strayed from the straight and narrow is very real. The experience serves to open his eyes to a deeper truth: he had thought he was virtuous, but instead he is guilty of the sins of pride and competitiveness. Interestingly, this important moral lesson is elided in the revised version of the play, *The Sheep and the Goats*.

A now familiar theme is the comparison between Nonconformism as a cultural blanket that alternately comforts and stifles, and 'real' Welsh culture identified with a pre-Nonconformist culture. Rebecca, a highly principled Nonconformist, is juxtaposed with Dicky and his natural ethics. Her attempt to turn him into a Calvinist Methodist is a comic highlight of the play as it merely serves to provide Dicky with the vocabulary to express his own philosophy of life. Alone, he struggles to say what it is: 'I, er, I've got the idea here in my head – if I could only bring it out. The birds, Twm: every bird is according to the egg. The plant is according to the root' (p. 29). When Micah clarifies to him the meaning of the term predestination, Dicky thinks he can explain his nature: 'It's no good trying to contradict what you've got inside you. And you call that – Predestination? . . . I can see *your* Predestination very clear, Mr. Morgan: poetry and insurance. For some of us others, it's game and fish' (p. 45). What he means to say is that everyone should be true to his or her nature. Dicky personifies in a literal way how Francis felt about culture, tradition and national identity: being true to one's nature is the one true source of identity as one's essence is an expression of the unchanging essence of a people over the centuries. As Fleure was measuring the external signs of such an unchanging, genetic trajectory, Francis was searching for a similarly unchanging inner truth. He, however, did not seek to actually describe what constituted that essence – he merely pointed out that more modern manifestations of culture might not truthfully describe it. Similarly, Dicky's way of life expresses *his* essence as someone who is only truly happy when living in harmonious coexistence with the natural world, but it is not a recipe for happiness for all – it certainly does not lead to *eudaimonia*. The ethical lesson to be absorbed by the audience is that true essences are determined by one's locality and one's genetic inheritance, and that a truly virtuous existence arises from being true to that essence, not by obeying imposed, seemingly moral, codes of conduct.

Tares in the Wheat was revised as *The Sheep and the Goats*, probably in 1951. Letters to the publisher, Samuel French, reveal that the former had not been popular with amateur drama companies. Francis looked at the play again and decided that the second act was

> rather 'bitty'. What was worse, the third act had two scenes, the first of them an exterior setting and the second an interior. That made a big stage management difficulty for small amateur companies. As a rule they like plays in a single unchanged set. Furthermore, the general story in the play struck me as being too slight for a full length play. . . . [46]

Reflecting thus on the needs of amateur companies reveals Francis's deep commitment to the world of amateur drama in Wales, as well as a consciousness that the play was unlikely to be picked up by a professional company and a clear understanding of the limits this imposed upon him as an artist.

In *The Sheep and the Goats* the story of the play is not markedly changed, but brought into sharper relief: it is now set in Cambrian House in the rural village of Trepant. Johnnie Bookworm, whose story had partly mirrored that of Micah Thomas, is excised and a new character, Bethan Pugh, a woman Twm Tinker had promised to marry in Glamorgan, is introduced, allowing for scenes of confrontation between Twm's two women. Micah Roberts, Rebecca Roberts's uncle, is now a retired headmaster and newly elected councillor, which makes his fall from grace more vivid. Interestingly, from the point of view of an ethics of place, Rebecca's attraction to and ultimate rejection of Twm Tinker is more clearly presented as the contrast between Glamorgan and rural mid-Wales.

When Twm first arrives to take on a job at Cambrian House, taking Dicky with him, the latter is awestruck by the village: 'I suppose we're in what they call civilisation – in now up to our necks?'[47] 'Civilisation' essentially means an ordered village community in which the inhabitants have no secrets from one another, where the community's moral life is still ruled over by the chapel, and which, in short, is comfortable but also slightly dull, just like Watkin Howells, Rebecca's suitor, who in this play is asthmatic to reinforce the contrast between him and the vigorous Twm Tinker.

Trepant is contrasted with Pentre Mabon, where Twm lived before he ran away from Bethan Pugh:

DICKY: Pity we didn't stay in the Four Valleys, Twm. There's – there's things happening here I don't understand. I was all right in Pentre Mabon. And this village, now we've been here a fortnight its getting rather dull. It's like Sunday all the week in this village. Pentre Mabon was full of fun and excitement.

TWM: Pentre Mabon's a very special place, Dicky.

DICKY: Special, Twm? Why?

TWM: There was a time when this little country of ours went through a big change. I think it was a sad change, very, very sad. The land of the harp turned into something quite different.

DICKY: Turned into what?

TWM: The land of the harmonium.

DICKY: (very anxious) Not Pentre Mabon?

TWM: No, Dicky – not Pentre Mabon. Pentre Mabon refused to make the change – refused with scorn. It kept the flag flying and clung to its old traditions. And there it is now – a great worry, perhaps, to the County Police, but still Pentre Mabon! (p. I–2–11)

The name of Twm's and Dicky's previous abode, Pentre Mabon, indicates that it is in the industrial valleys in Glamorgan and aligns its culture with the bygone era of Francis's youth – a time when the spirit of compromise was still tangible and the 'fun and excitement' of the town was still innocent. The industrial town of Pentre Mabon comes to exemplify a positive, free sense of Welshness that goes back to ancient times and is identified with a poetic culture, whereas Trepant symbolizes the bad change brought about in the nineteenth century by the rise of Nonconformity. *The Sheep and the Goats* thus brings together two main preoccupations that are visible in his oeuvre as a whole: a desire to show and give a voice to a Welshness that is perceived as 'real' because it apparently has an unbroken tradition going back to prehistoric times and which is contrasted favourably with a newer 'invention of tradition', which Francis perceives as less genuine and as stifling. Secondly, the place of this genuine, traditional sense of Welshness is (or can be) Glamorgan. Dicky's idiosyncratic understanding of the term 'predestination', which is kept in this version of the play, exemplifies the point.

THE BAKEHOUSE (1912) AND THE SEWING GUILD (c.1943)

Something that for this reader remains unsatisfactory in most of Francis's romance plots is the role of women, who seem only too keen to give up their independence and sometimes their money to marry. In *The Little Village* (discussed below), the wealthy Susannah Thomas is surprised into agreeing to marry the penniless layabout Shoni Dai Dai but apparently does not mind the fait accompli. In *The Dark Little People*, Teleri is a strong, almost fierce young woman. Initially she rejects Dai Williams's offers of marriage because 'I'd despise a husband who'd let me be master'.[48] At the end of the play, she does want to marry him, but she makes it sound as if she is giving in rather than exercising her free will: 'I know when I'm conquered'.[49] This almost Doris-Day-like stereotype of the tough-minded woman who is, nevertheless, liable to swoon helplessly at displays of manliness, runs through Francis's comic plays, but I would argue that the use of such stereotypical gendered behaviour is bound up with the romance element in comic drama rather than a general reflection on the scope for action/emotion of female characters in the work more generally. Women are not usually merely 're-actors' to male actors. This becomes clear in two unusual plays in Francis's oeuvre – unusual because they have all-female casts, are situated in totally female spheres, and thus display female behaviour when no men are there to observe.

The Bakehouse was written at the start of Francis's career and first performed at the same time as *The Poacher*. It is set in Mrs Evans's bakehouse in which a number of the married women in Aberpandy, the same fictional setting as in *Change*, bake their bread. It is a simple story about pettiness and jealousies among a tightly-knit community, but also about generosity and deftly administered justice. The recently married Mrs Morgan has brought her bread to the bakehouse for the first time. Unfortunately, she has married the man whom Mrs Richards had 'chosen' for her daughter Jinnie. As a result mother and daughter behave meanly towards her, despite making much of their moral superiority over the rest of the women because Mrs Richards's eldest daughter has married a preacher and Mr Richards has recently become a deacon. As poor Mrs Morgan's bread fails to rise, Mrs Howells, a kindly, matriarchal figure, quickly switches her own bread for that of Mrs Morgan to teach the Richardses a lesson:

> Mrs. Morgan may have brought in two tins of putty. But if Mrs. Richards is going to look on, Mrs. Morgan will be taking out as good bread as any in this blessed bakehouse to-night. And that's a slap in the face for old mother

Richards! . . . It takes a woman as wicked as me to deal with a woman as good as Mrs. Richards.[50]

Just like *The Poacher*, the main theme of this play is hypocrisy, which in this play, too, is linked with chapel culture rather than religion itself. On a deeper level the play also shows that an ethics based on virtue rather than on principles may sometimes deliver better justice. Indeed, it may support the case of moral particularism as described by Jonathan Dancy: 'Particularists think that moral judgement can get along perfectly well without any appeal to principles, indeed that there is no essential link between being a full moral agent and having principles'.[51] A principled stance would not have allowed Mrs Howells to pretend that her bread is, in fact, Mrs Morgan's bread and she would not have been able to lie to Mrs Richards because a woman of principle would have been duty-bound to tell the truth. However, in the logic of the play, a little lying in a good cause is, in fact, the virtuous thing to do as the immense false pride of the Richardses is punctured and the confidence of the shy, insecure Mrs Morgan is boosted. Of course, the play does not propose that this state of affairs is to continue: at the end of the play Mrs Morgan, who has an inkling of what occurred, invites Mrs Howells to tea and Mrs Howells agrees to visit her in order to teach her how to bake better bread.

The Sewing Guild, although written around thirty years later, covers similar moral territory.[52] The fact that it is set in a Women's Institute in the fictional market town of Aberton made it particularly suitable for Women's Institute dramatic competitions, and it is not a great leap of the imagination to suppose that it was written with such competitions in mind. Indeed, the play deals with a competition – a sewing competition. The action focuses on events immediately preceding the competition. The women have to sew a nightdress under supervision to ensure that nobody cheats. We see several of the competitors at work. By and by we learn that one of them, Georgina Lewis, has fallen upon hard times. Her husband turned out to be a gambler, his affairs are in disarray and he left town in a hurry. Their children are to live with her mother and she herself is forced to put her house on the market. Her main motivation for winning the prize is that it will virtually guarantee her a job at the Bon Marche department store, which will enable her to pay back the money owed by her husband. The favourite to win, however, is Emma Watts, an ambitious young woman who has always coveted winning the prize. The play focuses on the way Sarah Wheeler, this play's Mrs Howells, leans on Emma rather heavily to allow Georgina to win the prize:

SARAH: ... You see your duty now; see it quite plain, of course.

EMMA (*surprised*): *My* duty? ...

SARAH: You oughtn't to win this Prize now.

EMMA: (*with a rush of hot indignation*). Oughtn't? You dare stand there and –? Don't you know that to win this Bradley-Pugh Prize has been one of my greatest ambitions? ... And now, when I've got the Prize almost in my very grasp – d'you tell me I'm to let it go to someone else? To a Prosser Morgan of all people? The daughter of *that* woman? You're talking daft, Sarah. Crazy![53]

The moral argument is slightly more complex than in *The Bakehouse*. Although Georgina is poor now, she comes from a wealthy background and has a mother seemingly not unlike Mrs Richards in *The Bakehouse*. Furthermore, it has been one of Emma's keenest ambitions to win the prize and she is to lose it on somebody else's behalf just as she can be sure to win. Unlike *The Bakehouse*, where we never doubt the outcome, there are some genuine moments of tension in the play until Emma lets herself be persuaded to do the decent thing, makes some errors in her work and foregoes the prize. Georgina, of course, does not at once realize that Emma has given up her prize to aid her and is triumphant. But Sarah soon puts her right and Georgina impulsively thanks Emma. In the end Emma realizes that her prejudices regarding Georgina were false: 'I didn't know till tonight that you had so much of the human being in you. (...) And I certainly didn't know *I* had so much of the angel'.[54]

The group of women (excepting the judges for the prize) are realistically portrayed as closely interested in each other's welfare without, however, their giving up all self-interest. Emma and Georgina in particular gain significant moral knowledge and, as a consequence, understand each other better. Both consciously choose the path of virtue: Emma realizes that Georgina's motivation to win the prize is one of concern for others, notably her children, and she gives up what in this situation is excessive ambition. Georgina is inclined to be vain about her abilities as a seamstress, but is able to forget her own concerns and embrace Emma in an act of pure friendship and thankfulness.

It cannot be said that *The Bakehouse* and *The Sewing Guild* contain much feminist thought unless the fact that they contain strong parts for women and show them interacting with one another without overt reference to men is itself feminist.[55] The social framework is that of marriage and the settings of the bakehouse and the Women's Institute are limited by traditional expectations of the proper sphere for women. Arguably, Francis wrote these plays with amateur companies in mind, which were (and are) often struggling to find plays with enough female parts. And yet, when one strips away the genre conventions of romantic comedy and takes his serious plays into consideration, his works display an astonishing number of strong women who stand up for their beliefs and who can make their own way in the world. Indeed, women like Mrs Howells (*The Bakehouse*), Sarah Wheeler (*The Sewing Guild*), Shân Powell (*The Beaten Track*) or Gwen Price (*Change*) hold the family and the community together, thus contributing perhaps more than the male characters towards the building-up of tradition that is so highly prized in Francis's work.

LITTLE VILLAGE (1928)

The final play discussed in this chapter is *Little Village*, a full-length farce about marriage, local pride and jealousies, which also reveals Francis's conception of the ideal village community. It was first performed by the Trecynon Amateur Dramatic Society in the Public Hall in Trecynon, Aberdare, on 27 December 1928. At its centre are two marriage plots: Susannah Thomas, the owner of the tavern The Druid's Arms and of several local properties, is coming out of mourning after the death of her first husband and the local bachelors are preparing themselves for the contest for her hand, most prominent among them Shoni Dai Dai, a part-time sailor and full-time layabout, and Elias Watkins, a thoroughly respectable businessman from Little Village's biggest rival, Upper Village. The second marriage plot concerns Mary Morgan, the American-born daughter of Welsh émigré and millionaire Silas J. Morgan, and Mostyn Pryce, who has been studying for the bar. The marriage plots are linked with scenes of village life culminating in the competitions at the local Pontifor eisteddfod, which, so Mostyn proudly proclaims, 'is very old, and has a ritual of its own',[56] as well as Silas J. Morgan's purchase of the Maesgwyn Estate for his daughter, who steps into the shoes of the deceased last member of the local gentry, Mr Coleby-Pugh.

Little Village and Upper Village are situated in the borough of Pontifor, probably north Ceredigion. Little Village is, in many ways, an ideal Welsh village community: it has grown organically, has a long history and 'ancient customs' (p. 123). The law is upheld (more or less) by Bevan Bobby, who allows minor infringements such as serving alcohol before the official opening hours and supplying drinks on credit in The Druid's Arms because it helps the social cohesion of the village. There is no moral relativism implied, nor even a mild version of the moral particularism proposed by Jonathan Dancy. It is not as if the characters in Little Village, particularly Shoni Dai Dai and his cronies, lazy loafers to a man, are unprincipled, merely that their principles clash, on occasion, with '*the austere enactments of the House of Commons*' (p. 89). The village pub itself shows that Bevan Bobby's assessment of the Little Village community is correct: '*The general atmosphere, like that of many Welsh rural taverns, is friendly, decent and domestic, and has nothing of the crude harshness of the public-house of a modern industrial town*' (p. 89). Little Village is a rural idyll untouched by the purported harshness of life elsewhere.

Virtuous action in *Little Village* is identified with ensuring the continuing vitality of the village community according to its own peculiar rhythm of life. Life there is slow and it is devoted to art rather than business. In the local eisteddfod, Dai and his friends effortlessly beat the choir of his rival in love, Elias Watkins, a victory that ultimately wins him Susannah Thomas's affection. When they stand opposite each other, Elias declaring that 'I stand for the trade and the prosperity of the Borough', while Shoni aligns himself with 'Homer, Virgil, Dante, Shakespeare' (p. 115), Susannah is swayed in favour of the winner of the Pontifor Crown.

The eisteddfod Crown, it turns out, is an important symbol for positive, changeless tradition. Just prior to the eisteddfod, Mostyn fears that 'this is probably the last Crown that will ever be given at our Eisteddfod' (p. 52) because it had always been provided by the local gentry, the Coleby-Pughs of Maesgwyn. Now that the last Coleby-Pugh has died, the villagers worry that their way of life will change. Mostyn fears that Maesgwyn will be purchased by an anonymous 'syndicate' that will 'work it on strictly business lines. We can't expect them to spend a deal of money to keep up traditions they don't understand' (p. 53). Little Village is imagined as truly organic: it is the body and needs its head, the Maesgwyn Estate, for survival. Mostyn explains that the

> Parish swings round Maesgwyn. It's been the heart of the place for centuries. And the Maesgwyn people have always been very kind to Little Village. But, if this syndicate takes over the estate, all that old friendly Welsh feeling will vanish. They'll put up the rents. There'll be friction and bitterness. Some hardships, too, I daresay. The whole character of Little Village will change. I don't want it to change. I like it just as it is . . . It's a corner of bygone Wales unspoilt by the nineteenth century. There's no other place in the country like it. And now it's threatened. (pp. 100–1)

Local place and identity, the *bro*, is at the heart of this vision, which is regarded as somehow more real and meaningful than the kind of Welsh nationalism based on chapel, language and Liberal politics that emerged in the second half of the nineteenth century. As in *The Poacher* and the other plays featuring Dicky Bach Dwl and Twm Tinker, Nonconformism is not considered a constitutive part of that local Welsh identity: the vicar in this parish is an Anglican. It is unclear which language the characters are meant to speak: they use Welsh phrases and sing Welsh songs, but both have a ritualistic function. The American-born Mary Morgan can scarcely have learnt Welsh in the short time she has spent in Little Village. And yet, Mog Militia is worried about 'the recitations in English' at the eisteddfod, suggesting that recitation in Welsh might have been more congenial (p. 26). The place is untouched by politics other than village 'politics'. It is an ageless place, which is ruled by its own internal laws and customs.

The syndicate is experienced as threatening not simply because it comes from the outside, although that is a factor ('Birmingham! Cardiff would be bad enough. But Birmingham!', p. 14). It is a faceless, de-individualized company, which has no names associated with it except the local agent, Appleby. It has no stake in the community; instead, it is responsible to equally faceless stakeholders. It does, however, have the power to change life in Little Village, beginning with the utterly undemocratic 'ancient custom' that allows the owner of Maesgwyn to select the mayor of the village. This custom is not questioned: it is understood that the 'head' of the village will make a virtuous decision as he or she is just as committed to the village as its inhabitants are. The syndicate has no local knowledge but seems keen to continue with the custom. Based on its own business ethics, it is prepared to consider Elias Watkins, the businessman, as the best candidate for the job, however unsuitable he would be for 'poetic' Little Village.

The village is saved at the last minute by the intervention of Mary Morgan and her millionaire father. Similar to Owen's in *The Beaten Track*, Mary's stay in Little Village has been short, but she has quickly put down roots, something that emerges at the beginning of the play because she effortlessly relates to Shoni and his cronies. She belongs because she engages with the village, but this is no act of 'elective affinity'. Mary may be born in America, but she has 'Welsh blood in [her]' (p. 53), which enables her to belong. She is immediately accepted into the village as its new head, particularly as she and her husband-to-be, Mostyn Pryce, promise to 'keep the old customs of the Parish' (p. 123). Mary adds:

> This is a Welsh Borough. You are Welsh people. I am a Welsh woman. In my first official act, I want to show that I'm in sympathy with Welsh traditions. ... Who is the man to whom we give more honour than other nations give?

It's the poet. . . . And to show my true Welsh quality, I choose as Mayor-elect (. . .) the Crowned Bard of Little Village. (pp. 125–6)

Thus, a happy resolution is made possible in the true style of comedy: the likeable characters are rewarded and the unlikeable characters are punished. Yet the play's underlying assumptions point to a distinctive worldview that seems surprisingly conservative for an ex-member of the Fabian Society who may have wished to join the Labour Party in his youth. It is uncritical when displaying the power differential between gentry, church and people, although the days of the landed gentry are clearly over and they are being supplanted by a new, moneyed elite. Although the female characters in the play, Mary and Susannah, are strong characters who are independently wealthy, their main bargaining chip is their marriageability. Interestingly, Mary's speech claims that the local identity of the *bro* and national identity are the same, which puts 'Welshness' in opposition to an unscrupulous, grasping capitalism to which Cardiff has succumbed and which can only be resisted in the villages. This vision is not Conservative in the political sense, but it shares the assumptions about traditions and organic community of small-c conservative writers like G. K. Chesterton and Hilaire Belloc in England, as well as the rather more left-wing thought of the early Plaid Cymru. It also contradicts Francis's views about the 'real Welshness' of Glamorgan expressed in plays like *Change, King of the River* and essays like 'The glory of Glamorgan', although the point may, once again, be that tradition can be and is meaningful if it is lived local tradition. Once people lose touch with localized, lived tradition, they lose their sense of Welsh identity, too.[57]

Western Mail reviewers liked the play. The preview calls Francis 'the foremost of Welsh dramatists' who has written 'one of the finest farces written dealing with Welsh life'.[58] The premiere of the play was well received in Aberdare and Francis, who had been present, received a standing ovation. The review of the performance comments: 'The author is found in a new mood. No great issues are involved, but rather he has soared into a world of fantasy. The result is a delightful burlesque on some of the most popular, and may be the most important, institutions of Welsh life'.[59]

To conclude, Francis's comic plays, particularly the one-act plays, display the simplicity desired by critics and create the illusion of direct access to the world of the characters by setting the action in locations that would have been familiar to actors and audiences alike. Thus, they create group experiences that support and develop community cohesion. At the same time prevailing stereotypes are gently questioned and an ethics is postulated by which meaningful identity is derived from living local traditions. His ideas thus connect with the spirit of O. M. Edwards, who in *Cartrefi Cymru* skilfully evokes the spirit of a place by describing traditions past and present.[60] The difference lies in the fact that Edwards's selection of Welsh homesteads support his contention that the 'real' Wales could only be found in rural Wales. Francis, on the other hand, locates Welsh identity wherever a living tradition can be found in Wales. This ethical and political point is reinforced by Francis's non-fiction work, to which the following chapter is devoted.

5

A Pilgrim to St David's

Reading J. O. Francis's essays means going on journeys to Wales with him. Were one to map the journeys described in the essays one would discover a pattern: journeys leading into south Wales, past Newport and Cardiff into the Rhondda are voyages home into the well-remembered childhood past of the author, filled with vivid and concrete detail. By contrast, journeys that take us into north or west Wales have more in common with pilgrimages, and they take place in the author's present. The narrative pace is leisurely. Lacking concrete knowledge of the localities in question, Francis lets his imagination fill in the details and draws more abstract, general conclusions. It is this type of journey that can give rise to epiphanies – moments of clarity and understanding. A third kind of journey is more metaphorical, such as when the author describes the development of the drama in Wales, for instance, or muses upon the nature of national identity. Taking this body of work as a whole, one gets a tangible sense of the Wales of Francis's experience and of his imagination, a Wales that is often implicitly contrasted with the starting point of his journeys: London.

This chapter deals with the ethics of place in J. O. Francis's personal essays, primarily through considering the notion of responsibility of the author as mapped out by Wayne Booth in *The Company We Keep*. These are responsibilities regarding truth-telling coupled with an awareness of the provisionality of conclusions, and, above all, a stance of respect vis-à-vis the reader as well as the community and non-human environment described. The chapter examines how Francis used the form of the personal essay to explore the interrelationship between community and place and to examine the locus of national identity.

The art of the personal essay involves making it seem entirely transparent: its aesthetics lies in it appearing to be entirely artless, a direct, unmediated channel between the author's thoughts and the reader's. It creates, or appears to create, a relationship that has a direct ethical impact. Francis was aware of this relationship and successfully developed a tone of friendly companionship, writing with much humour and generally in a descriptive and sometimes in a persuasive vein. We seem to hear his voice directly and his 'personal experience [is] presented through a mind that gives it a personal imprint and interpretation'.[1] The aim is an attitude of friendship, a virtue in itself in Aristotle's *Nicomachean Ethics* and a central metaphor for ethical engagement in *The Company We Keep*.

Apart from his many plays, Francis wrote nearly seventy short essays and around sixteen 'radio talks' and features for radio. Most of these short non-fiction pieces are written in the form of the personal essay, a form that allows the writer to write in an apparently slight, merely entertaining way about incidents, characters or places, but which, at a second glance, often conveys a deeper meaning. On the surface, an essay like 'The village of merciful men'[2] is about the somewhat lenient court proceedings in a north Wales village and 'The legend of the Welsh'[3] is about the prevalent prejudice that the Welsh are 'artistic' while the English are rational people of action. However, the first essay is also a meditation on the nature of justice, arguing that the more intimate and less formal environment of a village court might deliver it in a more effective way than the pomp and circumstance of the Old Bailey. The latter essay makes us laugh, but in doing so it shows how erroneous national stereotyping can be. Recognizing the second, deeper meaning allows the reader to gain ethical knowledge and deepen understanding; anecdotes reveal universal meaning just beneath the surface.

Having achieved some fame as a playwright who wrote about the Welsh nation and who did so in a thoughtful, amusing and 'homely' way, Francis was approached by the popular press in Wales and asked to write short pieces. He wrote twenty essays for the *Welsh Outlook* between 1919 and 1924 and about thirty essays for the *Western Mail* between 1921 and 1924. All his essays were about Wales, which suggests that he worked to a (perhaps informal) brief. Topics were varied and included reflections on eisteddfodau, travel writing, meditations on his childhood, Welsh politics, and, intriguingly, several defences of the London Welsh. He also wrote articles that were not personal essays, such as those on the development of Welsh drama in the *Western Mail*, in Hugh Edwards's *Wales* (1913) and in *The Amateur Stage* (1926?). In the late 1940s and in the 1950s he was commissioned by the BBC Head of Welsh Programmes, Aneirin Talfan Davies, to write short radio talks – spoken radio essays, which he voiced himself. His radio talks included non-fiction radio essays, such as the ten-minute-long 'The Welshman takes to the stage',[4] which was broadcast as part of the BBC Welsh Service's *Arts Magazine* in 1949, radio essays that shaded over into the short story such as 'Johnnie Genteel' (1945),[5] a talk about a Dicky Bach Dwl-like character in the fictional village of Llanrafon but which employs the approach and tone that normally characterizes the familiar essay, and one forty-five-minute radio feature on the development of the drama in Wales entitled *Beginners Please!* (1955).[6] The following will focus on his personal essays, which still sound fresh and are as enjoyable as anything Robert Louis Stevenson or G. K. Chesterton ever wrote. Crucially, the 'vision of Wales' pictured in them complements the ethics of place explored in his plays.

Even though the personal essay has been a popular genre for centuries, there has been little research on the subject, G. Douglas Atkins's *Tracing the Essay* (2005) being a notable exception. Therefore, a brief excursus on the nature of the essay and its own specific ethics is warranted here. It seems that the lack of research may be a result of the uncertain place of the essay within 'English studies': should it be studied as background to creative writing or should it be studied for its own sake? Should students merely read or actively produce creative non-fiction?[7] There is a great variety in terminology: the phrase 'creative nonfiction' is used side by side with 'essay'.[8] Meic Stephens calls the essays collected in *Illuminations* 'short prose' in the subtitle to his volume of translations,[9] but then, in the 'Preface', prefers the term *ysgrifau*, 'writings', because he feels that they differ from essays in English.[10] The confusion in the terminology is mirrored by the tremendous variety within the genre itself. Essays can be short (for example most of Chesterton's early essays, such as those contained in *The Defendant*, 1901, or the ultra-short essays contained in J. B. Priestley's *Delight*, 1949) or long (de Quincey, 'On murder considered as one of the fine arts', 1827). They can be personal reflections, including personal reflections on the self (Montaigne's *essais*; Leigh Hunt, 'Getting up on cold mornings', 1820), personal reflections on an activity (Hazlitt, 'On going a journey', 1822) or personal reflections on place (John Galsworthy, 'The inn of tranquility', 1910; Hilaire Belloc's 'On Ely', 1906). They can eschew the personal voice for a more impersonal stance (Thomas Carlyle, 'Signs of the times', 1829; John Ruskin, *Sesame and Lilies*, 1865) or a stance that seeks to instruct rather than explore (Francis Bacon's essays). They are generally taken to be non-fiction in which, one assumes, the truth is told,[11] although they may include fictional elements. Some are entirely made up, such as Jonathan Swift's biting satire 'A modest proposal' (1729). Usually the essay has only one narrative voice, but occasionally essays have been written in the form of dialogues. One could arguably count Plato's dialogues among them, as well as Arno Schmidt's 'Der Triton mit dem Sonnenschirm: Überlegungen zu einer Lesbarmachung von *Finnegans Wake* von James Joyce' (1961)[12]. The dialogic form lends itself to a use in media other than the printed page, and Schmidt's dialogic essays as well as some of the dialogic talks by J. O. Francis were written to be broadcast on the radio. This, in turn, means that essays are not always written but can be spoken – delivered as lectures, for example, as in the case of Virginia Woolf's 'How should one read a book?' (1932), which was presented as a lecture at a school.

Focusing on the personal essay, Francis's preferred essay style, it is possible to define the genre more closely, however. According to Hesse, the characteristics of the personal essay are

> that reality is mediated and narrativized; that the particular subjectivities of authors are crucial and should be textually embodied rather than effaced; that language and form must have a surface and texture that remind readers the work is artificed; that even though some readers are considerably more adept and enculturated, the work is not reserved for a narrow specialist audience.[13]

Personal essays are personal narrative reflections for the non-specialist reader. Harris argues that 'the personal essay is the literary kind closest to the lyric. Personal essays, like lyrics, state individually determined and packaged attitudes, feelings, or beliefs; to the extent that authors are successful . . . readers are stimulated to consider their agreement'.[14] Dialogue between author and reader is thus characteristic of the genre.[15] Indeed, the essay's effect on the reader is the most immediate entry point for a criticism based on ethics, especially a consideration of ethical responsibility.

The linchpin of the personal and the familiar essay is the author – or rather the persona the author adopts, what Harris refers to as 'presence'.[16] Usually the author tends to wear a cloak of genuine or assumed modesty with regard to subject and audience.[17] This authorial modesty and humility also suffuses the language in which the essay is written. 'The ordinary, the common, the humble, the modest – they variously describe aspects of the essay, the essayistic character, and the form's space'.[18] This modesty exists in tension with an element of self-confidence: the essay-writer believes that her personal reflections are worth reading and that her observations may lead us to significant insights. For example, Chesterton's 'A piece of chalk' (1905) describes the author setting out for a walk to the coast to do some drawing. He arrives and wants to set to work but finds he has no white chalk. Just as he is about to curse his bad luck he glances up and notices the obvious:

> The landscape was made entirely of white chalk. White chalk was piled more miles until it met the sky. I stooped and broke a piece of the rock I sat on: it did not mark so well as the shop chalks do, but it gave the effect. And I stood there in a trance of pleasure, realizing that this Southern England is not only a grand peninsula, and a tradition and a civilization; it is something even more admirable. It is a piece of chalk.[19]

The simplicity of the narrative, which is meant to be read as a truthful account, and the writer's ready admission of his error, underscore his humble attitude towards the reader. It makes the epiphany – a revelation in the religious sense – all the more wonderful. In sharing his epiphany with the reader, Chesterton assumes the mantle of philosopher-teacher, although not obtrusively so. This type of essay allows the reader to gain ethical knowledge, specifically about the virtue of being alive to one's environment and what it has to give, even though it is not openly didactic. Conclusions are suggested, hinted at, because the 'more directly an essay tells readers how they should feel and what they should do, the less thought it is likely to evoke'.[20] The ethics of the personal essay is determined by an authorial stance that takes readers seriously as fellow thinking adults. Moreover, the type of learning described here does not necessarily involve gaining entirely new knowledge, if that is narrowly understood as conceptual knowledge. Instead, the essay helps readers explore what they already know by adding a 'knowledge what it would be like', which Carroll argues, serves to add to the quality, not merely the quantity of knowledge: the result is an increase in understanding,[21] in wisdom.[22]

Francis, a few years younger than Chesterton, seems to have shared his outlook. He was at times almost comically humble. In 'By the kitchen fire' he noted that he consented to becoming a contributor to *The Welsh Outlook* with some misgivings. 'Some weeks went by before I was able to provide the necessary copy, and, during much of that period, I sat paralysed before the unsoiled writing sheet, in mortal terror of the *Welsh Outlook*'s high tradition'.[23] The terror of the blank sheet of paper is common to many authors, but to describe his words as smudges, which are about to deface the pristine piece of paper, is taking authorial humility to ironic extremes. In 'A comment from Corwen', an essay that is critical of aspects of the ways the National Eisteddfod was 'staged', the author's humility served to counteract and deflate possible counter-criticism, particularly *ad hominem* criticism, which might have been levelled against a relatively new eisteddfodwr:

> Therefore, as one who, in a brief experience, has learnt to love the Eisteddfod and to see in it a scope of achievement only in part fulfilled, I take courage faithfully to set down certain comments; and, while I suspect that my small oracles will be entirely ignored, I have at least the comfort of knowing that, like a true Eisteddfodwr, I am already chin deep in dispute, though I pledge no allegiance either to the Old Bards or the New.[24]

Here the internal contradiction in the stance of the essay writer – he is both humble and self-confident – becomes obvious. On the one hand, Francis stakes his claim to speaking his mind. On the other hand he declares carefully that his views are relatively unimportant and that he merely behaves like any other eisteddfodwr in similar circumstances.

Modesty of stance goes hand in hand with a (real or assumed) role as layperson or amateur.[25] Even though the essayist can be a professional writer, somebody who makes a substantial part of their income by writing essays and other journalistic pieces like Robert Louis Stevenson, G. K. Chesterton, Grant Allen or H. G. Wells, the stance of the writer is that of a leisured amateur, of somebody who writes because he enjoys doing so. As a civil servant, Francis had no pressing need to earn a living by the pen and thus could perhaps indulge in the pose of the amateur author with some justification. Indeed, we get no sense of J. O. Francis, the London-based civil servant, when we read his essays. His stance is that of somebody who travels at leisure, who observes people and places with sympathetic detachment, who picks up books idly and who takes the time to recollect childhood memories. Only once does the mask slip. 'On a dramatic entry' begins: 'Casting about to find a subject for this paper, I am sorely tempted to write about a certain friend of mine. . . .'[26], thus revealing something of the strain of having to write a column of about 1,500 words for the *Western Mail* week after week.

The directness of address signals the author's basic honesty of purpose. Even though use may be made of hyperbole, exaggeration and other literary devices associated with humour, the reader gets a sense of 'the directness and sense of honesty that comes with a single voice telling things as they are seen by that person'.[27] Crucially it is a relationship of respect: 'essay conventions develop a respectful kind of relationship with a reader: an effective narrator comes off as honest, yet does not burden the reader with a confessional'.[28] Although Francis sometimes contradicts himself – he argues that it is good that the Welsh are quick to discard traditions and to 'follow new lamps' in 'The followers of new lamps',[29] but then bemoans the fact that the traditions of the old Welsh railways are not kept up because 'we must remember that, though [these] lamps are new, they may not give better light' in 'In praise of Avon Wen'[30] – the reader does not doubt that the author's own opinions are expressed. Harris notes that the 'personal essay often seems honest even though not comprehensive, and thus necessarily less than fully truthful'.[31] However, 'the whole truth' is probably impossible to deliver: what is important for the ethical compact between author and reader is that the author appears to be telling the truth honestly as he sees it.

In the essays Francis adopted the voice of a man much older than he was in reality. In pieces like 'A meditation on a pink ticket' or 'Knickerbocker politics'[32] it is the voice of someone in advanced middle age and yet they were published before he was thirty-nine years old. The choice of adopting the voice of an older man was probably influenced by the fact that he had experienced major upheavals at a relatively young age. He had seen the rise of Keir Hardie and socialism in Wales (see 'Knickerbocker politics'), experienced the last significant Nonconformist Revival in 1904/5 and had lived through the First World War. The exciting part of his life seemed to lie behind him in the early 1920s. However, this older voice is also encouraged by the genre itself. The authority of the essayist depends largely on her wisdom – and wisdom comes with age. Assumed age and real age of the author need not be the same: G. K. Chesterton, who published *The Defendant* (1901) at the young age of twenty-seven, adopted the voice of someone who has had the time to form the opinions he defends. Similarly, in 'The mowing of a field' (1906), Hilaire Belloc returns to the small farm where he grew up and finds to his delight that he can still use a scythe to mow a field as skillfully as ever.[33] The essay's rhythm echoes the swing of the scythe, which is contrasted with the pointless haste of modernity. The voice of the essayist is that of somebody in tune with an unchanging, ageless rural landscape. When the essay was published in 1906, Belloc was only thirty-six years old.

Connected to the stance of the leisured amateur is a writing style that has been likened to a taking a stroll.[34] As Haas notes, the image of the stroll also hints at the essay's provisionality, at the tentativeness at which conclusions are arrived. In Haas's words, 'the appropriate way of proceeding is a speculative circling of the probable truth. Truth is only ever action-bound and procedural, never constitutes finished and final insight'.[35] The essay form is paradoxically both polished final product and carries with it the suggestion that the author is 'in the act of thinking things out, feeling and finding a way' and searching for a way to express himself.[36]

Francis signals provisionality by a certain tentativeness in the phrasing of his conclusions, such as 'And in the night, and the wind, and that far space of the sea is, *perhaps*, the secret of the lonely village.'[37] Phrases like that signal that the author's conclusions may not be final and allow for differences in opinion between writer and reader. The ethics of provisionality is a measure of respect towards the reader. The author recognizes the reader as her 'other' whom she addresses and whom she may wish to convince of her point of view but whose compliance she does not take for granted.

Harris has noted that the personal essay experienced a 'strong resurgence' at the end of the nineteenth century after a dry spell in the Victorian period.[38] The most famous English and Scottish practitioners of the form in Francis's period include Robert Louis Stevenson, Max Beerbohm, E. V. Lucas, G. K. Chesterton, Hilaire Belloc, A. A. Milne and others. The tone and style of Francis's essays suggests that he was deeply influenced by the modern British school of popular essayists, particularly by Chesterton. John Gross has written that '[m]any other English writers have preached Democracy in the abstract; Chesterton is one of the very few who genuinely liked the common man (because he was sure there was no such thing)'.[39] Francis's essays display the same virtue: he does not seek to instruct but speaks to the reader as a friend. Nor does he make assumptions about the reader's level of education as, for instance, Virginia Woolf's essays do. Phrases of hers such as 'It is obvious ... that Greek literature is the impersonal literature'[40] assume that readers at least have a passing knowledge of the literature she is talking about. Woolf's stance is democratic because she addresses the readers of her *Common Reader* as equals, and yet her work is largely inaccessible to those who are not on her wavelength. Francis, by contrast, is a true populist like Chesterton whose work addresses everyone, regardless of knowledge or interest in (high) culture. He does, however, presume that his readers are Welsh or have an interest in Welsh matters.

The kind of personal essay Francis wrote for the *Western Mail* and *The Welsh Outlook* remained a rarity in Wales in the period under discussion. English-language cultural periodicals published broadly between 1910 and 1940, such as *Wales* or *The Welsh Outlook*, contain very few personal or familiar essays. Among the handful of writers providing such material for the *Outlook* was Francis's fellow dramatist R. G. Berry, who contributed two personal essays between 1920 and 1921 – one about his dog[41] and one about his library.[42] Another exception is the idiosyncratic travel sketch 'Souvenirs from Erin' by Idris Davies, which appeared in *Wales* in 1937.[43]

Francis was easily the most prolific writer of essays for the periodical at the time and his pieces were much appreciated by the magazine's editor Tom Jones, as a letter to Percy Watkins written in 1919 shows.[44] It is not entirely clear whether such writing was not encouraged by editors or whether authors rarely offered such pieces. The lack of personal essays contributed to the fact that publications like *The Welsh Outlook* had an overly serious air and were somewhat deficient in humour.[45]

According to Meic Stephens, the tradition of the personal essay, or *ysgrif*, in Welsh established itself after the First World War at about the same time that Francis published his first essays, which means, first, that Welsh-language writers seem to have been influenced by the same school of English-language personal essays and, secondly, that Francis was not influenced by his Welsh contemporaries directly.[46] T. H. Parry-Williams, the father of the personal essay in Welsh, began publishing his 'writings' (*ysgrifau*) a few years after Francis. This body of work established the genre in Wales and signalled a decisive break with the kind of essays that were published in nineteenth-century Welsh periodicals, which had mostly been didactic and had been published by the magazines of the various Nonconformist denominations, such as *Seren Cymru*, a Baptist periodical. Parry-Williams's essays replicate the manner of some of Chesterton's pieces but develop a light, humorous voice of their own that set the tone and style of the personal essay in Welsh for many years to come. Some of his essays were published in *Y Llenor* ['The writer'] in 1922 and his collection *Ysgrifau* appeared in 1928. Following Parry-Williams, the essay enjoyed a brief vogue in Welsh, and not only major writers like Saunders Lewis, Kate Roberts and T. Gwynn Jones but also people primarily known as academics and scholars, such as Iorwerth C. Peate and Ffransis G. Payne, contributed essays on a variety of subjects.

At the beginning of this chapter, I suggested that Francis's essays could be likened to journeys, which take the author and his readers from London to Wales – the first along the lines of the Great Western Railway into the south Wales of his boyhood memories, the second following the route of the erstwhile Cambrian Railway into the north and west Wales of his present (1919–21), and the third constituting more metaphorical journeys. The rest of the chapter will trace those journeys and provide a discussion of Francis's vision of Wales as it emerges from these essays.

FIRST JOURNEY: LONDON – NEWPORT – CARDIFF – RHONDDA

Francis's essays about his past are about 'the impressions [that are] most deeply written on [his] mind'.[47] The journeys into south Wales lead into the Rhondda of his boyhood years, the 1880s and 90s. They are nostalgic reminiscences, which converge on the 'Town of the martyr', Merthyr Tydfil, his hometown.[48] It is a bustling place, filled with warm-hearted, kindly people, who can be passionate when the occasion demands it, for example at election time.[49]

Place is not clearly remembered in these short sketches; it is always people that are in the foreground. Interestingly, the iconic symbols and features of south Wales, such as winding gear, industrial machinery, slag heaps with their attendant evils of pollution, overcrowding, and the ever-present grime and poverty are completely absent from Francis's imaginative reconstructions of the past. This landscape, which was to become so significant for the fiction emerging from south Wales in the 1930s and which dominated public consciousness to such an extent that it virtually came to symbolize 'Wales' as a whole,[50] simply does not appear in his memories. It is also absent from Francis's plays about industrial urban south Wales, *Change* and *The Devouring Fire*. Even though he did not come from a family of miners, the emblems of mining would have been all around him, so their absence is suggestive of a world-view in which human beings are subject to influences of place but are not completely dominated by the materiality of their environment.

The places that left lasting impressions are those that filled the young Francis with a sense of excitement and pleasure: the railway station,[51] the rugby pitch[52] and the Drill Hall where political hustings took place and where the teenager saw Keir Hardie before the latter was elected MP for Merthyr Tydfil and Aberdare in 1900.[53] In 'Knickerbocker politics', the excitement of elections is described as being so palpable as to have percolated down to the as yet uncomprehending ten-year-old Francis: 'I had no knowledge of what [the politicians] stood for. . . . But I did my duty, and, like many another political philosopher, I listened to discover which crowd sang loudest, and straightaway gave it the full weight of my ten-year-old support'.[54] With a few brushstrokes a bygone era is evoked: politicians 'then wore silk hats and frock-coats as necessary parts of their attire'. Mabon, who 'was one of the saints of the South Wales calendar', dominated the valley.[55] The reference is to William 'Mabon' Abraham, secretary of the Cambrian Miners' Association and later president of the

South Wales Miners' Federation, who was 'a canny bargainer, but one deeply committed to class collaboration and social harmony. His influence pervaded most of the coalfield'.[56] The miner's monthly holiday was appropriately named 'Mabon's Day'. The decline of Mabon's influence was a central symbol of the social change dramatized in Francis's play of the same title:

> The abolition of Mabon's Day after the six-month coal stoppage of 1898 was not only an error of monumental, if characteristic stupidity by the coalowners. It marked the end of an era in the coalfield in which the values of Welshness, of nonconformity, of class harmony and identification with the valley community would be rapidly eroded by new imperatives of class struggle and industrial conflict. Ethical priorities would be supplanted by economic, and Mabon's world brought crashing down.[57]

This enormous social and political change is here alluded to as a change in style – Keir Hardie, accompanied by his wife, appears in the Drill Hall wearing a 'shabby, careless suit' and 'against his soft-collar flared the challenge of a red neck-tie'.[58]

The Merthyr of his youth is at the centre of the past of Francis's imagination. Given that he is describing childhood memories, which are generally circumscribed by the location of home, this is not surprising. However, one of Francis's central aims in his work more generally is locating a genuine Welsh identity in south Wales. In 'The railways of romance', he contrasts the big metropolitan railway stations of Paddington and Euston, which are 'wondrous places' but which have a 'strenuous air', with the rather more comfortable ambience of Merthyr train station.[59] Similarly, in his memory the different trains that arrived in Merthyr have distinct personalities: 'the "London North Western" engine carried an air of restraint and culture, suggesting, perhaps an elegant curate. It came among us kindly, but it was never really of us'.[60] The Cardiff-bound 'Taff' suggested 'a robust representation of John Bull',[61] thus characterizing Cardiff as active and confident but also as a hybrid place whose intrinsic Welsh identity had been lost or given up. Real sympathy is reserved for the 'Brecon and Merthyr' train, which apparently was never on time. 'It was not even expected. People were, in the main, quite satisfied when it came on the proper day. . . . [W]hen it arrived at last the general relief was so charged with fine emotion that pity and forgiveness flowed easily to the top.'[62] Positive identification with Welshness is nearly always bound up with an idea of romance, of poetry: the train is described as inspiring the imagination and not being in thrall to prosaic notions of efficiency and punctuality. It is worth emphasizing that this romantic notion of national identity is not located in rural Wales, but in the centre of industrial, urban south Wales where it would have seemed incongruous to many.

The essays primarily evoke a concrete, localized past for readers who are encouraged to identify with the memories of the author or to contribute their own. Their narrative point of view is limited and by focusing on small details, Francis evokes a vivid picture of the past. One can feel the atmosphere and readers of the author's age will have recognized the incidents he writes about. It is a kind of documentary reportage, which is unsentimental despite the focus on his childhood past and the 'homely' narrative tone. But it is neither political analysis nor commentary.

SECOND JOURNEY: LONDON – BRECON – LLANIDLOES – ABERDOVEY – ABERYSTWYTH[63]

The second type of journey takes place in the writer's present: the starting point is Francis's home in London and he is usually on holiday, setting out for various holiday destinations (Corwen, Aberystwyth, St David's). He seems to be alone, in a Wordsworthian mood, observing his thoughts and feelings to recall them later 'in tranquillity'. However, the impression of the essay as a dialogue just between author and reader is not quite correct – occasionally he mentions a travelling companion and it is possible that the conclusions of his essays are not the product of his thought processes alone. However, the stance is that of a tête-à-tête conversation between author and reader. Importantly, Francis is aware of his status as outsider and, in describing landscape and people, he 'resists the lure of that false intimacy of unthinking assimilation of objects and people'[64] by retaining a characteristic humility and respect vis-à-vis the 'other', namely the place and community he is visiting.

Jane Bennett has argued in favour of a 'naive realism' when dealing with the challenge of recording the non-human 'other'. It is a response to Adorno's concept of the 'non-identical' (*das Nichtidentische*) developed in *Die Negative Dialektik* (1966),[65] a term for the way in which the materiality of the non-human can never completely be explained by human beings because they have no way of experiencing it. Bennett, however, argues that a

> naive realism (. . .) allows nonhumanity to appear on the ethical radar screen . . . [A] receptive mood with a moment of naivete is a useful counter to the tendency (. . .) to conclude the biography of an object by showing how it, like everything, is socially constituted.[66]

In other words, a 'naive realism' looks respectfully at the nonhuman other, takes into account its material difference and is aware of its own sense-making strategies. It allows the nonhuman other to be 'other', to have a real existence outside the discourse about it. Strangely perhaps, this post-postmodern concept of 'naive realism' describes Francis's pre-postmodern consciousness very well. He is familiar with this landscape and its people and travelling to Corwen, Borth, Aberystwyth or St David's always entails a partial homecoming. But it is only ever partial and, with the exception of Merthyr, he cannot and does not pretend to fully understand any of the places he visits.

'The village of the tides', in which Francis visits Borth, is a good example. The opening paragraph sets the tone and mood of the piece:

> Our old Welsh towns and villages have, almost always, a characteristic quality. In some that quality is elusive, like a faint fragrance hanging in the air. Others have the past so clearly written on their stones that the visitor needs no book to learn the essentials of their history.[67]

Francis agrees with the geographical thinking stemming from La Blanche that places have a particular personality. It is the task of the visitor to look beyond guidebooks – dismissed in '"Yr adsain"' because 'their revelations are all of the external' and reveal nothing of a place's 'spirit and its charm'[68] – and immerse himself in the place to discover its story. To do so is, in fact, an act of virtuous contemplation, of respectful listening: 'For those whose inward ear can catch the silent language of suggestion, down in the heart of this uncommunicating village lies a secret that must be more deeply sought'.[69]

The right frame of mind for virtuous contemplation is one of solitary meditation, alone on an evening in winter, with the full moon providing atmosphere. Only by consciously fading out the distractions of the day – bright light, noise – can Francis produce the conditions for the necessary shift in perspective that leads to understanding:

> And in the night, and the wind, and that far space of the sea is, perhaps, the secret of the lonely village. It stands on the verge of the waters of disaster. Many centuries have sped since the waves broke down the walls of Seithenyn, flooding the rich plain of the Cantref. ... [B]rooding alone by the sea that conquered, the village can never forget those 'sixteen fortified cities, the largest and finest that were in Wales, excepting only Caerleon upon Usk.'[70]

The essay refers to the legend of the drowning of Cantre'r Gwaelod (the 'lowland hundred'), Wales's own tale of Atlantis. According to this legend, the space now occupied by Cardigan Bay was made up of low-lying land with a hundred homesteads. Before of finding itself a lonely and isolated village on the edge of the water, Borth is imagined as having once been part of a thriving community. Thus the 'secret' of the village is that it is a survivor, with all the complex feelings that surviving entails, not least loneliness.

This conclusion, and the respectful provisionality at which it is arrived, is characteristic of this type of essay. Its object is to express the truth about Borth as it revealed itself to Francis after an act of contemplation similar to Chesterton's epiphany in 'A piece of chalk'. This means going beyond externalities straight to the essence of the place, which entails following its history down to its mythological foundations. His is a pre-constructionist view of the essence of place: place is not, as Doreen Massey has recently argued, 'relational'. The identity of place is not seen as a construct, a 'product of practices, trajectories, interrelations'[71]. Francis's Borth has a soul and it is this intrinsic 'personality' or 'character' of place that he seeks to discover and transmit to his readership.

This group of essays usually takes Francis on a journey to north Wales and to west Wales. Once, however, he travels home to the Rhondda: 'Against measuring heads' is part of an ongoing engagement with locating genuine Welshness in south Wales by presenting local people as being as rooted in their industrial locality as rural Welsh people reputedly are in theirs. The essay pretends to take up ironic cudgels against the 'new geography' of Patrick Geddes and H. J. Fleure and their contention that the 'natural units' of culture, landscape and identity do not neatly map on to political units.[72] He satirizes Fleure's longitudinal research project of 'measuring the types of Welsh people'[73] and good-humouredly invokes the court of public opinion:

> I refuse to yield to this upstart ethnology. What was good enough for our fathers is good enough for me. . . . I take the opportunity of laying testimony before the court of public opinion, and my testimony is the more reliable because it comes, not from the laboratory or the class-room (old breeding-grounds of error), but from the great temple of human truths – the public railway carriage.[74]

Francis's journey home is his 'research experiment'. Observing passengers on the train, he creates a dichotomy between English people, who are 'stiff, reserved and silent'[75] and create distance between themselves and others, and Welsh people, who are warm and in whose company '[c]onversation flows easily through the carriage'.[76] The representative of Welshness encountered on this journey home to Merthyr is a hard-bitten old collier, who sits before you with a pungent cloud of 'Ringer' or 'Franklin' trailing across the pallor of a blue-scarred visage. He must, of course, be one of the real old Valley breed, who remembers the 'Glorans'[77] – not a member of the new invading hosts of anywhere. He has been down to Pontypridd, and is now returning, dressed in his 'evening clothes' ('dillad dwetydd').[78]

Beyond the cliché, this choice of character who represents the 'other' to English reserve is interesting: his roots have long been established, his language is the local English dialect peppered with Welsh words and phrases and he works in the predominant industry of the area. He is contrasted with those who are not similarly rooted in place. Identification of Welshness by character is presented as more reliable than measuring cephalic indexes. The journey home to familiar characters like this is also the journey into the heart of Wales. It implicitly negates the equation of the identification of 'real Wales' with 'rural Wales' and claims his home as the home for a genuine Welsh identity based on the positive, even romantic, appraisal of the local.

THIRD JOURNEY: INTO THE HEART OF THE NATION

The third group of essays are not about literal journeys at all. Instead, they deal with ideas, concepts and ideologies and take the reader to the centre of Francis's imagined nation. 'The legend of the Welsh', for instance, begins by arguing against national stereotyping, ascribing it to mental laziness: 'In the old human dislike of the labour that goes to our understanding, we are always prone to make our definitions at the expense of truth'.[79] Stereotypes are wrong because they mask the contradictions inherent in national identity: 'A baffling fact in the character of nations is that, regularly and by immemorial habit, they combine qualities that seem mutually exclusive'.[80] Not only are national traits contradictory, they are also often less 'picturesque'[81] than stereotypes suggests. According to Francis's ironic pen, the English stereotype of the Welsh has a long history:

> As far as I can make out, the English assessment of the Welsh must have been arrived at, once and for all, in the far-off centuries of warfare between the two peoples. The bards who encouraged the Welsh in battle produced a deep and lasting impression on the English invaders; and from that time to this the English have insisted on regarding us as a race of artists, from whose lips immortal verse and deathless music flow in a steady stream. Our choral singing, our eisteddfodau, our religious festivals, and our delight in orators

have, of course, helped to maintain the English delusion regarding us. Indeed, we have long since come to accept that delusion ourselves. 'Ah yes!' says England, with its kindly, tolerant smile, 'The Welsh – a race of artists, poets, orators, and dreamers!' We think it rather nice of them, and, with a little encouragement, we are prepared to put on a look of Celtic melancholy.[82]

The stereotype of the Welsh as feminized, emotional and artistic, which tends to be juxtaposed against the stereotype of the English as rational, practical and unemotional has a long pedigree. It informs Matthew Arnold's treatment of Welsh culture in *On the Study of Celtic Literature* (1867). It is not only disseminated by English writers – Welsh writers, too, are in thrall to it. Katie Gramich has noted how in the Dau Wynne's novel *A Maid of Cymru* (1901) 'the English are seen as "materialistic" and "utilitarian", engaged in "conquest of the world", whereas the Welsh are seen as poetic, dreamy, liable to "abandon" themselves in impractical pursuits'.[83] And elsewhere, of course, Francis himself cannot resist the lure of the 'romance' of the stereotype, notably in 'The railways of romance' (discussed above) and 'A lament of the Cambrian railway'.[84] In this essay he likens the journey to Aberystwyth to a pilgrim's route to be undertaken in a meditative spirit:

> As it had ever been, Aberystwyth was still a place to be approached in the mood of the Wandering Friar – and at no greater pace than his. To draw near in the vulgar violence of speed would be to break the spell. The Cambrian Railway maintained the ancient glamour, and three parts of our delight in getting to Aberystwyth came – as it should – out of the fear that we might never arrive at all.[85]

Of course, the description is ironic, but it is a loving, sympathetic irony that does not demolish the stereotype but instead celebrates it. 'The legend of the Welsh' is different in that it tries to overturn the stereotype because the seemingly 'good' characterization of the Welsh as 'artistic' is now considered a double-edged compliment, which simultaneously flatters and controls the 'other' as real political power clearly should only be entrusted to 'the great practical nation', England, which, in contrast to Wales, 'plods on and "gets things done"'.[86] Toleration does not imply acceptance, it means being able to put up with difference, particularly when one's position of power is not seriously threatened by the 'other' being tolerated. Wales, Francis suggests, is colluding in this act of colonial toleration by playing up to the stereotype.

The essay then proceeds to dismantle the stereotype of Wales as 'artistic' ('Certain Greek cities, not as big as Cardiff, completely eclipse all we have done', p. 13) before going on to deliver the surprising thesis that the

'Welshman's gifts lie not in the realm of art, but in the brisk world of action. His line is not in the dream, but the business' (p. 13). It lists several examples before finishing with the triumphant assertion that, during 'Black Friday' (15 April 1921), when the leaders of the National Transport Workers' Federation and the National Union of Railwaymen decided not to support striking mineworkers, the fate of the nation was decided by a group of Welshmen:

> for the Government, Mr. Lloyd George, of Criccieth; for the mineowners, Mr. Evan Williams, of Pontardulais; for the railwaymen, Mr. J. H. Thomas, of Newport; for the transport workers, Mr. Robert Williams, of Swansea; and for the miners, Mr. Frank Hodges, born at Chepstow, but, by training a Welshman.[87]

Francis does not want to engage in a political discussion per se; the point of the list is to assert that Welsh people occupy key positions in the polity and exercise real power every day. By arguing against national stereotyping in this way, Francis is in danger of simply reversing it rather than acknowledging the true complexity of identity, thus leaving the original dichotomy intact. Interestingly, the examples he marshals in defence of his thesis are mainly taken from his present: he mentions the number of Welsh sea-captains and the fact that Welsh people have done well in the Civil Service. It seems that a recourse to history or, indeed, to myth would have been counter-productive in this context.

Francis is likewise focused on present-day reality in the series of 'London Welsh papers' comprising of seven essays published in *The Welsh Outlook* between October 1920 and April 1921,[88] which also discuss national stereotyping. This time, however, it is the prejudice of the Welsh against the London Welsh that is at issue. The first essay dismantles the prejudice that the London Welshman 'has left his father's home to go into a far country'[89] and now resides there without taking any further interest in his home country. The six essays that follow enumerate the contributions made by the London Welsh to the Welsh nation, particularly through the various cultural organizations such as the *Cymmrodorion* and the *Gwyneddigion*. Arguments in favour of the London Welsh are the following: first, Francis mentions their engagement in politics on behalf of Wales.[90] Secondly, he argues that London has 'the power of welding Northmen and Southerners into one solid race': a unified national identity without the inherent rivalry of north and south is, apparently, only possible in London. Finally, he takes in 'the broad sweep of our island story', casts his mind back to legendary, pre-Roman times 'when there was a City of King Lud'.[91] As in 'The village of the tides' a mythological past is key to his argument. It seems that the London Welsh have a much stronger claim to a true Welsh identity than Welsh people residing in Wales: 'It is not we who have wandered, but the others – the Cardiffians and the Carnarvonites, the hypochondriacs of Llandrindod and the pale ecclesiastics of Bangor. We are where our people dwelt in the beginning'.[92] This striking manoeuvre displaces the centre (or centres) of Welsh identity to London and yet remains true to the logic of *cydymdreiddiad* of community and place, although his argument entails the loss of the third variable of J. R. Jones's term, namely language.

Indeed, Francis does not usually thematize the issue of language. In '"Yr adsain"' he argues that visitors to Corwen should 'avoid the guidebook that brings in Corwen as an appendage to Llangollen'[93] and instead read *Yr Adsain*, the local newspaper, which is written in Welsh. If his advice is meant at all seriously, Francis presupposes a knowledge of Welsh on the part of the visitor. In 'Proselytes of the book'[94] he discusses a range of reasons why people might like to learn Welsh without, however, expressing any opinion on the role of Welsh for Welsh culture or commenting on the rapid decline in the number of Welsh speakers in the early decades of the twentieth century. The essays are conspicuously free from any expression of preference for either Welsh or English as carriers of national identity. It appears that his notion of an identity based on locality included whatever language was spoken there – English, Welsh or a mixture of the two.

Francis's conception of the interrelationship of place and identity, his search for an essence of what a 'national character' might consist of and his insistence that both the people of south Wales and the London Welsh are fully Welsh replicate some of the concerns of his plays, notably in *The Beaten Track*, *Little Village*, *The Dark Little People* and *King of the River*. In common with much critical and popular discourse around identity at this time, his assumptions about the nature of the identities of people and of place were essentialist and in line with the conclusions Fleure drew from his research. Fleure had looked at the archaeological evidence and compared this with his findings from his survey of cephalic indexes in Wales. He concluded that ethnic markers such as hair colour, form of skull and height were still visible in his day: 'both England and Wales undoubtedly retain many descendants of their pre-Roman peoples'[95] and they are 'to a considerable extent similar in both cases'. Types did not blend but existed side by side.[96] Despite Francis's joking dismissal of Fleure's work in 'Against measuring heads', his work shows a similar understanding of national characteristics as immutable. What he argues against is prejudice and the denial of the contradictions and complexities of national identity by both the Welsh and the English. The local – represented here by the old miner in 'Against measuring heads', by villages such as Borth, by local newspapers, and by the Welsh cultural societies in London – is privileged as the locus of real national identity.

The difficulty with his line of argument is, as Massey has noted, the 'association of the local with the good and the vulnerable . . . It contributes to a persistent romanticization of the local'.[97] This romanticization can be obvious, as in 'The village of the tides' or 'A lament of the Cambrian railway' where it is celebrated. It can also be more implicit as the local experience – the experience of living in a particular *bro* – is privileged over any other experience. The link between place and community is not a matter of chosen allegiance; it is an essentialist deeper truth. This essentialism runs into trouble when it comes to his argument for the 'Welshness' of the London Welsh. Ignoring his own admission that most of the London Welsh migrated to London relatively recently, he constructs a complex argument seeking to locate the origins of the London-Welsh community in the pre-Roman London of the legendary King Lud. This argument, taken at face value, is patently absurd, and yet his imagined interrelatedness of community and place necessitates it. It is also problematic because it denies migrants the right to an identity based on elective allegiance. Thus he excludes 'the new invading hosts of anywhere'[98] from his conceptualization of Welshness and similarly Cardiff is regarded as having no special place-identity because, like its railway station, it is a 'gathering-ground for all classes, creeds, and clans'.[99] It is also unclear how many generations it takes for national identity to take hold. Oddly, this means that he excludes himself – a recent migrant to London – from claiming the London-Welsh identity that he so strenuously defends.

Essentialist notions of identity were, however, part of the academic and popular consensus of the time in which Francis was writing. And, while he did not usually question mainstream opinion, essays like 'The legend of the Welsh' and the 'London Welsh papers' questioned the validity of some stereotypical representations of Welshness. The description of his *bro* served to complicate the notion that 'real Welshness' is rooted in a rural lifestyle. Crucially, his respectful stance towards the reader opens up the option of dissent: more often than not, Francis creates a vision that invites the reader to engage with it on her own terms rather than trying to deluge her with arguments. And finally, his description of the land and its community entails a similar respect for the 'otherness' of place's materiality and spirit, on which he declines to impose his interpretation, thus allowing it to retain its indigenous mystery.

Afterword

This book has argued that localizing ethics – incorporating notions of place into a discussion of the virtues – is crucial when one seeks to escape from a universalism that negates the importance of specific cultural, historical and other circumstances without, however, sliding into the quagmire of moral relativism. The specific characteristics of virtues may transcend cultures, but for them to make sense in a specific environment they have to be adapted to local circumstances. The virtues, as Aristotle understands them, are thus largely culturally determined.

However, an alternative view exists, according to which ethics is based on a moral sense that is biologically innate. If all human beings – and perhaps even non-human animals – share a moral sense, the foundations of ethical systems are universal, not place- and culture-specific. Charles Darwin, for example, thought that morality was an innate sense. In *The Descent of Man* (1871), he argued that the moral sense did not only distinguish human beings from non-human animals but also that a developed sense of morality distinguished more 'civilised' human beings from 'savages'.[1] Lately, James Q. Wilson argued for such an inborn quality, even though he admitted that he could not prove a biological origin of a moral sense.[2] Recent research in moral psychology suggests that the biological location of morality is – like most other things that make us human – in the brain.[3] John Mikhail in *Elements of Moral Cognition* (2011) adopts Chomsky's concept of the Universal Grammar, namely the underlying facility that enables all non-impaired human babies to learn any language on earth, and argues that human beings also have a Universal Moral Grammar.[4] Most excitingly, experimental moral psychologists are now able to use brain imaging technology such as functional Magnetic

Resonance Imaging (fRMI) to conclusively prove that certain parts of the brain are active when human beings think morally. Thus, in a recent paper on moral emotions, Jorge Moll et al. discovered that 'the orbital and medial sectors of the prefrontal cortex and the superior temporal sulcus region, which are critical regions for social behavior and perception, play a central role in moral appraisals', not just the amygdala, which is associated with primitive emotions, such as fear.[5] Morality is thus based on higher-level brain activity encompassing several brain areas. Do these recent findings that consider the human body in isolation thus invalidate an ethical approach that looks beyond the boundaries of the body to the world in which we live?

While the case for a biological origin of a moral sense is a strong one, it does not invalidate a case for a place-based ethics. After all, an understanding of ethics and morality must in some way originate in the brain otherwise we would not have the capacity to think in ethical terms at all. However, while the findings derived from fRMI imaging show us that the brain is active in contexts of moral emotion or decision making, they cannot show us what form these moral emotions or decisions take: our thoughts are still our own. More importantly, this research shows that human beings are predisposed to interpret certain actions morally, which gives rise to ethics, but it does not explain the form ethical systems take. This is why Mikhail's Universal Moral Grammar is a good analogy: just like the Universal Grammar, the concept of the Universal Moral Grammar is a faculty, a predisposition, but does not tell us anything about the specificities of the ethical framework a human being operates within or the moral rules she follows.

To respond to Socrates's question of how human being should live, it may thus be more helpful to consider the web of linkages that connect human beings within their social contexts, contexts that are inevitably determined by culture and place. Aristotle's own conception of the virtues is culturally specific as his framework is explicitly designed for aristocratic Greek men with disposable income.[6] It is also place-specific as these Greek aristocrats are envisioned as living in a polis, a city state not unlike Athens. The realization of the 'implaced' nature of Aristotelian ethics allows one to transfer its methodology to usefully examine other, equally place- and culture-based systems of ethics.

As a quintessentially Edwardian writer, J. O. Francis emerged from a Victorian Welsh cultural background that had been characterized by several crucial elements, namely by a growth in civic nationalism, by a tendency to understand Welsh politics in terms of Liberal politics, by a belief that the nation still adhered to a particular form of Nonconformist Christianity, by the assumption that Welsh culture was mediated through the Welsh language and by an understanding that a certain kind of social contract forged in the 1860s still held sway in the 1890s and after. By the time Francis and other contemporary playwrights started writing for the stage, these central assumptions were being eroded, including the Victorian ethical framework, a mixture of Bentham's, Mill's and Sidgwick's Utilitarianism tempered by Nonconformist Christian values.

As a non-believer who came to be progressively disillusioned with politics, Francis explored the notion of an ethics based on locality and on local traditions. At its core was the organically grown community – not necessarily but often a rural community. He extrapolated an understanding of culture, nation and national identity from what he regarded as a wholesome, local community-based ethics. His concept of tradition, place and community was essentialist. What mattered to him was that the development of a community's ethics was 'natural' and he opposed what he regarded as the impositions of Nonconformist culture as vigorously as Caradoc Evans but employed a much more conciliatory stance, preferring mild humour to satire.

This understanding of a place-based, culturally determined ethics permeates the form of his plays and his essays as much as their contents: throughout his career he remained wedded to a realism that apparently gives audiences and readers direct access to the thoughts and actions of his characters. Indeed, realism is part and parcel of the notion of ethics he developed: the medium is as 'natural' as the message, and, to (post)postmodern audiences and readers must be just as suspect as the essentialism of his ethical vision. Yet, despite the problems inherent in this particular type of mimesis, Francis's stance was progressive: at his time and in his hands, realism was new, exhilarating and often challenged received opinion.

J. O. Francis was among the pioneers of what became a national (amateur) drama movement. His plays became models for other playwrights to adopt or, in time, to write against. His place is among the founding fathers and mothers of Welsh Writing in English and his work should be part of the canonical texts of Welsh literature and drama. A reassessment of Francis's work should be part of a re-telling of the story of drama and theatre in Wales, one which focuses on statistical evidence of performances given all over Wales – amateur as well as professional. Having considered one key writer of the Welsh drama movement, the present volume constitutes one key element in an archaeology of Welsh drama and performance that is yet to be written.

List of Works by J. O. Francis

1 Published Plays
The Bakehouse: A Gossip's Comedy (in One Act) (Cardiff: Educational Publishing Co. Ltd, 1914).
The Beaten Track: A Welsh Play in Four Acts (London: Samuel French, 1927).
Birds of a Feather: A Welsh Wayside Comedy in One Act (Newtown: Welsh Outlook Press, 1927).
Change: A Glamorgan Play in Four Acts (Aberystwyth: William Jones, 1913).
Cross-Currents: A Play of Welsh Politics in Three Acts (Cardiff: Educational Publishing Co. Ltd, 1924).
The Crowning of Peace: A Short Pageant of the League of Nations (Cardiff: Educational Publishing Co. Ltd, 1922).
The Dark Little People: A Comedy of the Welsh Tribes (Cardiff, London: Educational Publishing Co. Ltd, 1922?).
His Shining Majesty: A One Act Comedy (Cardiff: William Lewis, ?)
Howell of Gwent: a Romantic Drama in Three Acts (Cardiff: Educational Publishing Co. Ltd, 1934).
Hunting the Hare: A One Act Comedy (Cardiff: William Lewis, 1943).
John Jones: An Episode in the History of Welsh Letters (Newtown: Welsh Outlook Press, 1928).
King of the River: A One Act Comedy (Cardiff: William Lewis, 1942).
Little Village: A Welsh Farce in Three Acts (Cardiff: Educational Publishing Co. Ltd., 1929).
The Perfect Husband: A Welsh Farce in One Act (Newtown: Welsh Outlook Press, 1927?).
The Poacher: A Comedy in One Act (Cardiff: Educational Publishing Co. Ltd, 1914?).
The Sewing Guild: A Woman's Comedy in One Act (Cardiff: William Lewis, 1943?).

LIST OF WORKS BY J. O. FRANCIS

Tares in the Wheat: A Country Comedy in Three Acts (Cardiff: William Lewis, 1942?).

2 Published Plays: Translations[1]

Adar o'r Unlliw: Comedi mewn Un Act (Drefnewydd: Welsh Outlook Press, 1928).
Y Bobl Fach Ddu: Comedi Ynghylch Llwythau Cymru mewn Tair Act (Cardiff: Educational Publishing Co. Ltd, 1923).
Deufor-Gyfarfod, tr. Magdalen Morgan (London: Samuel French, 1929).
Ffordd yr Holl Ddaear: Drama mewn Pedair Act, tr. Magdalen Morgan (London: Samuel French, 1926).
Gwyntoedd Croesion: Drama ar Wleidyddiaeth Cymru mewn Tair Act, tr. R. Silyn Roberts (Cardiff: Educational Publishing Co. Ltd, 1924).
John Jones: Pennod yn Hanes Llên Cymru (Drefnewydd: Welsh Outlook Press, 1928).
Y Potsier: Digrifawd mewn Un Act (London: Samuel French, 192?).
Ein Bischof auf Abwegen: eine walisische Straßenkomödie, tr. Clotilde Schenck zu Schweinsberg, Bäreneiter Spieltexte, No. 421 (Kassel: Bärenreiter-Verlag, 1970).

3 Unpublished plays

Antony Settles Down: A Farcical Comedy in Four Acts, no MS, 1922?
The Broken Reed, one-act play, c.1911, no MS.
Day of Glory: A South Wales Comedy in One Act, MS and TS, 1956.
The Devouring Fire, play in three acts, MS and TS, 1953?
Eiddo Caesar, translation into Welsh of *The Things that are Caesar's*, no MS., 1925.
For France: An Episode from the Franco-Prussian War, one-act play, October 1914/15, MS.
Forbidden Fruit: A Welsh Rural Comedy in One Act, MS, n.d.
The Guns of Victory: A Play in One Act, 1915, no MS.
In God's Good Time, submission for a television comedy, no record of broadcast, 1954?
Jack Edwards, one-act play, c.1911, no MS.
Mrs Howells Intervenes, earlier version/title of *The Bakehouse* c.1911, no MS.
The Old Adam, prob. earlier version of *Birds of a Feather*, no MS, c.1914.
Old Heath House: A Comedy in Three Acts, MS, n.d.
The Other Gods, performed at the college reunion in 1908, no MS.
The Renegade, play in three acts, MS, draft, n.d.
The Things that are Caesar's, no MS, 1923.
The Whirligig: A Comedy of Time's Revenges, MS and TS, c.1955/6.

4 Published essays and other non-fiction:
'A Friday paper. I. The village of the tides', *Western Mail*, 31 December 1920, 4.
'A Friday paper. II. The glory of Glamorgan', *Western Mail*, 7 January 1921, 4.
'A Friday paper. III. A meditation on a pink ticket', *Western Mail*, 14 January 1921, 6.
'A Friday paper. IV. Against measuring heads', *Western Mail*, 21 January 1921, 6.
'A Friday paper. V. The railways of romance', *Western Mail*, 28 January 1921, 10.
'A Friday paper. VI. An ex-politician in Cardiganshire', *Western Mail*, 4 February 1921, 6.
'A Friday paper. VII. A herald of our dramatists', *Western Mail*, 11 February 1921, 6.
'A Friday paper. VIII. A revelation in Cardiganshire', *Western Mail*, 18 February 1921, 6.
'A Friday paper. IX. Knickerbocker politics', *Western Mail*, 25 February 1921, 6.
'A comment from Corwen', *The Welsh Outlook*, 6/9, 1919, 228–31.
'A Friday paper. X. Proselytes of the book', *Western Mail*, 4 March 1921, 6.
'A Friday paper. XI. On a dramatic entry', *Western Mail*, 11 March 1921, 6.
'A Friday paper. XII. Mr. Hergesheimer's Welshmen', *Western Mail*, 18 March 1921, 6.
'A Friday paper. XIII. Dr. Williams's school, Dolgelly', *Western Mail*, 1 April 1921, 4.
'A Friday paper. XIV. The village of merciful men', *Western Mail*, 8 April 1921, 4.
'A Friday paper. XV. Conflict of Wales and Canterbury. An angry archdeacon', *Western Mail*, 15 April 1921, 4.
'A Friday paper. XVI. The legend of the Welsh', *Western Mail*, 22 April 1921, 4.
'A Friday paper. XVII. The followers of new lamps', *Western Mail*, 29 April 1921, 4.
'A lament of the Cambrian railway', *The Welsh Outlook*, 7/5 (1920), 113–15.
'A meditation on a pink ticket', *The Legend of the Welsh and Other Papers* (Cardiff: Educational Publishing Co. Ltd, 1924), pp. 65–8.
'A meditation on the Cambrian railway', *The Welsh Outlook*, 6/4 (1919), 105–6.
'A revelation in Cardiganshire', *The Legend of the Welsh and Other Papers* (Cardiff: Educational Publishing Co. Ltd, 1924), pp. 77–80.
A Short History: The University College of Wales, Aberystwyth, (Aberystwyth: Old Students' Association, 1920).
'A vagrant by the Dee. A chronicle of August, 1919', *The Welsh Outlook*, 6/10 (1919), 261–3.
'A vagrant by the Dee' cont., *The Welsh Outlook*, 6/12 (1919), 305–7.
'A vagrant by the Dee' cont., *The Welsh Outlook*, 7/1 (1920), 17–20.
'A vagrant by the Dee' cont., *The Welsh Outlook*, 6/11 (1919), 281–4.

LIST OF WORKS BY J. O. FRANCIS

'Against measuring heads', *The Legend of the Welsh and Other Papers* (Cardiff: Educational Publishing Co. Ltd, 1924), pp. 29–33.
'An angry archdeacon', *The Legend of the Welsh and Other Papers* (Cardiff: Educational Publishing Co. Ltd, 1924), pp. 105–9.
'An ex-politician in Cardiganshire', *The Legend of the Welsh and Other Papers* (Cardiff: Educational Publishing Co. Ltd, 1924), pp. 73–6.
'An observer at Pontypool: recollections of the 1924 eisteddfod, *The Welsh Outlook*, 11/9 (1924), 242–3.
'Antipholus of Tanybwlch", *The Dragon*, 32 (Aberystwyth: *Welsh Gazette* Printeries, 1909), 57–60.
'By the kitchen fire: an episode of the April "Welsh Outlook"', *The Welsh Outlook*, 6/5 (1919), 131–2.
'Dr. Williams's school, Dolgelley', *The Legend of the Welsh and Other Papers* (Cardiff: Educational Publishing Co. Ltd, 1924), pp. 97–100.
'Drama in Wales: the amateur rampant', *The Amateur Stage*, 10 (1926?), no page numbers.
'Eisteddfod week. Great national festival opens to-day. On the way to Ammanford', *Western Mail*, 7 August 1922, 7.
'Full moon', *The Legend of the Welsh and Other Papers* (Cardiff: Educational Publishing Co. Ltd, 1924), pp. 45–8.
'Gilbert collected', *The Welsh Outlook*, 13/6 (1926), 152–3.
'In praise of Avon Wen. Where travel is yet leisurely', *Western Mail*, 6 October 1922, 6.
'In praise of the London Welsh', *The Legend of the Welsh and Other Papers* (Cardiff: Educational Publishing Co. Ltd, 1924), pp. 91–5.
'Knickerbocker politics', *The Legend of the Welsh and Other Papers* (Cardiff: Educational Publishing Co. Ltd, 1924), pp. 81–4.
'Latinity Jones. A brief memorial', *Western Mail*, 13 October 1922, 6.
'Local newspapers', *The Legend of the Welsh and Other Papers* (Cardiff: Educational Publishing Co. Ltd, 1924), pp. 15–20; also *The Welsh Outlook*, 6/1 (1919), 14–15.
'London Welsh papers. No. IV: the Gwyneddigion', *The Welsh Outlook*, 8/1 (1921), 312–14.
'London Welsh papers. No. V: worthies of the Gwyneddigion', *The Welsh Outlook*, 8/2 (1921), 33–4.
'London Welsh papers. No. VII: three other societies', *The Welsh Outlook*, 8/4 (1921), 81–3.
'London Welsh papers. No. I: apologia', *The Welsh Outlook*, 7/10 (1920), 235–8.
'London Welsh papers. No. II: a proposal for a history of the London Welsh', *The Welsh Outlook*, 7/11 (1920), 257–9.
'London Welsh papers. No. III: the Cymmrodorion', *The Welsh Outlook*, 7/12 (1920), 284–8.
'London Welsh papers. No. VI: worthies of the Gwyneddigion. Pughe and Myfyr', *The Welsh Outlook*, 8/3 (1921), 57–9.

'Mr. Hergesheimer's Welshmen', *The Legend of the Welsh and Other Papers* (Cardiff: Educational Publishing Co. Ltd, 1924), pp. 69–72.
'Pageantry in Wales. Harlech castle pomp. Famous people in roles of the past. Opening speech by the archbishop', *Western Mail*, 22 August 1922, 4.
'Playwrights on Wales. Cymric vogue of the Elizabethan era', *Western Mail*, 24 November 1922, 6.
'Proselytes of the book', *The Legend of the Welsh and Other Papers* (Cardiff: Educational Publishing Co. Ltd, 1924), pp. 61–4.
'Reflections of a lonely voter', *Western Mail*, 16 November 1922, 6.
'The city of Cardiff', *The Legend of the Welsh and Other Papers* (Cardiff: Educational Publishing Co. Ltd, 1924), pp. 111–15.
'The deacon and the dramatist', *The Legend of the Welsh and Other Papers* (Cardiff: Educational Publishing Co. Ltd, 1924), pp. 55–60; also *The Welsh Outlook*, 6/6 (1919), 158–60.
'The forgotten isle', *The Legend of the Welsh and Other Papers* (Cardiff: Educational Publishing Co. Ltd, 1924), pp. 117–20.
'The glory of Glamorgan', *The Legend of the Welsh and Other Papers* (Cardiff: Educational Publishing Co. Ltd, 1924), pp. 35–9.
'The legend of the Welsh', *The Legend of the Welsh and Other Papers* (Cardiff: Educational Publishing Co. Ltd, 1924), pp. 11–14.
'The new Welsh drama', *Wales*, 5/31 (1913), 6–8.
'The railways of romance', *The Legend of the Welsh and Other Papers* (Cardiff: Educational Publishing Co. Ltd, 1924), pp. 25–8.
'The road to Plas yn Bonwm', *The Legend of the Welsh and Other Papers* (Cardiff: Educational Publishing Co. Ltd, 1924), pp. 41–4.
'The village of merciful men', *The Legend of the Welsh and Other Papers* (Cardiff: Educational Publishing Co. Ltd, 1924), pp. 101–4.
'The village of the tides', *The Legend of the Welsh and Other Papers* (Cardiff: Educational Publishing Co. Ltd, 1924), pp. 21–4.
'The worthy order of Dafydd-Shon-Dics', *The Welsh Outlook*, 7/6 (1920), 144–5.
'Wales and the London Welsh', *The Legend of the Welsh and Other Papers* (Cardiff: Educational Publishing Co. Ltd, 1924), pp. 85–90.
" 'Yr adsain'", *The Legend of the Welsh and Other Papers* (Cardiff: Educational Publishing Co. Ltd, 1924), pp. 49–53.

5 Work for radio[2]

Awkward Annie, story talk, 12 November 19??, 6.45 p.m. to 7.00 p.m., MS.
Beginners Please!, forty-five-minute radio feature about the Welsh national drama movement, broadcast 10 June 1955, MS.
Change, excerpt for the BBC Light Programme, Celebration of St David's Day, 1 March 1955, MS.
Climax in Merthyr, fifteen-minute radio talk, broadcast 24 February 1956, MS.

LIST OF WORKS BY J. O. FRANCIS

Clippety Clop!, BBC Radio talk, London studio, recorded on 9 July 1943, 3.30 p.m. to 3.45 p.m., MS.

Johnnie Genteel, story talk, BBC, 15 October 1945, 8.30 p.m. to 8.45 p.m., MS.

Night Birds (*The Poacher* and *Birds of a Feather*), BBC Midland Home Service, recorded in Birmingham on 25 September 1951, MS.

Saving and Spending in Full Swing, four radio talks, 16, 23, 30 March and 6 April 1952, BBC Home Service, London, no MS.

The Bloodhound of Llanrafon, story talk, broadcast by Welsh regional station, Cardiff, 5 September 1950, MS.

The Question of Benjy Pugh, story talk, BBC Welsh Home Service, 6 February 1947?, 10.05 p.m. to 10.20 p.m., MS.

The Scarecrows, radio story for five voices, BBC Welsh Service, Swansea studio, transmission 9 December 1953, 9.15 p.m. to 9.45 p.m., MS.

The Stage Play and its Limitations, second of three radio talks on Welsh drama, BBC Home Service, recorded 18 November 1952, MS.

The Welshman Takes to the Stage, in BBC Welsh Service *Arts Magazine*, about ten minutes between 9.15 p.m. and 9.45 p.m., 29 June 1949, no MS.

Uncle George, story talk, BBC, 22 October 1945, 8.45 p.m. to 9.00 p.m., MS.

Valley of Valleys, MS for a fifteen minute radio talk, n.d., MS.

Writing Stage Plays, first of three radio talks on Welsh drama, BBC Welsh Home Service, 5 December 1951, MS.

List of Performances of Plays by J.O. Francis[1]

Adar o'r Unlliw
1927, Grand Theatre, Swansea (Swansea Welsh Drama Society, annual Welsh Drama Week).

August 1929, Crane Hall, Liverpool (Cwmni y Gogleddwyr, National Eisteddfod).

March 1934, London (Undeb y Cymdeithasau Cymreig, London).

August 1946, Coliseum, Mountain Ash (Cwmni Peniel, Carmarthen, National Eisteddfod).

Antony Settles Down
17 December 1922, Shaftesbury Theatre, London (Repertory Players, professional production).

11 June 1923, Ambassador's Theatre, Southend (no company information).

1 December 1926, St James's Theatre, London (Repertory Players, professional production).

The Bakehouse
11 February 1926, Eglwys Dewi Sant schoolroom, Cardiff (Welsh Board of Health Amateur Dramatic Society, Cardiff).

30 May 1933, Scala Theatre, London (Radcliffe-on-Trent Women's Institute, Radcliffe-on-Trent, Nottinghamshire).

January 1936, Hounslow (London Hounslow Welsh Society, Hounslow).

November 1936 (Llangorse Women's Institute, Llangorse).

November 1937, Cowbridge (Cwmgorse Women's Institute).

March 1938 (Cwmgorse Women's Institute).

26 April 1947, Coliseum, Aberdare (Pontygwaith WEA, Pontygwaith).

1950, Abergavenny Town Hall, Abergavenny (Longtown Women's Institute, Longtown).

The Beaten Track
7, 8 and 9 August 1924, Theatre Royal, Pontypool (London Welsh amateurs, London, premiere).

8 February – ? February (seventeen performances), Frolic Theatre, Broadway, New York (prod. Gustav Blum).

December 1929, Oxford Playhouse, Oxford (Oxford Players, Oxford).

Birds of a Feather
March? 1933 (Mardy Dramatic Society. Maerdy, preliminary round for British Festival of Community Drama).

3 December 1936, Llanfair Church Hall, Penygraig (drama groups of Williamstown Social Centre and Tonypandy Unemployed Club).

2 April 1936, Treherbert (Blaencwm Dramatic Society, Blaencwm).

April 1948, Coliseum, Aberdare (Trecynon Dramatic Society, Aberdare).

17? June 1948, Scala Theatre, London (Trecynon Dramatic Society).

21 June 1948, Alexandra Palace, London (Trecynon Dramatic Society, televised performance).

12 July 1948, BBC Studios, Cardiff (Trecynon Dramatic Society, special radio broadcast).

15 July 1948, Coliseum, Aberdare (Trecynon Dramatic Society, Scala celebration night).

9 June 1953, National Theatre, Launceston, Tasmania, Australia (Launceston Technical High School).

23 June 1965, National Theatre, Launceston, Tasmania, Australia (St Patrick's College).

Y Bobl Fach Ddu
11 February 1926, Llewelyn Hall, Swansea (Henrietta Dramatic Society, Swansea).

20 February 1928 University College of Wales Aberystwyth, Aberystwyth (Cwmni Aberystwyth, Aberystwyth).

May 1928, Beaumaris (Menai Bridge Dramatic Society, Menai Bridge).

2 June 1928, Beaumaris (Menai Bridge Dramatic Society, Menai Bridge).

Change

Spring 1913, Aberystwyth (Ystwyth Players, premiere).

7, 8, 9 December 1913, Haymarket Theatre, London (Repertory Players).

27 January – February 1914, Booth Theatre, Broadway, New York (Repertory Players).

11, 13, 16 May 1914, New Theatre, Cardiff (National Theatre Company, National Drama Week).

18 May 1914, Theatre Royal, Merthyr Tydfil (National Theatre Company).

29 June 1914, Grand Theatre, Swansea (National Theatre Company, National Drama Week).

July 1914, Aberystwyth (National Theatre Company, National Drama Tour).

28 January 1920, Ton Pentre Workmen's Hall, Ton Pentre (Pontlottyn Dramatic Company, Pontlottyn).

21 February and 6 March 1920, Stacey Road Hall, Cardiff (Nelson Dramatic Society).

2 March 1920, Park and Dare Hall, Treorchy (Mardy Dramatic Society, Maerdy).

15 March 1920, St John's Hall, Cymmer (Glandwr Society, Taff's Well).

17 March 1920, Workmen's Institute, Cwmaman (Trecynon Dramatic Society, Trecynon).

19 March 1920, St John's Hall, Cymmer (Mardy Dramatic Society, Maerdy).

March 1920, Trecynon (Meirionydd Dramatic Society, Trecynon).

March 1920, Trecynon (Mardy Dramatic Society, Maerdy).

29 March 1920, Abergorky Workmen's Institute, Treorchy (Mardy Dramatic Society, Maerdy).

April 1920, Porth (Glandwr Society, Taff's Well).

April 1925, Pontyberem (Ponthenry Society, Ponthenry).

4 February 1928, Ysgol St John, Deansgate, Manchester (Cwmni Dewi Sant, Manchester).

October 1928, Dowlais (Trecynon Dramatic Society, Trecynon).

18 October 1928, Workmen's Hall, Tredegar (Trecynon Dramatic Society, Trecynon).

October 1928, New Theatre, Mountain Ash (Trecynon Dramatic Society, Trecynon).

26 October 1928, Graig Calvinistic Methodist Church, Pontypridd (Trecynon Dramatic Society, Trecynon).

27, 29, 30 January 1932, Little Theatre, Mumbles, Swansea (Little Theatre Company, Swansea).

21 May 1932, Jewin Chapel, London (Mardy Dramatic Society, Maerdy).

Cross-Currents
October 1923, Oddfellows Hall, Dowlais (Trecynon Dramatic Society, Trecynon).

30 April 1924, Grand Theatre, Swansea (Swansea Welsh Drama Society, Swansea).

The Crowning of Peace
9 August 1922, National Eisteddfod special pavilion, Ammanford (Pontardulais group, Pontardulais).

9 August 1922, National Eisteddfod special pavilion, Ammanford (Penygroes group, Penygroes).

10 August 1922, National Eisteddfod special pavilion, Ammanford (Pontardawe group, Pontardawe).

10 August 1922, National Eisteddfod special pavilion, Ammanford (Ystradgynlais group, Ystradgynlais).

The Dark Little People
21 April 1922, Parish Hall, Aberystwyth (past and present students, University College of Wales, Aberystwyth).

24 and 25 February 1924, Aldwych, London (Repertory Players, London).

Deufor Gyfarfod
16 and 19 April 1929, Grand Theatre, Swansea (Swansea Welsh Drama Society, Swansea).

28 January 1932, Little Theatre, Mumbles, Swansea (Little Theatre Company, Swansea).

August 1935, National Eisteddfod drama pavilion, Caernarvon (Cwmni Drama "Rhydallt", Llanrug).

Eiddo Caesar
25 April 1925, Grand Theatre, Swansea (Swansea Welsh Drama Society, Swansea).

Ffordd yr Holl Ddaear
2 and 6 August 1926, Grand Theatre, Swansea (Swansea Welsh Drama Society, Swansea).

August 1931, County Theatre, Bangor (Cymdeithas Ddrama Gymraeg Llandudno a'r Cylch, Llandudno).

6 and 8 April 1933, Grand Theatre, Swansea (Swansea Welsh Drama Society, Swansea).

Gwyntoedd Croesion
21 February 1924, County Theatre, Bangor (Welsh Dramatic Society, Bangor, university students).

His Shining Majesty
12 April 1956, National Theatre, Launceston, Tasmania, Australia (Launceston Technical High School).

Howell of Gwent
15 December 1932, University College of Wales, Aberystwyth (UCW Aberystwyth Dramatic Club, premiere).

6 July 1933, Gnoll Hall, Neath (Welsh National Theatre Company).

7 July 1933, Memorial Hall, Barry (Welsh National Theatre Company).

8 July 1933, Playhouse Theatre, Cardiff (Welsh National Theatre Company).

Hywel, Tywysog Gwent
26 February 1936, Cardiff (radio broadcast from Cardiff, presumably BBC).

John Jones: *Pennod yn Hanes Llên Cymru*
16 March 1928, Grand Theatre, Swansea (Swansea Welsh Drama Society, Swansea).

4 August 1930, Hippodrome, Llanelli (Cwmni Drama King's Cross, London, National Eisteddfod).

August 1941, National Eisteddfod drama pavilion (no company information).

2 November 1946, Talybont (London Welsh Dramatic Society, London, visit from London Welsh Dramatic Society to show appreciation for Cardiganshire support during the war).

Little Village
27 December 1928, Empire, Aberdare (Trecynon Dramatic Society, Trecynon, premiere).

The Perfect Husband
30 January 1926, St David's Welsh Church Hall, London (London Society of the Old Aberystwythians, London).

3 December 1936, Llanfair Church Hall, Penygraig (drama groups of Williamstown Social Centre and Tonypandy Unemployed Club).

The Poacher
15 and 16 May 1914, New Theatre, Cardiff (Welsh National Theatre Company, Welsh National Drama Week).

1 July 1914, Grand Theatre, Swansea (Welsh National Theatre Company, Welsh National Drama Week).

November 1915, Coliseum, London (Hopkins Players).

19 March 1921, Workingman's Hall, Treorchy (Mardy Dramatic Society, Maerdy).

28 March 1921, Town Hall, Pontypridd (Hopkins Players).

26 February 1924, Lyric Theatre, London (Portmadoc Players).

20 August 1924, Criccieth Memorial Hall, Criccieth (Portmadoc Players).

2 May 1925, Grand Theatre, Swansea (Swansea Welsh Drama Society, Swansea).

26 March 1926, Playhouse, National Union of Students Congress, Cambridge (students from University College of Wales, Aberystwyth).

1927 Birmingham, Midlands Final of the British Drama League Festival of Community Drama (Trecynon Dramatic Society, Trecynon).

6 February 1928, New Theatre, St Martin's Lane, London, Final of the British Drama League Festival of Community Drama (Trecynon Dramatic Society, Trecynon).

6 April 1932, Park and Dare Hall, Treorchy (Mardy Dramatic Society, Maerdy).

18 May 1932, Bethlehem Hall, Splott, Cardiff, Welsh Final British Drama League Festival of Community Drama (Mardy Dramatic Society, Maerdy).

23 May 1932, Garrick Theatre, London, Final British Drama League Festival of Community Drama (Mardy Dramatic Society, Maerdy).

April 1936, Newtown (Hodley Dramatic Society).

21 November 1936, Oxford House, Risca (Oxford House Players, Risca).

Y Potsier
20 April 1925, Grand Theatre, Swansea (Swansea Welsh Drama Society, Swansea).

4 August 1930, Hippodrome, Llanelli (Cwmni Drama Rhydlewis, Rhydlewis).

5 June 1933, Aberystwyth, Final of Welsh area of British Drama League Festival of Community Drama (Mardy Dramatic Society, Maerdy)

4 June 1936, Urdd Eisteddfod drama pavilion, Blaenau Ffestiniog (Tregaron, Seniors).

7 August 1937, National Eisteddfod drama pavilion, Machynlleth (Gland_r Dramatic Society.

April 1938, St George's Hall, London (no cast information).

The Sewing Guild
May 1950, Albert Hall, Llandrindod Wells (Crossgates Women's Institute, Crossgates).

The Things that are Caesar's
23 March 1923, London School of Economics, London (University of London Welsh Society, London).

Notes

Introduction

1. Editorial, 'Mr. Lloyd George and the Welsh drama', *Western Mail*, 16 May 1914, 6.
2. Editorial, 'Welsh national drama', *Western Mail*, 9 May 1914, 6.
3. Owen Rhoscomyl, 'Venture in drama. The appeal to Welsh nationalism', *Western Mail*, 8 May 1914, 4.
4. Ibid.
5. Ioan Williams's *Y Mudiad Drama yng Nghymru, 1880–1940* goes some way to address this question. He focuses mainly on Welsh-language drama, although J. O. Francis's *Change* is discussed in detail. See Ioan Williams, *Y Mudiad Drama yng Nghymru, 1880–1940* (Caerdydd: Gwasg Prifysgol Cymru, 2006).
6. Stephen Knight, *A Hundred Years of Fiction* (Cardiff: University of Wales Press, 2004), pp. 25–31.
7. Editorial, 'Welsh national drama at Cardiff theatre', *Western Mail*, 11 May 1914, 4.
8. Peter Levine, *Reforming the Humanities: Literature and Ethics from Dante through Modern Times* (Basingstoke: Palgrave Macmillan, 2009), p. 11; Daniel T. O'Hara, 'The return to ethics: a report from the front', *boundary 2*, 24/2 (1997), 145–56, 149–50.
9. Gregory Currie, 'The moral psychology of fiction', *Australasian Journal of Philosophy*, 73 (1995), 250–9; Noël Carroll, 'Art and ethical criticism: an overview of recent directions of resarch', *Ethics*, 110/2 (2000), 350–87; Noël Carroll, 'The wheel of virtue: art, literature and moral knowledge', *The Journal of Aesthetics and Art Criticism*, 60/1 (2002), 3–26.
10. Robert Eaglestone, *Ethical Criticism: Reading after Levinas* (Edinburgh: Edinburgh University Press, 1997), p. 47.
11. After postmodernism, academic authors have become wary of ideas like *the good* and it is almost incumbent on authors to note their scepticism about such

apparently universal categories by putting quotation marks around them. However, I would like to argue in this volume that ideas of the good are always particular, specific. I will, therefore, not use quotation marks.

[12] Through the Christian influence, the word virtue has substantially changed its meaning. The *Oxford English Dictionary* defines virtue as 'conformity of life and conduct with the principles of morality; voluntary observance of the recognized moral laws or standards of right conduct; abstention on moral grounds from any form of wrong-doing or vice'. In the classical world, the word meant 'excellence' and did not necessarily have moral connotations. It is in this sense that I use the word 'virtue' in what follows. See *Oxford English Dictionary*, online at http://www.oed.com/view/Entry/223835?rskey=41rrSc&result=1#eid [accessed 5 August 2013].

[13] Arguments why an ethical approach based on Aristotelian virtue ethics is better suited to an analysis of literature than either a Utilitarian or a Kantian approach is discussed in Nussbaum's *Love's Knowledge*. She argues that both Utilitarian and Kantian approaches curtail the possible range of inquiry because they start off with focused questions ('How can I maximise utility?' and 'What is my moral duty?' respectively) rather than the much more open 'How shall one live?', which, as Nussbaum argues convincingly, lies at the heart of a great deal of imaginative literature. See Martha Nussbaum, *Love's Knowledge: Essays on Philosophy and Literature* (Oxford: Oxford University Press, 1990), p. 24.

[14] Bernard Williams, *Ethics and the Limits of Philosophy* (London: Routledge, repr. 2011), p. 49.

[15] Julia Annas, 'Aristotle on virtue and happiness', in Nancy Sherman (ed.), *Aristotle's Ethics: Critical Essays* (Lanham: Rowman & Littlefield, 1999), pp. 35–55, p. 36.

[16] Ibid., p. 37.

[17] For a list of Aristotelian virtues, see Peter Vardy and Paul Grosch, *The Puzzle of Ethics* (London: Fount, 1999), pp. 26–9.

[18] Ibid.

[19] The challenge to supposedly universal assumptions about race by Edward Said may suffice as an example. See Edward Said, *Orientalism: Western Conceptions of the Orient* (Harmondsworth: Penguin, repr. 1991).

[20] Martha Nussbaum, 'Non-relative virtues: an Aristotelian approach', in James P. Sterba (ed.), *Ethics: The Big Questions* (London: Blackwell, 1998), pp. 259–76, p. 269.

[21] Nussbaum, *Love's Knowledge*, p. 38.

[22] Alasdair MacIntyre, *After Virtue*, 3rd ed. (London: Duckworth, 2007), p. 148.

[23] Ibid., pp. 194–5, my emphasis.

[24] Levine, *Reforming the Humanities*, p. 8.

[25] See Wayne C. Booth's discussion of the responsibilities of author and reader in *The Company We Keep: An Ethics of Fiction* (Berkeley: University of California Press, 1988). See also Levine, who argues for the importance of 'context', but interprets this as 'cultural context' not location. Levine, *Reforming the Humanities*, pp. 10–11.

NOTES   159

[26] Edward S. Casey, *Getting Back into Place: Toward a Renewed Understanding of the Place-World* (Bloomington: Indiana University Press, 1993), pp. 3–21.
[27] Rob Shields, *Places on the Margin Alternative Geographies of Modernity* (London: Routledge, 1991), p. 7.
[28] Language here refers mainly to the English dialects of Wales. However, Francis also wrote plays set in Welsh-speaking areas and presumably representing spoken Welsh in English.
[29] Edward S. Casey, *The Fate of Place: A Philosophical History* (Berkeley: University of California Press, 1997), p. xiv.
[30] Following Bernard Williams, I also differentiate between ethics and morality. According to Williams, 'morality should be understood as a particular development of the ethical. . . . It peculiarly emphasizes certain ethical notions rather than others, developing in particular a special notion of obligation'. Williams, *Ethics and the Limits of Philosophy*, p. 7. See also Kwame Anthony Appiah, *The Ethics of Identity* (Princeton: Princeton University Press, 2005), p. xiii.
[31] A Correspondent, 'J. O. Francis – the gentle satirist', *Merthyr Express*, 20 October 1956, no page numbers.
[32] William Griffiths, 'Profile of the month: J. O. Francis', *Y Ddinas*, November 1954, 4 and 9.
[33] Ibid., 4.
[34] John Davies, *A History of Wales*, rev. ed. (Harmondsworth: Penguin, 2007).
[35] Griffiths, 4.
[36] J. O. Francis, 'New Welsh play. Presentation last night in London. Applying drama to new purposes', *Western Mail*, 7 July 1924, 9.
[37] T. Gwynn Jones, draft of letter sent to J. O. Francis dated 16 February 1923. T. Gwynn Jones Papers, B 131 (Aberystwyth: National Library of Wales).
[38] J. O. Francis, 'Foreword', *Cross-Currents* (Cardiff: Educational Publishing Co. Ltd, 1922), pp. 5–10, p. 9.
[39] '. . . yn gyfrifol am ddenu sylw a brwdfrydedd y dosbarth canol newydd (athrawon, gweinidogion, diwydianwyr ac yn y blaen) a'r dosbarth gweithiol fel ei gilydd'. Emyr Wyn Jenkins, *Y Ddrama Gymraeg yn Abertawe a'r Cylch* (Abertawe: W. Walters a'i Fab, 1985), p. 10. This and all following translations are my own.
[40] J. O. Francis, *Glider Notes*, non-paginated MS, 1956. J. O. Francis Papers, Box 3 (Aberystwyth University: Hugh Owen Library).
[41] Montrose J. Moses, 'Introduction', J. O. Francis, *Change* (Garden City: Doubleday, 1915), pp. v–xviii.
[42] Ibid., pp. xii–xiii.
[43] J. O. Francis, *A Short History of the University College of Wales, Aberystwyth* (Aberystwyth: Old Students' Association, 1920), p. 3.
[44] Anon., 'Re-union dramatics', *The Dragon*, 1908/9, 220–2, 221. Cf. also Hywel Teifi Edwards, who notes that Francis wrote a farce called *The Other Gods* for the reunion of 1908. I have not been able to trace the play. Hywel Teifi Edwards, *Wythnos yn Hanes y Ddrama yng Nghymru, 11–16 Mai 1914* (Bangor: Cymdeithas Theatr Cymru, 1984), p. 22.
[45] Griffiths, 'Profile of the month: J. O. Francis', 4. There seems to be some confusion with regard to Francis's time in France. *Welsh Biography Online* has him

spend time as a student at the Sorbonne, a detail that I found impossible to verify. See Mary Auronwy James, 'John Oswald Francis', online at *http://wbo.llgc.org. uk/en/s2-FRAN-OSW-1882.html?query=john+oswald+francis&field=content* [accessed 20 May 2013].

[46] E. A. Baughan, 'The drama of the year', in L. Carson (ed.), *'The Stage' Yearbook 1914* (New York: The Stage, 1914), pp. 1–6, p. 4.

[47] Owen Rhoscomyl, 'Historic week. Welsh national drama. A few reflections. The players, manager and the public', *Western Mail*, 19 May 1914, 7.

[48] Unfortunately, this play was not published and the script seems to be lost.

[49] Lord Chamberlain's Archive, correspondence, 'Antony Settles Down', date of license: 30 May 1923 (London: British Library).

[50] Brian Owen, Curator, Royal Welch Fusiliers Museum, personal email communication (10 February 2011).

[51] Griffiths, 'Profile of the month: J. O. Francis', 9.

[52] Letter from Raymond Edwards dated 23 June 1955 thanking Francis for his visit to the college and asking him to come back in the next session to address the students. J. O. Francis Papers, Box 2 (Aberystwyth University: Hugh Owen Library).

[53] J. O. Francis, entry for 21 September 1956, *Glider Notes*, p. 31.

[54] Paul Rosé, 'Mr. J. O. Francis', *The Times*, 10 October 1956, 13.

[55] G. C. Ager, 'Mr. J. O. Francis', *The Times*, 11 October 1956, 14.

[56] Griffiths, 'Profile of the month: J. O. Francis', 4.

[57] '[y]r oedd Mr Francis yn ymddangos megis petai'n cytuno â'm syniadau i'; 'O, ydwyf wedi meddwl dros ein hymddiddan neithiwr, a nid wyf yn cytuno â chi. Yr wyf yn gweld yr ochr arall yn awr.' Saunders Lewis, 'Dramâu J. O. Francis', Saunders Lewis, *Meistri A'u Crefft: Ysgrifau Llenyddol gan Saunders Lewis*, ed. Gwynn ap Gwilym (Caerdydd: Gwasg Prifysgol Cymru, 1981), pp. 263–5, p. 263.

[58] Some of J. O. Francis's plays were performed in England, particularly in London (*The Poacher* at the Coliseum in November 1915, *The Things that are Caesar's* on 23 March 1923, at the LSE, *The Dark Little People* on 24 and 25 February 1924 at the Aldwych Theatre etc.) but also elsewhere, such as Cambridge (*The Poacher* at Playhouse, 26 March 1926 etc.), Manchester (*Change* at Ysgol St John in Deansgate, Manchester, 4 February 1928) or Oxford (*The Beaten Track*, Oxford Playhouse, December 1929). Some plays were performed outside the UK, such as *Change* and *The Beaten Track*, which received Broadway performances (for details see chapter 3). A few plays were even performed at the National Theatre, Launceston, Tasmania/Australia (*Birds of a Feather*, which was performed on two occasions by different companies (Launceston Technical High School, 9 June 1953, and St Patrick's College, 23 June 1965; *His Shining Majesty*, Launceston Technical High School, 12 April 1956). In what follows, I will concentrate on performances of the plays in Wales.

[59] Anon., 'Drama in Wales. £50 prize offered for Powys eisteddfod', *Western Mail*, 19 April 1924, 6.

[60] Our Own Correspondent, 'Mr. J. O. Francis on Welsh drama. Plea for pure comedy movement', *Western Mail*, 20 January 1923, 10.

NOTES

161

[61] Morag Bell, 'Reshaping boundaries: international ethics and environmental consciousness in the early twentieth century', *Transactions of the Institute of British Geographers*, 23/2 (1998), 151–75, 154.

[62] Davies, *A History of Wales*, p. 460.

[63] Thomas Jones, 'Foreword', *The Welsh Outlook*, 1/1 (1914), 1–2, 1.

[64] Ibid., 2.

[65] J. O. Francis, *Beginners Please!*, TS (Cardiff: BBC Welsh Home Service, 1955), J. O. Francis Collection Box 2 (Aberystwyth: Hugh Owen Library), p. 13.

[66] J. P. Wearing, *The London Stage 1910–1919: A Calendar of Plays and Players*, vol. 1 (Metuchen, NJ: Scarecrow, 1982), pp. 144–6, p. 251.

[67] Gwyn A. Williams, *When Was Wales?* (Harmondsworth: Penguin, repr. 1991), pp. 237–40.

[68] Pyrs Gruffudd, 'Remaking Wales: nation-building and the geographical imagination, 1925–50', *Political Geography*, 14/3 (1995), 219–39.

[69] Pyrs Gruffudd, 'Back to the land: historiography, rurality and the nation in interwar Wales', *Transactions of the Institute of British Geographers*, 19/1 (1994), 61–77, 61.

[70] Cf. Dorian Llywelyn, *Sacred Place, Chosen People: Land and National Identity in Welsh Spirituality* (Cardiff: University of Wales Press, 1999), p. 66.

[71] 'Diese sah die Natur in einem dauernden schöpferischen Werden, nach ihr innewohnenden Gesetzen sich organisch entwickelnd, ein für sich bestehendes Ganzes, das nicht für den Menschen geschaffen ist, dem dieser vielmehr angehört, da in ihm dieselben göttlichen Kräfte wirksam sind.' Paul Kluckhohn, *Das Ideengut der Deutschen Romantik*, 3rd ed. (Tübingen: Niemeyer, 1953), p. 24.

[72] Ralph Waldo Emerson, *Nature*, in Nina Baym et al. (eds), *The Norton Anthology of American Literature*, vol. 1, 4th ed. (New York: Norton, 1994), pp. 993–1021, p. 995.

[73] Henry Thoreau, *Walden* (1854), in Carl Bode (ed.), *The Portable Thoreau* (Harmondsworth: Penguin, 1981), pp. 258–572, pp. 260–3 and *passim*.

[74] Mike Crang, *Cultural Geography* (London: Routledge, 1998), p. 17.

[75] Ibid., p. 18.

[76] Aldo Leopold, 'The land ethic', *A Sand County Almanac; and Sketches here and there* (Oxford: Oxford University Press, repr. 1977), pp. 201–26, p. 204.

[77] Ibid.

[78] Bell, 'Reshaping boundaries', 158.

[79] Gruffudd, 'Back to the land', 63.

[80] Ibid., 67.

[81] R. F. Wright, 'Bathing', *The Welsh Outlook*, 1/8 (1914), 358–9; Anon., 'Brunaerau open-air school', *The Welsh Outlook*, 1/4 (1914), plate between 161 and 162; T. H. Morris, 'The need for open air schools', supplement to the February number, *The Welsh Outlook*, 6/2 (1919), 7.

[82] Bell, 'Reshaping boundaries', 153.

[83] Anon., 'Housing', *The Welsh Outlook*, 1/1 (1914), plates between 30 and 31; Anon., 'Housing: town planning – 60 years ago', *The Welsh Outlook*, 1/2 (1914), plates between 16 and 17.

[84] Thoreau, 'Walden', p. 270.

[85] For an interesting discussion of the notion of practical wisdom, see Barry Schwartz and Kenneth Sharpe, *Practical Wisdom: The Right Way to Do the Right Thing* (Harmondsworth: Riverhead, 2010).

Chapter 1

[1] E. E., 'Some recent Welsh plays', *The Welsh Outlook*, 1/6 (1914), 29–30.
[2] Cecil Price, *The English Theatre in Wales in the Eighteenth and Nineteenth Centuries* (Cardiff: University of Wales Press, 1948); Cecil Price, *The Professional Theatre in Wales* (Llandysul: Gomer and University College of Wales Swansea, 1984).
[3] O. Llew Owain, *Hanes y Ddrama yng Nghymru, 1850–1943* (Lerpwl: Gwasg y Brython, 1948).
[4] Anwen Jones, *National Theatres in Context: France, Germany, England and Wales* (Cardiff: University of Wales Press, 2007).
[5] R. A. Griffiths (Elphin), 'The prospect of the Welsh drama', *The Transactions of the Honourable Society of Cymmrodorion*, session 1912–13 (London: Cymmrodorion, 1914), 129–39.
[6] Price, *The English Theatre in Wales*, pp. 153–4.
[7] Ibid., p. 157.
[8] St John Ervine, *The Theatre in My Time* (London: Rich & Cowan Ltd, 1933), p. 94 and *passim*.
[9] J. O. Francis, 'The drama in Wales: the amateur rampant', *The Amateur Stage*, 10 (1926?), no page numbers.
[10] Price, *The Professional Theatre in Wales*, p. 17.
[11] Anon., 'Llandudno', *North Wales Chronicle*, 27 May 1865, 8.
[12] Anon., 'Portmadoc eisteddfod', *North Wales Chronicle*, 31 August 1872, 3.
[13] Anon., 'Bethesda', *North Wales Chronicle*, 30 April 1887, 6.
[14] Jones, *National Theatres in Context*, p. 142.
[15] Owen Morgan (Morien), 'The revival of the drama in Wales: splendid reception at Pontypridd', *Western Mail*, 29 December 1986, 2.
[16] Abel J. Jones, 'Does Wales need the drama?', *The Welsh Outlook*, 6/1 (1914), 255–6, 255.
[17] Ibid., 256.
[18] Nicholas Ridout, *Theatre and Ethics* (Basingstoke: Macmillan, 2009), p. 19.
[19] There is no doubt that Plato's was an extreme view even in ancient Greece – Aristotle, for one, strongly disagreed. However, to put Plato's views into perspective, one needs to perhaps remember that going to the theatre was not merely a leisure activity. Plays were performed as part of religious festivities and were thus a part of civic and political life. In this context, Plato's fears of the potentially powerful effects of plays on the citizens of Athens make more sense. Similar worries about the potentially dangerous effects of art are at the heart of all state censorship of the arts, for example the theatre censorship in Britain that was only abandoned in 1968.

NOTES

[20] Jonas Barish, *The Antitheatrical Prejudice* (Berkeley: University of California Press, 1981), p. 323.
[21] Loren Kruger, *The National Stage: Theatre and Cultural Legitimation in England, France, and America* (Chicago: University of Chicago Press, 1992), p. 90.
[22] Sally Ledger, 'Naturalism: "Dirt and Horror Pure and Simple"', in Matthew Beaumont (ed.), *A Concise Guide to Realism* (Oxford: Wiley-Blackwell, 2010), pp. 86–101, p. 86.
[23] Joseph Donohue, 'What is Edwardian Theatre?', in Michael R. Booth and Joel H. Kaplan (eds), *The Edwardian Theatre: Essays on Performance and the Stage* (Cambridge: Cambridge University Press, 1996), pp. 10–35, pp. 14–15.
[24] Ervine, *The Theatre in My Time*, p. 102.
[25] See Jones, *National Theatres in Context*, p. 151.
[26] Bernard Shaw, 'The author's apology', *Dramatic Opinions and Essays with an Apology* (New York: Brentano's, 1910), pp. xxi–xxv, pp. xxii–xxiii.
[27] D. T. Davies, 'Ton Pentre success. Adjudication to be made on Tuesday', *Western Mail*, 2 February 1920, 6.
[28] Anon., 'The Welsh drama. Rev. R. G. Berry on needs of Welsh literature', *Western Mail*, 22 January 1920, 7.
[29] Emyr Wyn Jenkins, *Y Ddrama Gymraeg yn Abertawe a'r Cylch* (Abertawe: W. Walters a'i Fab, 1985), p. 7.
[30] Griffiths, 'The prospect of the Welsh Drama', pp. 136–7.
[31] Llewelyn Williams, 'A transformation and a revelation', *Western Mail*, 16 May 1914, 7.
[32] J. O. Francis, 'The deacon and the dramatist', *The Legend of the Welsh and Other Papers* (Cardiff: Educational Publishing Co. Ltd, 1924), pp. 55–60, p. 59.
[33] The *Brad y Llyfrau Gleision*, the 'Treachery of the Blue Books' was the reaction to the government-sponsored reports on the state of Welsh education published in 1847. The report made some valid points regarding the uneven education provision in Wales. However, the English authors had significantly overstepped their brief by commenting negatively on the state of Welsh morals, particularly on that of Welsh women, and ascribing the 'backwardness' of Wales to the persistent use of the Welsh language. The results were not only the Education Acts and the provision of a new school system for Wales (discussed in chapter 1) but a furious backlash in Wales. Communities began rigorously policing themselves in order to show that their morals were beyond reproach. It is this cultural climate that the deacons in Francis's plays emerge from and that he and his contemporaries criticized. For a discussion of the scandal, see John Davies, *A History of Wales*, rev. ed. (Harmondsworth: Penguin), pp. 378–81.
[34] William Archer cited in Robert Hogan, Richard Burnham and Daniel P. Poteet, *The Rise of the Realists, 1910–1915* (Dublin: Dolmen, 1975), p. 21.
[35] Hogan et al., *The Rise of the Realists*, p. 17.
[36] Ibid., p. 76.
[37] Ibid., pp. 26–34.
[38] Ibid., p. 34.
[39] '... gwthiodd y ddrama ei hun i bron bob ardal yng Nghymru'. Jenkins, *Y Ddrama Gymraeg*, p. 9.

40 'roedd *Y Beirniad, Tarian y Gweithiwr, Y Brython, Y Genedl Gymreig, Wales, Young Wales, The Welsh Outlook, Western Mail, South Wales Daily News* a'r *South Wales Daily Post* yn tystio i ddiddordeb cynyddol ym mhosibiliadau'r ddrama yng Nghymru'. Hywel Teifi Edwards, *Wythnos yn Hanes y Ddrama yng Nghymru, 11–16 Mai 1914* (Bangor: Cymdeithas Theatr Cymru, 1984), p. 8.

41 J. Hugh Edwards, 'The month in Wales', Editorial, *Wales*, 5/34 (February 1914), 183–4.

42 E. E., 'Some recent Welsh plays', 29.

43 Howard de Walden cited in Owain, *Hanes y Ddrama yng Nghymru*, p. 121.

44 J. Saunders Lewis, 'The drama in Wales. Over seventy plays in competition', *Western Mail*, 6 August 1920, 4.

45 D. T. Davies, 'Welsh Drama Week. "Serch Hudol" played at Ton Pentre', *Western Mail*, 29 January 1920, 7.

Chapter 2

1 Thomas J. Hatton, *Playwriting for Amateurs: How to Become a Published Playwright* (Colorado Springs: Meriwether Publishing Ltd, 1981), p. 5.

2 Ibid., p. 6.

3 Ibid., p. 7.

4 Anon., 'John Oswald Francis', in Meic Stephens (ed.), *The New Companion to the Literature of Wales* (Cardiff: University of Wales Press, 1998), p. 253.

5 J. O. Francis, *'The Whirligig'. Comments by Theatre Managers*, undated TS, c.1954, J. O. Francis Collection Box 3 (Aberystwyth University: Hugh Owen Library).

6 J. O. Francis, personal letter to Arthur Elsbury (Samuel French Ltd) dated 2 May 1954, J. O. Francis Collection Box 4 (Aberystwyth University: Hugh Owen Library).

7 See, for example, Christopher Innes's discussion of David Edgar's early work. Christopher Innes, *Modern British Drama: The Twentieth Century* (Cambridge: Cambridge University Press, repr. 2002), pp. 178–9.

8 Interestingly, in some ways professional theatre companies now have to show evidence of community engagement to be eligible for public funding – and they may, of course, be genuinely interested in fostering links with local communities. An example would be the National Theatre Wales's production of *The Passion*. The play was staged at several locations in Port Talbot and invited audiences to engage actively with the play, to discuss it and even to take part. Lyn Gardner described the play as 'uplifting' and was sure that 'over the last three days, Port Talbot was one of the happiest places on Earth', thus neatly capturing some of the central goals of community drama. See Lyn Gardner, 'The Passion – review', *The Guardian*, 24 April 2011, online at *http://www.guardian.co.uk/stage/2011/apr/24/the-passion-port-talbot-review* [accessed 28 June 2013].

9 Percy MacKaye, *Community Drama: Its Motive and Method of Neighborliness* (Boston: Houghton Mifflin, 1917).

10 Ibid., pp. 12–15.

[11] Ibid., pp. 20–1.
[12] Ibid., p. 25.
[13] Ibid., p. 40.
[14] Hijinx Theatre, 'Odyssey Theatre', online at *http://www.hijinx.org.uk/Odyssey* [accessed 21 December 2011].
[15] Sydney Box, 'The drama festival', in Patrick Carleton (ed.), *The Amateur Stage: A Symposium* (London: Geoffrey Bles, 1939), pp. 63–108.
[16] Lawrence du Garde Peach, 'Village drama', in Patrick Carleton (ed.), *The Amateur Stage: A Symposium* (London: Geoffrey Bles, 1939), pp. 139–58.
[17] For an example, see G. W. Bishop (ed.), *The Amateur Dramatic Year Book and Community Theatre Handbook, 1928–9* (London: A. & C. Black Ltd, 1929).
[18] Don Chapman, *Oxford Playhouse: High and Low Drama in a University City* (Hatfield: University of Hertfordshire Press, 2008).
[19] Ethel Ross, *Dylan Thomas and the Amateur Theatre* (Swansea: Swansea Little Theatre, 1985), no page numbers, eight pages, p. 3.
[20] Ibid.
[21] D. T. Davies, 'Ton Pentre success. Adjudication to be made on Tuesday', *Western Mail*, 2 February 1920, 6.
[22] Rhondda Cynon Taf Library Service, 'The Aberdare Little Theatre Company', 2006, online at *http://webapps.rhondda-cynon-taff.gov.uk/heritagetrail/english/cynon/aberdare_little-theatre.html* [accessed 3 December 2011].
[23] Ross, *Dylan Thomas*, p. 3.
[24] Neath Little Theatre, 'About us', no date, online at *http://www.neathlittletheatre.co.uk/#!about-us* [accessed 3 December 2011].
[25] D. T. Davies, 'Welsh Drama Week. "Serch Hudol" played at Ton Pentre', *Western Mail*, 29 January 1920, 7.
[26] D. T. Davies, 'Drama in Wales. Notable productions at Merthyr', *Western Mail*, 13 April 1920, 6.
[27] Content analysis is a method borrowed from mass communication studies. It enables the reader to analyse large numbers of texts reliably. See Klaus Krippendorf, *Content Analysis: An Introduction to its Methodology*, 2nd ed. (London: Sage, 2004).
[28] D. T. Davies, 'Ton Pentre success', 6.
[29] Hatton, *Playwriting for Amateurs*, passim.
[30] Anne I. Miller, *The Independent Theatre in Europe, 1887 to the Present* (New York: Bloomberg, 1966), p. 320.
[31] Anon., 'Dramatist's defence. "Cwm Glo" author replies to critics. "Sex is not its Theme"', *Western Mail*, 24 August 1934, 11.
[32] D. T. Davies, 'Welsh drama. Some principles of play-writing', *Western Mail*, 30 July 1920, 9.
[33] Richard Posner, 'Against ethical criticism', *Philosophy and Literature*, 2/1 (1999), 1–27.
[34] *Taffy* will be discussed in chapter 5.
[35] J. Kitchener Davies, 'An analysis of present day Welsh literary effort', *Western Mail*, 17 October 1936, 11.

[36] Cited in J. T. Jones, 'Welsh pioneer in drama. Interview with the Rev. R. G. Berry. Wales wants its own J. M. Synge', *Western Mail*, 9 July 1924, 6.
[37] M. Morris-Roberts, 'Welsh plays overdo the kitchen drama', *Western Mail*, 17 April 1936, 8.
[38] The fact that Gruffydd was the least-performed out of the first generation of authors is also interesting, considering that he is the only author out of the four mentioned who is still remembered at all – as a poet.
[39] J. Eddie Parry, 'Welsh drama. Brilliant close to Swansea Week. Is a national theatre practicable?', *Western Mail*, 3 May 1924, 9.
[40] Patrick Carleton, 'Amateur and professional acting', in Patrick Carleton (ed.), *The Amateur Stage: A Symposium* (London: Geoffrey Bles, 1939), pp. 1–43, p. 33.
[41] Anon., 'Drama competition. Not one play about Welsh life', *Western Mail*, 3 November 1936, 5.
[42] Anon., 'One-act play writing competition: an encouraging number of entries', *Western Mail*, 16 March 1932, 5.
[43] Anon., 'Drama contest winners. Lord Howard de Walden and play writing', *Western Mail*, 22 August 1936, 10.
[44] J. O. Francis, letter to Cyril Hogg, Samuel French, 3 February 1952. J. O. Francis Collection Box 4 (Aberystwyth University: Hugh Owen Library).
[45] Francis was not inclined to leave the success or failure of his plays up to chance: he assiduously promoted his plays by sending manuscripts to theatre companies and producers. For example, he sent a copy of *The Sheep and the Goats* to Douglas Neil, the General Manager of the Royalty Theatre in Chester, because, he argued 'Wales being very near to your city your audiences might find interest in the play'. When Neil did not answer for some time, Francis pressed him, and he finally responded by saying that he had enjoyed the play and was going to suggest it to the director of the company. No further letters exist, so it is unclear whether the Royalty Theatre ever did perform the play. Francis tried to promote his late comedy *The Whirligig* in a similar way and meticulously typed up the polite rejection notes he received from various English repertory theatres. The apparent failure to have his plays produced at this later stage in his career by companies other than Welsh amateur dramatic companies shows the strictly limited appeal of the play of Welsh life and perhaps also Francis's failure to reinvent his form and style to suit the professional stage of the 1950s. See J. O. Francis, letter to Douglas Neil, 18 January 1954; Douglas Neil, letter to J. O. Francis, February 1954, J. O. Francis Collection Box 4; J. O. Francis, 'comments by theatre managers re. *The Whirligig*, J. O. Francis Collection Box 3 (Aberystwyth University: Hugh Owen Library).
[46] Anon., 'Awards in Welsh drama. Pontardulais & Mardy gain first prizes', *Western Mail*, 22 March 1920, 8.
[47] Anon., 'Drama week for church funds. South Wales companies in competition', *Western Mail*, 21 April 1936, 6.
[48] Box, 'The drama festival', p. 71.
[49] Ibid., pp. 99–100.
[50] Our Drama Critic, 'Welsh actors' venture in Shakespeare. Mountain Ash Drama Week players' work', *Western Mail*, 27 October 1932, 9.

NOTES   167

[51] Anon., 'A County Drama Festival. Monmouthshire League innovation', *Western Mail*, 5 December 1932, 7.
[52] J. O. Francis, '*National drama in Wales*', radio talk, TS, recorded 19 November 1952, J. O. Francis Collection Box 2 (Aberystwyth University: Hugh Owen Library), pp. 6–7.
[53] Ibid., p. 7.

Chapter 3

[1] Martha Nussbaum, *Love's Knowledge: Essays on Philosophy and Literature* (Oxford: Oxford University Press, 1990), pp. 4–5.
[2] Ann Marie Adams, 'Look back in realism: the making and unmaking of dramatic form in the reception of the British new wave', *The Journal of the Midwest Modern Language Association*, 40/1 (2007), 75–86, 77.
[3] Nussbaum, *Love's Knowledge*, p. 5.
[4] Ibid., p. 37.
[5] J. O. Francis, *Change: A Glamorgan Play in Four Acts*, marked acting copy (Cardiff: Educational Publishing Co. Ltd, 1914), J. O. Francis Collection Box 1 (Aberystwyth University: Hugh Owen Library), p. 133.
[6] '[d]ie Namen von Fürsten und Helden können einem Stücke Pomp und Majestät geben; aber zur Rührung tragen sie nichts bei. Das Unglück derjenigen, deren Umstände den unsrigen am nächsten kommen, muß natürlicherweise am tiefsten in unsere Seele dringen'. Gotthold Ephraim Lessing, *Hamburgische Dramaturgie* (Berlin: Deutscher Verlag der Wissenschaften, 1952), p. 58.
[7] William Archer, *Play-making: A Manual for Craftsmanship* (Boston: Small, Maynard and Company, 1918), p. 64.
[8] Keir Elam, *The Semiotics of Theatre and Drama* (London: Routledge, repr. 1997), p. 13.
[9] Christopher Innes (ed.), *A Sourcebook on Naturalist Theatre* (London: Routledge, 2000).
[10] See O. Llew Owain, *Hanes y Ddrama yng Nghymru, 1850–1943* (Lerpwl: Gwasg y Brython, 1948), plate between pp. 84 and 85.
[11] Anon., 'The play of the month', *The Playgoer and Society Illustrated: A Magazine of the Drama, Fashion and Society*, 7/37 (1912) (London: Kingshurst Publishing Co. 1913), 1–19.
[12] J. P. Wearing, *The London Stage 1910–1919: A Calendar of Plays and Players*, vol. 1: 1910–16 (Metuchen, NJ: Scarecrow, 1982), p. 174 and p. 407.
[13] E. E., 'Some recent Welsh plays', *The Welsh Outlook*, 1/6 (1914), 29–30, 29.
[14] Karen Vandevelde, '"What's All the Stir About": Gerald MacNamara, Synge and the early Abbey Theatre', *New Hibernia Review/Iris Éireannach Nua*, 10/3 (2006), 108–21, 110.
[15] For a discussion of the symbol of the house, see Martin Rhys, 'Keeping it in the family: *Change* by J. O. Francis, *The Keep* by Gwyn Thomas and *House of America* by Ed Thomas', in Katie Gramich and Andrew Hiscock (eds), *Dangerous*

Diversity: The Changing Faces of Wales. Essays in Honour of Tudor Bevan (Cardiff: University of Wales Press, 1998), pp. 111–28.

[16] M. Wynn Thomas, 'All change: the new Welsh drama before the Great War', *Internal Difference: Twentieth-Century Writing in Wales* (Cardiff: University of Wales Press, 1992), pp. 1–14, p. 15.

[17] John Davies, *A History of Wales*, rev. ed. (Harmondsworth: Penguin, 2007), pp. 478–9; Kenneth O. Morgan, *Rebirth of a Nation: A History of Modern Wales* (Oxford: Oxford University Press, 1998), pp. 146–8; Gwyn A. Williams, *When Was Wales? A History of the Welsh* (Harmondsworth: Penguin, repr. 1991).

[18] Hywel Teifi Edwards, *Wythnos yn Hanes y Ddrama yng Nghymru, 11–16 Mai 1914* (Bangor: Cymdeithas Theatr Cymru, 1984), p. 25; Tim Evans, 'The Llanelli riots', *Planet*, 203 (2011), 80–90, 84.

[19] Alasdair MacIntyre, *After Virtue*, 3rd ed. (London: Duckworth, 2007), p. 222.

[20] Loren Kruger, *The National Stage: Theatre and Cultural Legitimation in England, France, and America* (Chicago, IL: University of Chicago Press, 1992), pp. 109, 114, 116.

[21] Ibid., p. 110.

[22] Naunton Davies, *The Human Factor: A Play in Four Acts* (Cardiff: Educational Publishing Co. Ltd, 1920).

[23] D. T. Davies, *Ble Ma Fa? Drama Mewn Un Act yn Nhafodiaith Cwm Rhondda* (Aberystwyth: Ddraig Goch, 1913).

[24] Martha Nussbaum, 'Non-relative virtues: an Aristotelian approach', in James P. Sterba (ed.), *Ethics: The Big Questions* (London: Blackwell, 1998), pp. 259–76, p. 264.

[25] Anon., 'Notes of the month', *The Welsh Outlook*, 1/2 (1914), 8–9.

[26] Innes, *A Sourcebook on Naturalist Theatre*, pp. 65–71.

[27] See Nicholas Grene, *The Politics of Irish Drama: Plays in Context from Boucicoult to Friel* (Cambridge: Cambridge University Press, 1999), pp. 18–34.

[28] John D. Lewis, 'Welsh dramatists. No. 3. Work of J. O. Francis', *Western Mail*, 21 December 1921, 9.

[29] Cited in Hazel Walford Davies, *Y Theatr Genedlaethol yng Nghymru* (Caerdydd: Gwasg Prifysgol Cymru, 2007), p. 7. See also Edwards, *Wythnos yn Hanes Ddrama yng Nghymru*, p. 18.

[30] D. T. Davies, 'Welsh Drama Week. Assured success at Ton Pentre. "Change" the best effort of recent years', *Western Mail*, 30 January 1920, 8.

[31] Anon., 'Chancellor and the Welsh drama. Delighted with plays. "Success Assured". Suffragettes create a diversion', *Western Mail*, 16 May 1914, 7.

[32] Anon., 'Welsh drama. New national movement. Successful start. "Change" produced at Cardiff. Capable artistes', *Western Mail*, 12 May 1914, 6.

[33] John D. Lewis, 'Welsh drama. The untouched field of romance', *Western Mail*, 23 October 1920, 10.

[34] J. O. Francis, *Cross-Currents: A Play of Welsh Politics in Three Acts* (Cardiff: Educational Publishing Co. Ltd, 1924), p. 100.

[35] Francis, 'Foreword', *Cross-Currents: A Play of Welsh Politics in Three Acts*, pp. 9–10.

NOTES

36 See Aristotle, *Nicomachean Ethics*, Book X, esp. 1177a12 onwards. Aristotle, *The Nicomachean Ethics* (Harmondsworth: Penguin, 2004).
37 J. Graham Jones, 'Lloyd George, Cymru Fydd and the Newport meeting of 1896', *Cylchgrawn Llyfrgell Genedlaethol Cymru/National Library of Wales Journal*, 29/4 (1996), 435–53.
38 Morgan, *Rebirth of a Nation: A History of Modern Wales*, pp. 32–4; Davies, *A History of Wales*, pp. 441–2.
39 See John Rawls, *A Theory of Justice* (Cambridge, MA: Harvard University Press, 1999), pp. 118–23 and *passim*.
40 T. Gwynn Jones, draft of a letter sent to J. O. Francis, dated 16 February 1923, T. Gwynn Jones Papers, B 131 (Aberystwyth: National Library of Wales).
41 R. G. Berry, 'New play by Mr. J. O. Francis. Study of modern Welsh hamlet', *Western Mail*, 20 February 1923, 9.
42 Ibid.
43 J. Eddie Parry, 'Drama week. A disappointment at Swansea. The weakness of "Cross Currents"', *Western Mail*, 1 May 1924, 12.
44 J. Eddie Parry, 'Drama week. Moliere in Welsh at Swansea. A dull performance of "Cross Currents"', *Western Mail*, 2 May 1924, 10.
45 T. Huws Davies, 'Some recent Welsh literature and the limitations of realism', *Y Cymmrodor*, 27 (London: Cymmrodorion, 1917), 186–205, 196.
46 Harri Roberts, 'The body and the book: Caradoc Evans's *My People*', *Welsh Writing in English: A Yearbook of Critical Essays*, 11 (2006/7), 32–50.
47 Caradoc Evans, *Taffy: A Play of Welsh Village Life* (London: Andrew Melrose, 1924), p. 22.
48 M. Wynn Thomas, *In the Shadow of the Pulpit: Literature and Nonconformist Wales* (Cardiff: University of Wales Press, 2010), p. 150.
49 John D. Lewis, 'Libel on life in Wales. Mr. Caradoc Evans' new play. "Taffy". applauded by London audience', *Western Mail*, 27 February 1923, 6.
50 Cited in Our Own Correspondent, 'New attack on Wales. "Caradoc" explains his revised play. Revelations for London. Expects bricks, but pleads for tolerance', *Western Mail*, 2 September 1925, 7.
51 J. O. Francis, *The Beaten Track: A Welsh Play in Four Acts* (London: Samuel French, 1927), p. 17.
52 Anon., '"The Beaten Track." Mr. J. O. Francis's new play at Pontypool', *Western Mail*, 6 August 1924, 9.
53 D. T. Davies, 'The Beaten Track. A new Welsh play of distinction. Another triumph for Mr. J. O. Francis', *Western Mail*, 8 August 1924, 7.
54 Cited in Robert Hogan, Richard Burnham and Daniel E. Poteet, *The Rise of the Realists, 1910–1915* (Dublin: Dolmen, 1975), p. 1979.
55 Davies, 'The Beaten Track. A new Welsh play of distinction', 7.
56 Simone Weil, *The Need for Roots*, tr. Arthur Wills (Abingdon: Routledge, repr. 2002), p. 43.
57 Davies, 'The Beaten Track. A new Welsh play of distinction', 7.
58 Ibid.
59 J. O. Francis, 'An observer at Pontypool: recollections of the 1924 eisteddfod', *The Welsh Outlook*, 11/9 (1924), 242–3.

[60] Anon., 'Notes of the month', *The Welsh Outlook*, 16/9 (1924), 229–30.
[61] Amanda Smith, editorial director at Samuel French, personal email communication regarding Samuel French stock, 24 September 2009.
[62] Curtis Brown Ltd, letter to J. O. Francis, 15 October 1953, J. O. Francis Collection Box 1 (Aberystwyth University: Hugh Owen Library).
[63] Arthur O. Roberts, 'Cloudbreak', Amy Key Clarke, A. O. Roberts and L. du Garde Peach, *Three One-Act Plays* (Oxford: Basil Blackwell, 1925), p. 74.
[64] Ifan Kyrle Fletcher, '"Cloudbreak." A Welsh monograph play', *Western Mail*, 17 November 1925, 9.
[65] Richard Hughes, 'The Sisters' Tragedy', *Plays* (London: Chatto & Windus, 1928), pp. 2–35, p. 6. The setting and characters are strongly reminiscent of Elizabeth Inglis-Jones's first novel *Strange Fields* (1929).
[66] Ibid., p. 4.
[67] Ibid., p. 5.
[68] D. R. Davies, 'Welsh national theatre movement', MS, n.d., D. R. Davies Collection, scrapbook No. 101/1 – Welsh National Theatre Movements No. 1, Press Cuttings, 1900–1914, 14 August 1931 – August 1934, 1937 (Aberystwyth: National Library of Wales).
[69] J. O. Francis, letter to D. R. Davies, 1932, D. R. Davies Collection, scrapbook No. 101/1 – Welsh National Theatre Movements No. 1, Press Cuttings, 1900–1914, 14 August 1931 – August 1934, 1937 (Aberystwyth: National Library of Wales).
[70] Our Own Correspondent, 'Welsh national theatre. Ready to perform in barns if Necessary', *Western Mail*, 14 March 1933, 7; see also chapter 2.
[71] Our Own Correspondent, 'National theatre company. First production in Wales. Play Secret', *Western Mail*, 4 February 1933, 7.
[72] Our Own Correspondent, 'Welsh national theatre', 7.
[73] Richard Hughes, 'A Comedy of Good and Evil', *Plays* (London: Chatto & Windus, 1928), pp. 36–141, p. 43.
[74] Ibid., p. 39.
[75] Our Own Correspondent, 'National theatre. Movement hopes to have a professional company', *Western Mail*, 27 January 1933, 9.
[76] John Glyn Roberts, 'National theatre. A venture worthy of Wales's support', letter to the Editor, *Western Mail*, 6 February 1933, 11.
[77] J. Eddie Parry, '"Howell of Gwent". Performance at Neath to-night', *Western Mail*, 6 July 1933, 11.
[78] Romantic love is a theme in many of Francis's plays, notably the comic plays, but they are, as it were, requirements of the genre. In *Howell of Gwent*, romantic love is a carrier of meaning and is fully imagined and enacted.
[79] J. O. Francis, *Howell of Gwent: A Romantic Drama in Three Acts* (Cardiff: Educational Publishing Co. Ltd, 1934), p. 22.
[80] A Welsh M.A., 'Epstein and "Howell of Gwent": a comparison. "Mauve trying to be Purple"', *Western Mail*, 19 July 1933, 8.
[81] Ibid.
[82] J. Eddie Parry, '"Howell of Gwent"', 11.
[83] Our Drama Critic, 'Romance of Old Wales. Native writer's triumph', *Western Mail*, 10 July 1933, 9.

NOTES   171

[84] J. O. Francis, letter to Aneirin Talfan Davies, 11 October 1953, J. O. Francis Collection Box 1 (Aberystwyth University: Hugh Owen Library).
[85] Ibid.
[86] J. O. Francis, *The Devouring Fire: Play in Three Acts*, unpublished TS, J. O. Francis Collection Box 1 (Aberystwyth University: Hugh Owen Library), p. II. 33. Idiosyncratic numbering in original.
[87] J. O. Francis, 'National drama in Wales', radio talk, TS, recorded 19 November 1952, J. O. Francis Collection Box 2 (Aberystwyth University: Hugh Owen Library), p. 2.
[88] Ibid., p. 4.
[89] Rachel Bowlby, 'Foreword', in Matthew Beaumont (ed.), *A Concise Guide to Realism* (Oxford: Wiley-Blackwell, 2010), pp. xiv–xxi, p. xviii.

Chapter 4

[1] J. W. Marriott, 'Preface', *Great Modern British Plays* (London: George Harrap & Co., 1929), pp. 5–10, p. 6.
[2] Ibid., p. 7.
[3] See chapter 2.
[4] J. W. Marriott, 'Foreword', in J. W. Marriott (ed.), *One-Act Plays of To-Day*, third series (London: George Harrap & Co., 1926), pp. 5–7, p. 5.
[5] Helen Louise Cohen, 'Introduction', in Helen Louise Cohen (ed.), *One-Act Plays by Modern Authors* (New York: Harcourt, Brace and Co., 1927), pp. xiii–lxi, p. xiv. See a similar comparison in B. Louise Schafer, 'The one-act play and the short story', *The Sewanee Review*, 27/2 (1919), 151–62, 151.
[6] Schafer, 'The one-act play and the short story', 152.
[7] Harold Chapin, 'The Philosopher of Butterbiggins', in John Hampden (ed.), *Nine Modern Plays* (London: Thomas Nelson & Sons, 1926), pp. 29–42.
[8] Lord Dunsany (Edward John Moreton Drax Plunkett), 'The Flight of the Queen', in J. W. Marriott (ed.), *One-Act Plays of To-Day*, fourth series (London: George Harrap & Co., 1928), pp. 101–32, p. 102.
[9] F. Sladen-Smith, 'St Simeon Stylites', in J. W. Marriott (ed.), *One-Act Plays of To-Day*, fourth series (London: George Harrap & Co., 1928), pp. 133–69.
[10] W. F. Phillips, *The Lost Legacy: A Play of Welsh Domestic Life* (Liverpool: Walton, 1918).
[11] This emphasis of 'simplicity' does not just apply in the Welsh context. J. W. Marriott in the 'Foreword' to his third selection of *One-Act Plays of To-Day* commented that '[s]implicity [is] the keynote of the best modern work'. Marriott, 'Foreword', *One-Act Plays of To-Day*, pp. 5–7, p. 6.
[12] W. D. P., '"The Lost Legacy"', review, *The Welsh Outlook*, 5/3 (1918), 101–2, 102.
[13] Anthony Roche, 'Re-working *The Workhouse Ward*: McDonagh, Beckett, and Gregory', *Irish University Review*, 34/1 (2004), 171–84, 171.
[14] Schafer, 'The one-act play and the short story', 151.
[15] Ibid., 154.

[16] Gregory Currie, 'The moral psychology of fiction', *Australasian Journal of Philosophy*, 73/2 (1995), 250–9. On the issue of identifying with literary characters by 'simulation', I agree with Noël Carroll, who argues that readers (and, presumably, audiences) do not so much vicariously live through characters, experiencing their experiences, as empathize with them. However, it is an apt description of Schafer's point of view. See Noël Carroll's discussion of Currie's article in Noël Carroll, 'Art and ethical criticism: an overview of recent directions of research', *Ethics*, 110/2 (2000), 350–87, 371–4.

[17] Martha Nussbaum, *Love's Knowledge: Essays in Philosophy and Literature* (Oxford: Oxford University Press, 1990), p. 40.

[18] Amanda Smith, editorial director at Samuel French, personal email communication regarding Samuel French stock, 24 September 2009.

[19] J. O. Francis, *The Poacher: A Comedy in One Act* (Cardiff: Educational Publishing Co. Ltd, 1914?), pp. 13–14.

[20] J. Eddie Parry, 'Welsh drama. Brilliant close to Swansea Week. Is a national theatre practicable?', *Western Mail*, 3 May 1924, 9.

[21] John D. Lewis, 'Welsh dramatists. No. 3 work of Mr. J. O. Francis', *Western Mail*, 21 December 1921, 9.

[22] M. Wynn Thomas, *In the Shadow of the Pulpit: Literature and Nonconformist Wales* (Cardiff: University of Wales Press, 2010), p. 192.

[23] Geraint Goodwin, *The Heyday in the Blood* (Harmondsworth: Penguin, 1954), p. 17.

[24] Menna Gallie, *Strike for a Kingdom* (Aberystwyth: Honno, repr. 2010).

[25] George Ewart Evans, 'Let Dogs Delight', in Gwyn Jones and Islwyn Ffowc Elis (eds), *Classic Welsh Short Stories* (Oxford: Oxford University Press, repr. 1992), pp. 31–7. See also fictional settings by Leslie Norris and Glyn Jones.

[26] Thomas, *In the Shadow of the Pulpit*, p. 192.

[27] J. O. Francis, *Birds of a Feather: A Welsh Wayside Comedy in One Act* (Newtown: Welsh Outlook Press, 1927), p. 17.

[28] As a true child of nature, Dicky is terrified by the workhouse. In *The Sheep and the Goats* we learn that he was born in the workhouse and has tried to escape its shadow ever since. This detail makes him a cousin of Huckleberry Finn, another free spirit whose unconventional ways enable him (and the reader) to question established truths.

[29] J. O. Francis, correspondence, J. O. Francis Collection Box 2 (Aberystwyth University: Hugh Owen Library).

[30] Glyndwr Griffiths, '"Birds of a Feather" was acted in twenty-five square feet. Splash from the bishop's shirt on arc-lamp meant disaster!', *Aberdare Leader*, 3 July 1948. In D. R. Davies Collection, scrapbook 5–2: Wales and the British Drama League (1946–), pp. 55–6.

[31] J. O. Francis, correspondence, J. O. Francis Collection Box 3 (Aberystwyth University: Hugh Owen Library).

[32] For this discussion see, for example, Victor Caston, 'Aristotle's two intellects: a modest proposal', *Phronesis*, 44/3 (1999), 199–227, or David Charles and Dominic Scott, 'Aristotle on well-being and intellectual contemplation', *Proceedings of the Aristotelian Society*, supplementary volumes, 73 (1999), 205–23 and 225–42.

NOTES

[33] Francis, *Birds of a Feather*, p. 26.
[34] Ibid., p. 21.
[35] Ibid., p. 17.
[36] J. O. Francis, *King of the River: A One Act Comedy* (Cardiff: William Lewis, 1942), pp. 9–10.
[37] Ibid., p. 18.
[38] See Allen Raine, *A Welsh Witch: A Romance of Rough Places* (Aberystwyth: Honno, repr. 2013).
[39] J. O. Francis, *The Dark Little People: A Comedy of the Welsh Tribes* (Cardiff: Educational Publishing Co. Ltd, 1922?), p. 8.
[40] Thomas, *In the Shadow of the Pulpit*, p. 187.
[41] H. J. Fleure, 'The Welsh people', *Wales*, 10 (1939), 265–9, 267.
[42] Anon., '"Dark Little People". New Welsh play by Mr. J. O. Francis', *Western Mail*, 22 April 1922, 6.
[43] Anon., 'London letter. New play by Mr. J. O. Francis', *Western Mail*, 11 January 1924, 6.
[44] Our Own Correspondent, '"The Dark Little People." Charming comedy of Welsh tribes. Notable success won by Mr. J. O. Francis', *Western Mail*, 25 February 1924, 8.
[45] J. O. Francis, *Tares in the Wheat: A Country Comedy in Three Acts* (Cardiff: William Lewis, 1942?).
[46] J. O. Francis, letter to Cyril Hogg, Samuel French, 3 February 1952, J. O. Francis Collection Box 4 (Aberystwyth University: Hugh Owen Library).
[47] J. O. Francis, *The Sheep and the Goats*, TS, J. O. Francis Collection Box 4 (Aberystwyth University: Hugh Owen Library), p. I–1–9. Pagination according to MS.
[48] Francis, *The Dark Little People*, p. 25.
[49] Ibid., p. 91.
[50] J. O. Francis, *The Bakehouse: A Gossip's Comedy (in One Act)* (Cardiff: Educational Publishing Co. Ltd, 1914), p. 32.
[51] Jonathan Dancy, *Ethics without Principles* (Oxford: Oxford University Press, 2004), p. 1.
[52] J. O. Francis, *The Sewing Guild: A Woman's Comedy in One Act* (Cardiff: William Lewis, 1943?).
[53] Ibid., pp. 21–2.
[54] Ibid., p. 30.
[55] By this measure, both plays meet the criteria of the Bechdel test. It is applied to mainstream cinema films. The three criteria are: 'It has to have at least two [named] women in it; 2. Who talk to each other; 3. About something besides a man'. Surprisingly few contemporary films meet those simple criteria. See Anon., 'The Bechdel test', online at *http://bechdeltest.com* [accessed 1 July 2013].
[56] J. O. Francis, *Little Village: A Welsh Farce in Three Acts* (Cardiff: Educational Publishing Co. Ltd, 1929), p. 22.
[57] For a discussion of *Change*, see chapter 3. For a discussion of 'The glory of Glamorgan', see chapter 5.

[58] Anon., 'The Little Village. Latest play by J. O. Francis at Aberdare', *Western Mail*, 27 December 1928, 5.
[59] Our Own Correspondent, 'Welsh author's new play. First night enthusiasm at Trecynon', *Western Mail*, 28 December 1928, 8.
[60] O. M. Edwards, *Cartrefi Cymru* (Wrecsam: Hughes a'i Fab, 1896).

Chapter 5

[1] Wendell V. Harris, 'Reflections on the peculiar state of the personal essay', *College English*, 58/8 (1996), 934–53, 941.
[2] J. O. Francis, 'The village of merciful men', *Western Mail*, 8 April 1921, 4.
[3] J. O. Francis, 'The legend of the Welsh', *The Legend of the Welsh and Other Papers* (Cardiff: Educational Publishing Co. Ltd, 1924), pp. 11–14.
[4] J. O. Francis, 'The Welshman takes to the stage', TS, broadcast script 1949, J. O. Francis Collection Box 2 (Aberystwyth: Hugh Owen Library).
[5] J. O. Francis, 'Johnnie Genteel', TS (Cardiff: BBC, 1945), J. O. Francis Collection Box 2 (Aberystwyth University: Hugh Owen Library).
[6] J. O. Francis, *Beginners Please!*, TS (Cardiff: BBC Welsh Home Service, 1955), J. O. Francis Collection Box 2 (Aberystwyth University: Hugh Owen Library).
[7] Douglas Hesse, 'The place of creative nonfiction', *College English*, 65/3 (2003), 237–40, 238–9.
[8] Robert L. Root and Michael J. Steinberg (eds), *The Fourth Genre: Contemporary Writers of/on Creative Nonfiction*, 6th ed. (London: Longman, 2011).
[9] Meic Stephens (tr. and ed.), *Illuminations: An Anthology of Welsh Short Prose* (Cardiff: Welsh Academic Press, 1998).
[10] Meic Stephens, 'Preface', *Illuminations*, pp. vii–ix, p. vii.
[11] G. Douglas Atkins, *Tracing the Essay: Through Experience to Truth* (Athens: University of Georgia Press, 2005).
[12] Translation: The Triton with the Sunshade: reflections on a way of making James Joyce's *Finnegans Wake* readable. Arno Schmidt, 'Der Triton mit dem Sonnenschirm: Überlegungen zur Lesbarmachung von *Finnegans Wake* von James Joyce', *Dialoge 3* (Zürich: Haffmanns, 1991), 31–70.
[13] Hesse, 'The place of creative nonfiction', 239.
[14] Harris, 'Reflections on the peculiar status of the personal essay', 937.
[15] Gerhard Haas, *Essay* (Stuttgart: Metzler, 1969), p. 48.
[16] Harris, 'Reflections on the peculiar status of the personal essay', 934 *et passim*.
[17] Ibid., 14–18 *et passim*.
[18] Ibid., 20.
[19] G. K. Chesterton, 'A Piece of chalk', *Tremendous Trifles* (London: Methuen, 1909), 1–7, 7.
[20] Harris, 'Reflections on the peculiar status of the personal essay', 945.
[21] Noël Carroll, 'Art and ethical criticism: an overview of recent directions of research', *Ethics*, 110/2 (2000), 350–87, 361–2. As an example Carroll discusses the reading of *Uncle Tom's Cabin*: 'If one says that the moral knowledge available in *Uncle Tom's Cabin* is that slavery is evil, then the skeptic can say: (1) that was

already known by morally sensitive readers before the book was published; (2) it was knowledge that was or could have been stated in other than artistic forms, such as treatises, pamphlets, and sermons; and (3) the novel scarcely proved the case, since all the examples were made up. The ethical critic, however, might agree with all these points, but then continue by saying that the novel still afforded knowledge, namely, knowledge of what slavery was like. By providing richly particularized episodes of cruelty and inhumanity . . . the novelist engages the reader's imagination and emotions, thereby giving the reader a "feel" for what it was like to live in slave times.' It can be argued that, given that essays are narrativized and at least partly fictionalized accounts, this argument also applies.

[22] Wisdom here means *phronēsis*, practical wisdom as well as the wisdom defined as the ability to recognize patterns as a way of assimilating new knowledge. See Barry Schwartz and Kenneth Sharpe, *Practical Wisdom: The Right Way to Do the Right Thing* (Harmondsworth: Riverhead, 2010); Elkhonon Goldberg, *The Wisdom Paradox* (London: Pocket, 2007).

[23] J. O. Francis, 'By the kitchen fire: an episode of the April "Welsh Outlook"', *The Welsh Outlook*, 6/5 (1919), 131–2.

[24] J. O. Francis, 'A comment from Corwen', *The Welsh Outlook*, 6/9 (1919), 228–31, 228.

[25] Atkins, *Tracing the Essay*, p. 42.

[26] J. O. Francis, 'On a dramatic entry', *Western Mail*, 11 March 1921, 6.

[27] Leigh Howard Holmes, 'Linkages of nonfiction and selfhood: the places of personal essays', *The English Journal*, 91/4 (2002), 64–8, 64.

[28] Ibid., 65.

[29] J. O. Francis, 'A Friday paper. XV. The followers of new lamps', *Western Mail*, 29 April 1921, 4.

[30] J. O. Francis, 'In praise of Avon Wen. Where travel yet is leisurely', *Western Mail*, 6 October 1922, 6.

[31] Harris, 'Reflections on the peculiar status of the personal essay', 937.

[32] J. O. Francis, 'Knickerbocker politics', *The Legend of the Welsh and Other Papers* (Cardiff: Educational Publishing Co. Ltd, 1924), pp. 81–4.

[33] Hilaire Belloc, 'The mowing of a field', *Hills and the Sea* (London: Methuen, 1941), pp. 176–88, p. 181.

[34] Haas, *Essay*, p. 47.

[35] 'die angemessene Form des Vorgehens ist . . . das die wahrscheinliche Wahrheit umkreisende Vermuten. Wahrheit erscheint immer nur aktional und prozessural, nie als fertige und endgültige Erkenntnis', ibid., p. 50.

[36] William Gass, 'Emerson and the essay', *Habitations of the Word:* Essays (New York: Simon and Schuster, 1985), pp. 9–49, pp. 19–20.

[37] J. O. Francis, 'The village of the tides', *The Legend of the Welsh and Other Papers* (Cardiff: Educational Publishing Co. Ltd, 1924), pp. 21–24, p. 24, my emphasis.

[38] Harris, 'Reflections on the peculiar status of the personal essay', 940.

[39] John Gross, *The Rise and Fall of the Man of Letters: Aspects of English Literary Life since 1800* (Harmondsworth: Penguin, 1991), p. 236.

[40] Virginia Woolf, 'On not knowing Greek', *The Common Reader* (Harmondsworth: Penguin, 1938), pp. 32–47, p. 32.

[41] R. G. Berry, 'Moss – and others', *The Welsh Outlook*, 7/2 (1920), 41–3.
[42] R. G. Berry, 'Meditations among my tomes', *The Welsh Outlook*, 8/8 (1921), 178–80.
[43] Idris Davies, 'Souvenirs from Erin', *Wales*, 2 (1937), 56–60.
[44] Thomas Jones, letter to Percy Watkins, 3 September 1919, Thomas Jones Collection, Class H: Wales. Vol. 4. Welsh Outlook 1913–1919. (Aberystwyth: National Library of Wales).
[45] Gwyn Jenkins, 'The Welsh Outlook, 1914–1933', *Cylchgrawn Llyfrgell Genedlaethol Cymru/The National Library of Wales Journal*, 24 (1985–86), 463–96; Malcolm Ballin, 'Welsh periodicals in English, 1880–1965: literary form and cultural substance', *Welsh Writing in English Yearbook*, 9 (2004), 1–32; Malcolm Ballin, *Irish Periodical Culture, 1937–1972: Genre in Ireland, Wales, and Scotland* (Basingstoke: Palgrave Macmillan, 2008); Alyce von Rothkirch, 'Visions of Wales: The Welsh Outlook, 1914–1933', *Almanac: A Yearbook of Welsh Writing in English*, 14 (2010), 65–92.
[46] Stephens, 'Preface', *Illuminations*, pp.vii–ix.
[47] Francis, 'The railways of romance', *The Legend of the Welsh and Other Papers* (Cardiff: Educational Publishing Co. Ltd, 1924), p. 25.
[48] Ibid.
[49] Francis, 'Knickerbocker politics', *passim*.
[50] One need only think of the way slag heaps are integrated into the landscape in Lewis Jones's *Cwmardy* (1937) and in Menna Gallie's *Strike for A Kingdom* (first published in 1959, but set in 1926) and the way idle machinery, the image of slag heaps and unemployed miners are used to great effect in the film *Today We Live* (1937). See Lewis Jones, *Cwmardy, We Live* (Cardigan: Parthian, repr. 2006); Menna Gallie, *Strike for a Kingdom* (Aberystwyth: Honno, repr. 2010); BBC Wales Arts, 'Welsh film history 1930–39', online at *http://www.bbc.co.uk/wales/arts/sites/film/pages/history-1930–1939.shtml* [accessed 15 June 2013].
[51] Francis, 'The railways of romance'.
[52] J. O. Francis, 'A meditation on a pink ticket', *The Legend of the Welsh and Other Papers* (Cardiff: Educational Publishing Co. Ltd, 1924), pp. 65–8.
[53] Francis, 'Knickerbocker politics'.
[54] Ibid., p. 81.
[55] Ibid., p. 83.
[56] Kenneth O. Morgan, *Rebirth of a Nation: A History of Modern Wales* (Oxford: Oxford University Press, repr. 1998), p. 73.
[57] Ibid.
[58] Ibid., p. 84.
[59] Francis, 'The railways of romance', pp. 25, 26.
[60] Ibid., p. 27.
[61] Ibid., p. 27.
[62] Ibid., p. 28.
[63] This suggested journey does not correspond to any of the journeys described in the essays; it merely gives a suggestion of a possible journey.
[64] Daniel O'Hara, 'The return to ethics: a report from the front', *boundary 2*, 24/2 (1997), 156.

NOTES

[65] Theodor Adorno, *Negative Dialektik; Jargon der Eigentlichkeit*, gesammelte schriften (Frankfurt/M.: Suhrkamp, 1990).
[66] Jane Bennett, 'The force of things: steps towards an ecology of matter', *Political Theory*, 32/3 (2004), 347–72, 357–8.
[67] Francis, 'The village of the tides', p. 21.
[68] J. O. Francis, '"Yr adsain"', *The Legend of the Welsh and Other Papers* (Cardiff: Educational Publishing Co. Ltd, 1924), pp. 49–53, p. 49.
[69] Francis, 'The village of the tides', p. 22.
[70] Ibid., p. 24.
[71] Doreen Massey, 'Geographies of responsibility', *Geografisker Annaler, Series B. Human Geography*, 86/1 (2004), 5–18, 5.
[72] Morag Bell, 'Reshaping boundaries: international ethics and environmental consciousness in the early twentieth century', *Transactions of the Institute of British Geographers*, 23/2 (1998), 159.
[73] H. J. Fleure, 'The Welsh people', *Wales*, 10 (1939), 265–9, 269. The research project Fleure refers to in his article seems to have begun in 1934. 'The village of the tides' was published in 1920. It appears that Fleure engaged in a series of similar projects on a similar theme, all of which provided material for his central theses.
[74] J. O. Francis, 'Against measuring heads', *The Legend of the Welsh and Other Papers* (Cardiff: Educational Publishing CO. Ltd, 1924), pp. 29–33.
[75] Ibid.
[76] Ibid., p. 31.
[77] *Gwŷr y Gloran* (the men/people of the Gloran) were the small tenant or yeomen farmer families of the Rhondda before the coming of the mines. See E. D. Lewis, *The Rhondda Valleys: A Study on Industrial Development from 1800 to the Present Day* (London: Phoenix House, 1959).
[78] Ibid., p. 32.
[79] Francis, 'The legend of the Welsh', p. 11.
[80] Ibid.
[81] Ibid., p. 12.
[82] Ibid.
[83] Katie Gramich, *Twentieth-Century Women's Writing in Wales: Land, Gender Belonging* (Cardiff: University of Wales Press, 2007), p. 20.
[84] J. O. Francis, 'A lament of the Cambrian railway', *The Welsh Outlook*, 7/5 (1920), 113–15.
[85] Ibid., 113.
[86] Francis, 'The legend of the Welsh', p. 14.
[87] Ibid., p. 14.
[88] The first two essays of the series were reprinted in *The Legend of the Welsh and Other Papers*. In the following, I will focus on these two essays.
[89] J. O. Francis, 'Wales and the London Welsh', *The Legend of the Welsh and Other Papers* (Cardiff: Educational Publishing Co. Ltd, 1924), pp. 85–90, p. 85.
[90] J. O. Francis, 'In praise of the London Welsh', *The Legend of the Welsh and Other Papers* (Cardiff: Educational Publishing Co. Ltd, 1924), pp. 91–5, p. 91.
[91] Ibid., p. 94.

[92] Ibid., p. 95.
[93] Francis, '"Yr adsain"', p. 49.
[94] J. O. Francis, 'Proselytes of the book', *The Legend of the Welsh and Other Papers* (Cardiff: Educational Publishing Co. Ltd, 1924), pp. 61–4.
[95] Fleure, 'The Welsh people', 266.
[96] Ibid., 267.
[97] Massey, 'Geographies of responsibility', 14.
[98] Francis, 'Against measuring heads', p. 32.
[99] Ibid., p. 31.

Afterword

[1] See chapter V of Charles Darwin's *The Descent of Man and Selection in Relation to Sex*, vol. 1 (New York: Appleton and Co., 1871), pp. 152–77.
[2] James Q. Wilson, *The Moral Sense* (New York: Free Press, 1997), p. 26.
[3] This is not to suggest that a sense of morality necessarily distinguishes human beings from other animals. Mark Rowlands offers a stringent philosophical argument for the fact that animals can act morally in *Can Animals Be Moral?* (Oxford: Oxford University Press, 2012). However, the famous 'guilty' look dogs adopt when they have done something 'wrong' is not evidence of a moral sense – they simply react to their owners' signals of disapprobation; see Alexandra Horowitz, *Inside of a Dog: What Dogs See, Smell and Know* (London: Simon & Schuster, 2009), pp. 228–35.
[4] John Mikhail, *Elements of Moral Cognition: Rawls' Linguistic Analogy and the Cognitive Science of Moral and Legal Judgment* (Cambridge: Cambridge University Press, 2011).
[5] Jorge Moll, Ricardo de Oliveira-Souza, Paul J. Eslinger, Ivanei E. Bramanti, Janaína Mourão-Miranda, Pedro Angelo Andreioulo and Luiz Pessoa, 'The neural correlates of moral sensitivity: a functional magnetic resonance imaging investigation of basic and moral emotions', *The Journal of Neuroscience*, 22/7 (2002), 2730–6, 2730.
[6] See Julia Annas's discussion of the necessity of 'external goods' as a prerequisite to *eudaimonia*: 'goods of the body, like health, strength, beauty; goods like money and power; the health of others; good external circumstances like a peaceful and flourishing environment'. Morover, Irwin notes that 'Aristotle suggests that someone who is physically repulsive (not merely undistinguished) or of low birth, or solitary or childless is a poor candidate for happiness'. It is the Christian influence that makes the unapologetic emphasis on 'goods' like beauty, strength, money and power peculiarly difficult to stomach for many Western readers today, as is the implicit assumption that the philosophically active person cannot be a woman or a slave. Julia Annas, 'Aristotle on virtue and happiness', in Nancy Sherman (ed.), *Aristotle's Ethics: Critical Essays* (Lanham: Rowman & Littlefield, 1999), pp. 35–55, p. 37; T. H. Irwin, 'Permanent happiness: Aristotle and Solon', in Nancy Sherman (ed.), *Aristotle's Ethics: Critical Essays* (Lanham: Rowman &

Littlefield, 1999), pp. 1–33, p. 6; Peter Vardy and Paul Grosch, *The Puzzle of Ethics* (London: Fount, 1999), p. 33–4.

List of Works by J. O. Francis and List of Performances of his Plays

1 This list is indicative, as the Index Translationum only lists recent translations. It is likely that more plays were translated than appear here.
2 BBC Welsh Home Service unless otherwise indicated.

List of Performance of Plays by J. O. Francis

1 Given the difficulties in finding performance information, this list is indicative and not complete.

Bibliography

A Correspondent, 'J. O. Francis – the gentle satirist', *Merthyr Express*, 20 October 1956, no page numbers.
Adams, Ann Marie, 'Look back in realism: the making and unmaking of dramatic form in the reception of the British new wave', *The Journal of the Midwest Modern Language Association*, 40/1 (2007), 75–86.
Adorno, Theodor, *Negative Dialektik; Jargon der Eigentlichkeit*, gesammelte schriften (Frankfurt/M.: Suhrkamp, 1990).
Ager, G. C., 'Mr. J. O. Francis', *The Times*, 11 October 1956, 14.
Annas, Julia, 'Aristotle on virtue and happiness', in Nancy Sherman (ed.), *Aristotle's Ethics: Critical Essays* (Lanham: Rowman & Littlefield, 1999), pp. 35–55.
Anon., 'A county drama festival. Monmouthshire League innovation', *Western Mail*, 5 December 1932, 7.
Anon., 'Awards in Welsh drama. Pontardulais & Mardy gain first prizes', *Western Mail*, 22 March 1920, 8.
Anon., 'Bethesda', *North Wales Chronicle*, 30 April 1887, 6.
Anon., 'Brunaerau open-air school', *The Welsh Outlook*, 1/4 (1914), plate between 161 and 162.
Anon., 'Chancellor and the Welsh drama. Delighted with plays. "Success Assured". Suffragettes create a diversion', *Western Mail*, 16 May 1914, 7.
Anon., '"Dark Little People". New Welsh play by Mr. J. O. Francis', *Western Mail*, 22 April 1922, 6.
Anon., 'Drama competition. Not one play about Welsh life', *Western Mail*, 3 November 1936, 5.
Anon., 'Drama contest winners. Lord Howard de Walden and play writing', *Western Mail*, 22 August 1936, 10.
Anon., 'Drama in Wales. £50 prize offered for Powys eisteddfod', *Western Mail*, 19 April 1924, 6.
Anon., 'Drama week for church funds. South Wales companies in competition', *Western Mail*, 21 April 1936, 6.

BIBLIOGRAPHY

Anon., 'Dramatist's defence. "Cwm Glo" author replies to critics. "Sex is not its theme"', *Western Mail*, 24 August 1934, 11.
Anon., 'Housing', *The Welsh Outlook*, 1/1 (1914), plates between 30 and 31.
Anon., 'Housing: town planning – 60 years ago', *The Welsh Outlook*, 1/2 (1914), plates between 16 and 17.
Anon., 'John Oswald Francis', in Meic Stephens (ed.), *The New Companion to the Literature of Wales* (Cardiff: University of Wales Press, 1998).
Anon., 'Llandudno', *North Wales Chronicle*, 27 May 1865, 8.
Anon., 'London letter. New play by Mr. J. O. Francis', *Western Mail*, 11 January 1924, 6.
Anon., 'Notes of the month', *The Welsh Outlook*, 1/2 (1914), 8–9.
Anon., 'Notes of the month', *The Welsh Outlook*, 16/9 (1924), 229–30.
Anon., 'One-act play writing competition: an encouraging number of entries', *Western Mail*, 16 March 1932, 5.
Anon., 'Portmadoc eisteddfod', *North Wales Chronicle*, 31 August 1872, 3.
Anon., 'Re-union dramatics', *The Dragon*, 1908/9, 220–2.
Anon., '"The Beaten Track." Mr. J. O. Francis's new play at Pontypool', *Western Mail*, 6 August 1924, 9.
Anon., 'The Bechdel test', online at *http://bechdeltest.com* [accessed 1 July 2013].
Anon., 'The Little Village. Latest play by J. O. Francis at Aberdare', *Western Mail*, 27 December 1928, 5.
Anon., 'The play of the month', *The Playgoer and Society Illustrated: A Magazine of the Drama, Fashion and Society*, 7/37 (1912) (London: Kingshurst Publishing Co. 1913).
Anon., 'The Welsh drama. Rev. R. G. Berry on needs of Welsh literature', *Western Mail*, 22 January 1920, 7.
Anon., 'Welsh drama. New national movement. Successful start. "Change" produced at Cardiff. Capable artistes', *Western Mail*, 12 May 1914, 6.
Appiah, Kwame Anthony, *The Ethics of Identity* (Princeton: Princeton University Press, 2005).
Archer, William, *Play-making: A Manual for Craftsmanship* (Boston: Small, Maynard and Company, 1918).
Aristotle, *The Nicomachean Ethics* (Harmondsworth: Penguin, 2004).
Atkins, G. Douglas, *Tracing the Essay: Through Experience to Truth* (Athens: University of Georgia Press, 2005).
Ballin, Malcolm, 'Welsh periodicals in English, 1880–1965: literary form and cultural substance', *Welsh Writing in English Yearbook*, 9 (2004), 1–32.
——, *Irish Periodical Culture, 1937–1972: Genre in Ireland, Wales, and Scotland* (Basingstoke: Palgrave Macmillan, 2008).
Barish, Jonas, *The Antitheatrical Prejudice* (Berkeley: University of California Press, 1981).
Baughan, E. A., 'The drama of the year', in L. Carson (ed.), *'The Stage' Yearbook 1914* (New York: The Stage, 1914), pp. 1–6.

BBC Wales Arts, 'Welsh film history 1930–39', online at *http://www.bbc.co.uk/wales/arts/sites/film/pages/history-1930-1939.shtml* [accessed 15 June 2013].

Bell, Morag, 'Reshaping boundaries: international ethics and environmental consciousness in the early twentieth century', *Transactions of the Institute of British Geographers*, 23/2 (1998), 151–75.

Belloc, Hilaire, 'The mowing of a field', *Hills and the Sea* (London: Methuen, 1941), pp. 176–88.

Bennett, Jane, 'The force of things: steps towards an ecology of matter', *Political Theory*, 32/3 (2004), 347–72.

Berry, R. G., 'Meditations among my tomes', *The Welsh Outlook*, 8/8 (1921), 178–80.

——, 'Moss – and others', *The Welsh Outlook*, 7/2 (1920), 41–3.

——, 'New play by Mr. J. O. Francis. Study of modern Welsh hamlet', *Western Mail*, 20 February 1923, 9.

Bishop, G. W. (ed.), *The Amateur Dramatic Year Book and Community Theatre Handbook, 1928–9* (London: A. & C. Black Ltd, 1929).

Booth, Wayne C., *The Company We Keep: An Ethics of Fiction* (Berkeley: University of California Press, 1988).

Bowlby, Rachel, 'Foreword', in Matthew Beaumont (ed.), *A Concise Guide to Realism* (Oxford: Wiley-Blackwell, 2010), pp. xiv–xxi.

Box, Sydney, 'The drama festival', in Patrick Carleton (ed.), *The Amateur Stage: A Symposium* (London: Geoffrey Bles, 1939), pp. 63–108.

Carleton, Patrick, 'Amateur and professional acting', in Patrick Carleton (ed.), *The Amateur Stage: A Symposium* (London: Geoffrey Bles, 1939), pp. 1–43.

Carroll, Noël, 'Art and ethical criticism: an overview of recent directions of resarch', *Ethics*, 110/2 (2000), 350–87.

——, 'The wheel of virtue: art, literature and moral knowledge', *The Journal of Aesthetics and Art Criticism*, 60/1 (2002), 3–26.

Casey, Edward S., *Getting Back into Place: Toward a Renewed Understanding of the Place-World* (Bloomington: Indiana University Press, 1993).

——, *The Fate of Place: A Philosophical History* (Berkeley: University of California Press, 1997).

Caston, Victor, 'Aristotle's two intellects: a modest proposal', *Phronesis*, 44/3 (1999), 199–227.

Chapin, Harold, 'The Philosopher of Butterbiggins', in John Hampden (ed.), *Nine Modern Plays* (London: Thomas Nelson & Sons, 1926), pp. 29–42.

Chapman, Don, *Oxford Playhouse: High and Low Drama in a University City* (Hatfield: University of Hertfordshire Press, 2008).

Charles, David and Dominic Scott, 'Aristotle on well-being and intellectual contemplation', *Proceedings of the Aristotelian Society*, supplementary volumes, 73 (1999), 205–23 and 225–42.

Chesterton, G. K., 'A piece of chalk', *Tremendous Trifles* (London: Methuen, 1909), pp. 1–7.

BIBLIOGRAPHY

Cohen, Helen Louise, 'Introduction', in Helen Louise Cohen (ed.) *One-Act Plays by Modern Authors* (New York: Harcourt, Brace and Co., 1927), pp. xiii–lxi.

Crang, Mike, *Cultural Geography* (London: Routledge, 1998).

Currie, Gregory, 'The moral psychology of fiction', *Australasian Journal of Philosophy*, 73/2 (1995), 250–9.

Curtis Brown Ltd letter to J. O. Francis, 15 October 1953, J. O. Francis Collection Box 1 (Aberystwyth University: Hugh Owen Library).

Dancy, Jonathan, *Ethics without Principles* (Oxford: Oxford University Press, 2004).

Darwin, Charles, *The Descent of Man and Selection in Relation to Sex*, vol. 1 (New York: Appleton and Co., 1871).

Davies, D. T., *Ble Ma Fa? Drama Mewn Un Act yn Nhafodiaith Cwm Rhondda* (Aberystwyth: Ddraig Goch, 1913).

——, 'Drama in Wales. Notable productions at Merthyr', *Western Mail*, 13 April 1920, 6.

——, 'The Beaten Track. A New Welsh play of distinction. Another triumph for Mr. J. O. Francis', *Western Mail*, 8 August 1924, 7.

——, 'Ton Pentre success. Adjudication to be made on Tuesday', *Western Mail*, 2 February 1920, 6.

——, 'Welsh drama. Some principles of play-writing', *Western Mail*, 30 July 1920, 9.

——, 'Welsh Drama Week. Assured success at Ton Pentre. "Change' the best effort of recent years', *Western Mail*, 30 January 1920, 8.

——, 'Welsh Drama Week. "Serch Hudol" played at Ton Pentre', *Western Mail*, 29 January 1920, 7.

——, 'Welsh national theatre movement', MS, n.d., D. R. Davies Collection, scrapbook No. 101/1 – Welsh National Theatre Movements No. 1, Press Cuttings, 1900–1914, 14 August 1931 – August 1934, 1937 (Aberystwyth: National Library of Wales).

Davies, Hazel Walford, *Y Theatr Genedlaethol yng Nghymru* (Caerdydd: Gwasg Prifysgol Cymru, 2007).

Davies, Idris, 'Souvenirs from Erin', *Wales*, 2 (1937), 56–60.

Davies, J. Kitchener, 'An analysis of present day Welsh literary effort', *Western Mail*, 17 October 1936, 11.

Davies, John, *A History of Wales*, rev. ed. (Harmondsworth: Penguin, 2007).

Davies, Naunton, *The Human Factor: A Play in Four Acts* (Cardiff: Educational Publishing Co. Ltd, 1920).

Davies, T. Huws, 'Some recent Welsh literature and the limitations of realism', *Y Cymmrodor*, 27 (London: Cymmrodorion, 1917), 186–205.

Donohue, Joseph, 'What is Edwardian theatre?', in Michael R. Booth and Joel H. Kaplan (eds), *The Edwardian Theatre: Essays on Performance and the Stage* (Cambridge: Cambridge University Press, 1996), pp. 10–35.

Dunsany, Lord (Edward John Moreton Drax Plunkett), 'The Flight of the Queen', in J. W. Marriott (ed.), *One-Act Plays of To-Day*, fourth series (London: George Harrap & Co., 1928), pp. 101–32.

E., E., 'Some recent Welsh plays', *The Welsh Outlook*, 1/ 6 (1914), 29–30.

Eaglestone, Robert, *Ethical Criticism: Reading after Lévinas* (Edinburgh: Edinburgh University Press, 1997), p. 47.

Editorial, 'Mr. Lloyd George and the Welsh drama', *Western Mail*, 16 May 1914, 6.

Editorial, 'Welsh national drama', *Western Mail*, 9 May 1914, 6.

Editorial, 'Welsh national drama at Cardiff theatre', *Western Mail*, 11 May 1914, 4.

Edwards, Hywel Teifi, *Wythnos yn Hanes y Ddrama yng Nghymru, 11–16 Mai 1914* (Bangor: Cymdeithas Theatr Cymru, 1984).

Edwards, J. Hugh, 'The month in Wales', Editorial, *Wales*, 5/34 (February 1914), 183–4.

Edwards, O. M., *Cartrefi Cymru* (Wrecsam: Hughes a'i Fab, 1896).

Edwards, Raymond, letter dated 23 June 1955, J. O. Francis Papers Box 2 (Aberystwyth University: Hugh Owen Library).

Elam, Keir, *The Semiotics of Theatre and Drama* (London: Routledge, repr. 1997).

Emerson, Ralph Waldo, *Nature*, in Nina Baym et al. (eds), *The Norton Anthology of American Literature*, vol. 1, 4th ed. (New York: Norton, 1994), pp. 993–1021.

Ervine, St John, *The Theatre in My Time* (London: Rich & Cowan Ltd, 1933).

Evans, Caradoc, *Taffy: A Play of Welsh Village Life* (London: Andrew Melrose, 1924).

Evans, George Ewart, 'Let Dogs Delight', in Gwyn Jones and Islwyn Ffowc Elis (eds), *Classic Welsh Short Stories* (Oxford: Oxford University Press, repr. 1992), pp. 31–7.

Evans, Tim, 'The Llanelli riots', *Planet*, 203 (2011), 80–90.

Fletcher, Ifan Kyrle, '"Cloudbreak." A Welsh monograph play', *Western Mail*, 17 November 1925.

Fleure, H. J., 'The Welsh people', *Wales*, 10 (1939), 265–9.

Francis, J. O., 'A comment from Corwen', *The Welsh Outlook*, 6/9 (1919), 228–31.

——, 'A Friday paper. XV. The followers of new lamps', *Western Mail*, 29 April 1921, 4.

——, 'A lament of the Cambrian railway', *The Welsh Outlook*, 7/5 (1920), 113–15.

——, 'A meditation on a pink ticket', *The Legend of the Welsh and Other Papers* (Cardiff: Educational Publishing Co. Ltd, 1924), pp. 65–8.

——, *A Short History of the University College of Wales, Aberystwyth* (Aberystwyth: Old Students' Association, 1920).

BIBLIOGRAPHY

——, 'An observer at Pontypool: recollections of the 1924 eisteddfod', *The Welsh Outlook*, 11/9 (1924), 242–3.

——, *Beginners Please!*, TS (Cardiff: BBC Welsh Home Service, 1955), J. O. Francis Collection Box 2 (Aberystwyth: Hugh Owen Library).

——, *Birds of a Feather: A Welsh Wayside Comedy in One Act* (Newtown: Welsh Outlook Press, 1927).

——, 'By the kitchen fire: an episode of the April "Welsh Outlook"', *The Welsh Outlook*, 6/5 (1919), 131–2.

——, *Change: A Glamorgan Play in Four Acts*, marked acting copy (Cardiff: Educational Publishing Co. Ltd, 1914), J. O. Francis Collection Box 1 (Aberystwyth University: Hugh Owen Library), p.133.

——, correspondence, J. O. Francis Collection Box 2 (Aberystwyth University: Hugh Owen Library).

——, correspondence, J. O. Francis Collection Box 3 (Aberystwyth University: Hugh Owen Library).

——, *Cross-Currents: A Play of Welsh Politics in Three Acts* (Cardiff: Educational Publishing Co. Ltd, 1924).

——, 'Foreword', *Cross-Currents* (Cardiff: Educational Publishing Co. Ltd, 1922), pp. 5–10.

——, *Glider Notes*, non-paginated MS, 1956, J. O. Francis Papers Box 3 (Aberystwyth University: Hugh Owen Library).

——, *Howell of Gwent: A Romantic Drama in Three Acts* (Cardiff: Educational Publishing Co. Ltd, 1934).

——, 'In praise of Avon Wen. Where travel yet is leisurely', *Western Mail*, 6 October 1922, 6.

——, 'In praise of the London Welsh', *The Legend of the Welsh and Other Papers* (Cardiff: Educational Publishing Co. Ltd, 1924), pp. 91–5.

——, 'Johnnie Genteel', TS (Cardiff: BBC, 1945), J. O. Francis Collection Box 2 (Aberystwyth University: Hugh Owen Library).

——, *King of the River: A One Act Comedy* (Cardiff: William Lewis, 1942).

——, 'Knickerbocker politics', *The Legend of the Welsh and Other Papers* (Cardiff: Educational Publishing Co. Ltd, 1924), pp. 81–4.

——, letter to Aneirin Talfan Davies, 11 October 1953, J. O. Francis Collection Box 1. Aberystwyth University: Hugh Owen Library.

——, letter to Cyril Hogg, Samuel French, 3 February 1952, J. O. Francis Collection Box 4 (Aberystwyth University: Hugh Owen Library).

——, letter to D. R. Davies, 1932, D. R. Davies Collection, scrapbook No. 101/1 – Welsh National Theatre Movements No. 1, Press Cuttings, 1900–1914, 14 August 1931 – August 1934, 1937 (Aberystwyth: National Library of Wales).

——, letter to Douglas Neil, 18 January 1954; Douglas Neil, letter to J. O. Francis, February 1954, J. O. Francis Collection Box 4; J. O. Francis, 'comments by theatre managers re. *The Whirligig*, J. O. Francis Collection Box 3 (Aberystwyth University: Hugh Owen Library).

——, *Little Village: A Welsh Farce in Three Acts* (Cardiff: Educational Publishing Co. Ltd, 1929).

——, *National Drama in Wales*, radio talk, TS, recorded 19 November 1952, J. O. Francis Collection Box 2 (Aberystwyth University: Hugh Owen Library), pp. 6–7.

——, 'New Welsh play. Presentation last night in London. Applying drama to new purposes', *Western Mail*, 7 July 1924, 9.

——, 'On a dramatic entry', *Western Mail*, 11 March 1921, 6.

——, personal letter to Arthur Elsbury (Samuel French Ltd), dated 2 May 1954, J. O. Francis Collection Box 4 (Aberystwyth University: Hugh Owen Library).

——, 'Proselytes of the book', *The Legend of the Welsh and Other Papers* (Cardiff: Educational Publishing Co. Ltd, 1924), pp. 61–4.

——, *Tares in the Wheat: A Country Comedy in Three Acts* (Cardiff: William Lewis, 1942?).

——, *The Bakehouse: A Gossip's Comedy (in One Act)* (Cardiff: Educational Publishing Co. Ltd, 1914).

——, *The Beaten Track: A Welsh Play in Four Acts* (London: Samuel French, 1927).

——, *The Dark Little People: A Comedy of the Welsh Tribes* (Cardiff: Educational Publishing Co. Ltd, 1922?).

——, 'The deacon and the dramatist', *The Legend of the Welsh and Other Papers* (Cardiff: Educational Publishing Co. Ltd, 1924), pp. 55–60.

——, *The Devouring Fire: Play in Three Acts*, unpublished TS, J. O. Francis Collection Box 1 (Aberystwyth University: Hugh Owen Library), p. II. 33. Idiosyncratic numbering in original.

——, 'The drama in Wales: the amateur rampant', *The Amateur Stage*, 10 (1926?), no page numbers.

——, 'The legend of the Welsh', *The Legend of the Welsh and Other Papers* (Cardiff: Educational Publishing Co. Ltd, 1924), pp. 11–14.

——, *The Poacher: A Comedy in One Act* (Cardiff: Educational Publishing Co. Ltd, 1914?).

——, *The Sewing Guild: A Woman's Comedy in One Act* (Cardiff: William Lewis, 1943?).

——, *The Sheep and the Goats*, TS, J. O. Francis Collection Box 4 (Aberystwyth University: Hugh Owen Library), p. I–1–9. Idiosyncratic pagination according to MS.

——, *The Welshman Takes to the Stage*, TS, broadcast script 1949, J. O. Francis Collection Box 2 (Aberystwyth: Hugh Owen Library).

——, 'The village of merciful men', *Western Mail*, 8 April 1921, 4.

——, 'The village of the tides', *The Legend of the Welsh and Other Papers* (Cardiff: Educational Publishing Co. Ltd, 1924), pp. 21–4.

——, *'The Whirligig'. Comments by theatre managers*, undated TS, c.1954, J. O. Francis Collection Box 3 (Aberystwyth University: Hugh Owen Library).

——, 'Wales and the London Welsh', *The Legend of the Welsh and Other Papers* (Cardiff: Educational Publishing Co. Ltd, 1924), pp. 85–90.
——, '"Yr Adsain"', *The Legend of the Welsh and Other Papers* (Cardiff: Educational Publishing Co. Ltd, 1924), pp. 49–53.
Gallie, Menna, *Strike for a Kingdom* (Aberystwyth: Honno, repr. 2010).
Garde Peach, Lawrence du, 'Village Drama', in Patrick Carleton (ed.), *The Amateur Stage: A Symposium* (London: Geoffrey Bles, 1939), pp. 139–58.
Gardner, Lyn, 'The Passion – review', *The Guardian*, 24 April 2011, online at *http://www.guardian.co.uk/stage/2011/apr/24/the-passion-port-talbot-review* [accessed 28 June 2013].
Gass, William, 'Emerson and the essay', *Habitations of the Word: Essays* (New York: Simon and Schuster, 1985), pp. 9–49.
Goldberg, Elkhonon, *The Wisdom Paradox* (London: Pocket, 2007).
Goodwin, Geraint, *The Heyday in the Blood* (Harmondsworth: Penguin, 1954).
Gramich, Katie, *Twentieth-Century Women's Writing in Wales: Land, Gender Belonging* (Cardiff: University of Wales Press, 2007).
Grene, Nicholas, *The Politics of Irish Drama: Plays in Context from Boucicault to Friel* (Cambridge: Cambridge University Press, 1999).
Griffiths, Glyndwr, '"Birds of a Feather" was acted in twenty-five square feet. Splash from the bishop's shirt on arc-lamp meant disaster!', *Aberdare Leader*, 3 July 1948. In D. R. Davies Collection, scrapbook 5–2: Wales and the British Drama League (1946–), pp. 55–6.
Griffiths, R. A. (Elphin), 'The prospect of the Welsh drama', *The Transactions of the Honourable Society of Cymmrodorion*, session 1912–13 (London: Cymmrodorion, 1914), 129–39.
Griffiths, William, 'Profile of the month: J.O. Francis', *Y Ddinas*, November 1954, 4 and 9.
Gross, John, *The Rise and Fall of the Man of Letters: Aspects of English Literary Life since 1800* (Harmondsworth: Penguin, 1991).
Gruffudd, Pyrs, 'Back to the land: historiography, rurality and the nation in interwar Wales', *Transactions of the Institute of British Geographers*, 19/1 (1994), 61–77.
——, 'Remaking Wales: nation-building and the geographical imagination, 1925–50', *Political Geography*, 14/3 (1995), 219–39.
Haas, Gerhard, *Essay* (Stuttgart: Metzler, 1969).
Harris, Wendell V., 'Reflections on the peculiar status of the personal essay', *College English*, 58/8 (1996), 934–53.
Hatton, Thomas J., *Playwriting for Amateurs: How to Become a Published Playwright* (Colorado Springs: Meriwether Publishing Ltd, 1981).
Hesse, Douglas, 'The place of creative nonfiction', *College English*, 65/3 (2003), 237–40.
Hijinx Theatre, 'Odyssey Theatre', online at *http://www.hijinx.org.uk/Odyssey* [accessed 21 December 2011].

Hogan, Robert, Richard Burnham and Daniel P. Poteet, *The Rise of the Realists, 1910–1915* (Dublin: Dolmen, 1975).
Holmes, Leigh Howard, 'Linkages of nonfiction and selfhood: the places of personal essays', *The English Journal*, 91/4 (2002), 64–8.
Horowitz, Alexandra, *Inside of a Dog: What Dogs See, Smell and Know* (London: Simon & Schuster, 2009).
Hughes, Richard, 'A Comedy of Good and Evil', *Plays* (London: Chatto & Windus, 1928), pp. 36–141.
——, 'The Sisters' Tragedy', *Plays* (London: Chatto & Windus, 1928), pp. 2–35.
Innes, Christopher, *Modern British Drama: The Twentieth Century* (Cambridge: Cambridge University Press, repr. 2002).
—— (ed.), *A Sourcebook on Naturalist Theatre* (London: Routledge, 2000).
Irwin, T. H., 'Permanent happiness: Aristotle and Solon', in Nancy Sherman (ed.), *Aristotle's Ethics: Critical Essays* (Lanham: Rowman & Littlefield, 1999), pp. 1–33.
James, Mary Auronwy, 'John Oswald Francis', online at *http://wbo.llgc.org.uk/en/s2-FRAN-OSW-1882.html?query=john+oswald+francis&field=content* [accessed 20 May 2013].
Jenkins, Emyr Wyn, *Y Ddrama Gymraeg yn Abertawe a'r Cylch* (Abertawe: W. Walters a'i Fab, 1985).
Jenkins, Gwyn, 'The Welsh Outlook, 1914–1933', *Cylchgrawn Llyfrgell Genedlaethol Cymru/The National Library of Wales Journal*, 24 (1985–6), 463–96.
Jones, Abel J., 'Does Wales need the drama?', *The Welsh Outlook*, 6/1 (1914), 255–6.
Jones, Anwen, *National Theatres in Context: France, Germany, England and Wales* (Cardiff: University of Wales Press, 2007).
Jones, J. Graham, 'Lloyd George, Cymru Fydd and the Newport meeting of 1896', *Cylchgrawn Llyfrgell Genedlaethol Cymru/National Library of Wales Journal*, 29/4 (1996), 435–53.
Jones, J. T., 'Welsh pioneer in drama. Interview with the Rev. R. G. Berry. Wales wants its own J. M. Synge', *Western Mail*, 9 July 1924, 6.
Jones, Lewis, *Cwmardy, We Live* (Cardigan: Parthian, repr. 2006).
Jones, T. Gwynn, draft of letter sent to J. O. Francis dated 16 February 1923, T. Gwynn Jones Papers, B 131 (Aberystwyth: National Library of Wales).
Jones, Thomas, 'Foreword', *The Welsh Outlook*, 1/1 (1914), 1–2.
——, letter to Percy Watkins, 3 September 1919, Thomas Jones Collection, Class H: Wales. Vol. 4. Welsh Outlook 1913–1919 (Aberystwyth: National Library of Wales).
Kluckhohn, Paul, *Das Ideengut der Deutschen Romantik*, 3rd ed. (Tübingen: Niemeyer, 1953).
Knight, Stephen, *A Hundred Years of Fiction* (Cardiff: University of Wales Press, 2004).

Krippendorf, Klaus, *Content Analysis: An Introduction to its Methodology*, 2nd ed. (London: Sage, 2004).
Kruger, Loren, *The National Stage: Theatre and Cultural Legitimation in England, France, and America* (Chicago: University of Chicago Press, 1992).
Ledger, Sally, 'Naturalism: "Dirt and Horror Pure and Simple"', in Matthew Beaumont (ed.), *A Concise Guide to Realism* (Oxford: Wiley-Blackwell, 2010), pp. 86–101.
Leopold, Aldo, 'The land ethic', *A Sand County Almanac; and Sketches here and there* (Oxford: Oxford University Press, repr. 1977), pp. 201–26.
Lessing, Gotthold Ephraim, *Hamburgische Dramaturgie* (Berlin: Deutscher Verlag der Wissenschaften, 1952).
Levine, Peter, *Reforming the Humanities: Literature and Ethics from Dante through Modern Times* (Basingstoke: Palgrave Macmillan, 2009).
Lewis, E. D., *The Rhondda Valleys: A Study on Industrial Development from 1800 to the Present Day* (London: Phoenix House, 1959).
Lewis, Saunders, 'Dramâu J. O. Francis', in Saunders Lewis, *Meistri A'u Crefft: Ysgrifau Llenyddol gan Saunders Lewis*, ed. Gwynn ap Gwilym (Cardiff: University of Wales Press, 1981), pp. 263–5.
Lewis, J. Saunders, 'The drama in Wales. Over seventy plays in competition', *Western Mail*, 6 August 1920, 4.
Lewis, John D., 'Libel on life in Wales. Mr. Caradoc Evans' new play. "Taffy". Applauded by London audience', *Western Mail*, 27 February 1923, 6.
——, 'Welsh drama. The untouched field of romance', *Western Mail*, 23 October 1920, 10.
——, 'Welsh dramatists. No. 3 work of Mr. J. O. Francis', *Western Mail*, 21 December 1921, 9.
Llywelyn, Dorian, *Sacred Place, Chosen People: Land and National Identity in Welsh Spirituality* (Cardiff: University of Wales Press, 1999).
Lord Chamberlain's Archive, correspondence, 'Antony Settles Down' date of license: 30 May 1923 (London: British Library).
MacIntyre, Alasdair, *After Virtue*, 3rd ed. (London: Duckworth, 2007).
MacKaye, Percy, *Community Drama: Its Motive and Method of Neighborliness* (Boston: Houghton Mifflin, 1917).
Marriott, J. W., 'Foreword', in J. W. Marriott (ed.), *One-Act Plays of To-Day*, third series (London: George Harrap & Co., 1926), pp. 5–7.
——, 'Preface', *Great Modern British Plays* (London: George Harrap & Co., 1929), pp. 5–10.
Massey, Doreen, 'Geographies of responsibility', *Geografisker Annaler, Series B. Human Geography*, 86/1 (2004), 5–18.
Mikhail, John, *Elements of Moral Cognition: Rawls' Linguistic Analogy and the Cognitive Science of Moral and Legal Judgment* (Cambridge: Cambridge University Press, 2011).

Miller, Anne I., *The Independent Theatre in Europe, 1887 to the Present* (New York: Bloomberg, 1966).
Moll, Jorge, Ricardo de Oliveira-Souza, Paul J. Eslinger, Ivanei E. Bramanti, Janaína Mourão-Miranda, Pedro Angelo Andreioulo and Luiz Pessoa, 'The neural correlates of moral sensitivity: a functional magnetic resonance imaging investigation of basic and moral emotions', *The Journal of Neuroscience*, 22/7 (2002), 2730–6.
Morgan, Kenneth O., *Rebirth of a Nation: A History of Modern Wales* (Oxford: Oxford University Press, 1998).
Morgan, Owen, 'The revival of the drama in Wales: splendid reception at Pontypridd', *Western Mail*, 29 December 1986, 2.
Morris, T. H., 'The need for open air schools', supplement to the February number, *The Welsh Outlook*, 6/2 (1919), 7.
Morris-Roberts, M., 'Welsh plays overdo the kitchen drama', *Western Mail*, 17 April 1936, 8.
Moses, Montrose J., 'Introduction', in J. O. Francis, *Change* (Garden City: Doubleday, 1915), pp. v–xviii.
Neath Little Theatre, 'About us', n.d., online at *http://www.neathlittletheatre.co.uk/#!about-us* [accessed 3 December 2011].
Nussbaum, Martha, *Love's Knowledge: Essays on Philosophy and Literature* (Oxford: Oxford University Press, 1990).
——, 'Non-relative virtues: an Aristotelian approach', in James P. Sterba (ed.), *Ethics: The Big Questions* (London: Blackwell, 1998), pp. 259–76.
O'Hara, Daniel T., 'The return to ethics: a report from the front', *boundary 2*, 24/2 (1997), 145–56.
Our Drama Critic, 'Romance of old Wales. Native writer's triumph', *Western Mail*, 10 July 1933, 9.
Our Drama Critic, 'Welsh actors' venture in Shakespeare. Mountain Ash Drama Week players' work', *Western Mail*, 27 October 1932, 9.
Our Own Correspondent, 'Mr. J. O. Francis on Welsh drama. Plea for pure comedy movement', *Western Mail*, 20 January 1923, 10.
Our Own Correspondent, 'National theatre company. First production in Wales. Play secret', *Western Mail*, 4 February 1933, 7.
Our Own Correspondent, 'National theatre. Movement hopes to have a professional company', *Western Mail*, 27 January 1933, 9.
Our Own Correspondent, 'New attack on Wales. "Caradoc" explains his revised play. Revelations for London. Expects bricks, but pleads for tolerance', *Western Mail*, 2 September 1925, 7.
Our Own Correspondent, '"The Dark Little People." Charming comedy of Welsh tribes. Notable success won by Mr. J. O. Francis', *Western Mail*, 25 February 1924, 8.
Our Own Correspondent, 'Welsh author's new play. First night enthusiasm at Trecynon', *Western Mail*, 28 December 1928, 8.

Our Own Correspondent, 'Welsh national theatre. Ready to perform in barns if necessary', *Western Mail*, 14 March 1933, 7.
Owain, O. Llew, *Hanes y Ddrama yng Nghymru, 1850–1943* (Lerpwl: Gwasg y Brython, 1948).
Owen, Brian, Curator, Royal Welch Fusiliers Museum, personal email communication (10 February 2011).
P., W. D., '"The Lost Legacy."', review, *The Welsh Outlook*, 5/3 (1918), 101–2.
Parry, J. Eddie, 'Drama week. A disappointment at Swansea. The weakness of "Cross Currents"', *Western Mail*, 1 May 1924, 12.
——, 'Drama week. Moliere in Welsh at Swansea. A dull performance of "Cross Currents"', *Western Mail*, 2 May 1924, 10.
——, '"Howell of Gwent". Performance at Neath to-night', *Western Mail*, 6 July 1933, 11.
——, 'Welsh drama. Brilliant close to Swansea week. Is a national theatre practicable?', *Western Mail*, 3 May 1924, 9.
Phillips, W. F., *The Lost Legacy: A Play of Welsh Domestic Life* (Liverpool: Walton, 1918).
Posner, Richard, 'Against ethical criticism', *Philosophy and Literature*, 2/1 (1999), 1–27.
Price, Cecil, *The English Theatre in Wales in the Eighteenth and Nineteenth Centuries* (Cardiff: University of Wales Press, 1948)
——, *The Professional Theatre in Wales* (Llandysul: Gomer and University College of Wales Swansea, 1984).
Raine, Allen, *A Welsh Witch: A Romance of Rough Places* (Aberystwyth: Honno, repr. 2013).
Rawls, John, *A Theory of Justice* (Cambridge, MA: Harvard University Press, 1999).
Rhondda Cynon Taf Library Service, 'The Aberdare Little Theatre Company', 2006, online at http://webapps.rhondda-cynon-taff.gov.uk/heritagetrail/english/cynon/aberdare_little-theatre.html [accessed 3 December 2011].
Rhoscomyl, Owen 'Historic week. Welsh national drama. A few reflections. The players, manager and the public', *Western Mail*, 19 May 1914, 7.
——, 'Venture in drama. The appeal to Welsh nationalism', *Western Mail*, 8 May 1914, 4.
Rhys, Martin, 'Keeping it in the family: *Change* by J. O. Francis, *The Keep* by Gwyn Thomas and *House of America* by Ed Thomas', in Katie Gramich and Andrew Hiscock (eds), *Dangerous Diversity: The Changing Faces of Wales. Essays in Honour of Tudor Bevan* (Cardiff: University of Wales Press, 1998), pp. 111–28.
Ridout, Nicholas, *Theatre and Ethics* (Basingstoke: Macmillan, 2009), p. 19.
Roberts, Arthur O., 'Cloudbreak', Amy Key Clarke, A. O. Roberts and L. du Garde Peach, *Three One-Act Plays* (Oxford: Basil Blackwell, 1925).
Roberts, Harri, 'The body and the book: Caradoc Evans's *My People*', *Welsh Writing in English: A Yearbook of Critical Essays*, 11 (2006/7), 3–50.

Roberts, John Glyn, 'National theatre. A venture worthy of Wales's support', letter to the Editor, *Western Mail*, 6 February 1933, 11.
Roche, Anthony, 'Re-working *The Workhouse Ward*: McDonagh, Beckett, and Gregory', *Irish University Review*, 34/1 (2004), 171–84.
Root, Robert L., and Michael J. Steinberg (eds), *The Fourth Genre: Contemporary Writers of/on Creative Nonfiction*, 6th ed. (London: Longman, 2011).
Rosé, Paul, 'Mr. J. O. Francis', *The Times*, 10 October 1956, 13.
Ross, Ethel, *Dylan Thomas and the Amateur Theatre* (Swansea: Swansea Little Theatre, 1985).
Rothkirch, Alyce von, 'Visions of Wales: *The Welsh Outlook*, 1914–1933', *Almanac: A Yearbook of Welsh Writing in English*, 14 (2010), 65–92.
Rowlands, Mark, *Can Animals Be Moral?* (Oxford: Oxford University Press, 2012).
Said, Edward, *Orientalism: Western Conceptions of the Orient* (Harmondsworth: Penguin, repr. 1991).
Schafer, B. Louise, 'The one-act play and the short story', *The Sewanee Review*, 27/2 (1919), 151–62.
Schmidt, Arno, 'Der Triton mit dem Sonnenschirm: Überlegungen zur Lesbarmachung von *Finnegans Wake* von James Joyce', *Dialoge 3* (Zürich: Haffmanns, 1991), 31–70.
Schwartz, Barry, and Kenneth Sharpe, *Practical Wisdom: The Right Way to Do the Right Thing* (Harmondsworth: Riverhead, 2010).
Shaw, Bernard, 'The author's apology', *Dramatic Opinions and Essays with an Apology* (New York: Brentano's, 1910), pp. xxi–xxv.
Shields, Rob, *Places on the Margin: Alternative Geographies of Modernity* (London: Routledge, 1991).
Sladen-Smith, F., 'St Simeon Stylites', in J. W. Marriott (ed.), *One-Act Plays of To-Day*, fourth series (London: George Harrap & Co., 1928), pp. 133–69.
Smith, Amanda, editorial director at Samuel French, personal email communication regarding Samuel French stock, 24 September 2009.
Stephens, Meic (ed.), 'John Oswald Francis', *The New Companion to the Literature of Wales* (Cardiff: University of Wales Press, 1998), p. 253.
——, (tr. and ed.), *Illuminations: An Anthology of Welsh Short Prose* (Cardiff: Welsh Academic Press, 1998).
——, 'Preface', *Illuminations: An Anthology of Welsh Short Prose* (Cardiff: Welsh Academic Press, 1998), pp. vii–ix.
Thomas, M. Wynn, 'All change: the new Welsh drama before the Great War', *Internal Difference: Twentieth-Century Writing in Wales* (Cardiff: University of Wales Press, 1992), pp. 1–14.
——, *In the Shadow of the Pulpit: Literature and Nonconformist Wales* (Cardiff: University of Wales Press, 2010).
Thoreau, Henry, *Walden* (1854), in Carl Bode (ed.), *The Portable Thoreau* (Harmondsworth: Penguin, 1981), pp. 258–572.

Vandevelde, Karen, '"What's all the stir about": Gerald MacNamara, Synge and the early Abbey Theatre', *New Hibernia Review/Iris Éireannach Nua*, 10/3 (2006), 108–21.

Vardy, Peter, and Paul Grosch, *The Puzzle of Ethics* (London: Fount, 1999).

Wearing, J. P., *The London Stage 1910–1919: A Calendar of Plays and Players*, vol. 1: 1910–16 (Metuchen, NJ: Scarecrow, 1982), pp. 144–6.

Weil, Simone, *The Need for Roots*, tr. Arthur Wills (Abingdon: Routledge, repr. 2002).

Welsh M.A., A, 'Epstein and "Howell of Gwent": a comparison. "Mauve trying to be Purple"', *Western Mail*, 19 July 1933, 8.

Williams, Bernard, *Ethics and the Limits of Philosophy* (London: Routledge, repr. 2011).

Williams, Gwyn A., *When Was Wales? A History of the Welsh* (Harmondsworth: Penguin, repr. 1991).

Williams, Ioan, *Y Mudiad Drama yng Nghymru, 1880–1940* (Caerdydd: Gwasg Prifysgol Cymru, 2006).

Williams, Llewelyn, 'A transformation and a revelation', *Western Mail*, 16 May 1914, 7.

Wilson, James Q., *The Moral Sense* (New York: Free Press, 1997).

Woolf, Virginia, 'On not knowing Greek', *The Common Reader* (Harmondsworth: Penguin, 1938), pp. 32–47.

Wright, R. F., 'Bathing', *The Welsh Outlook*, 1/8 (1914), 358–9.

Index

Abbey Theatre, Dublin, *also* Irish National Theatre *and* Irish National Theatre Company 3, 17, 32, 33, 63, 83, 99, 104
Aberdare Little Theatre 41, 54
Abergavenny W.E.A. Dramatic Society 42
Abraham, William 'Mabon' 131–2
Accent on Youth (Sampson Raphaelson) 50
Adorno, Theodor W. 133
Aeres Maesfelin (R. Rhys Evans) 50
Allan, Laurence 40
Allen, Grant 127
amateur drama
  in Wales, *also* amateur theatre 2, 15, 22, 24, 26, 32, 37–59, 86, 97, 100, 112
  companies, *also* amateur theatre companies 2, 10, 13, 31, 35, 38, 40, 42, 53, 55, 81, 82, 85, 86, 91, 93, 97, 112, 116
  competitions, *also* amateur drama festivals *and* drama weeks 25, 43, 54–8
  festivals, *see* amateur drama competitions
  drama weeks, *see* amateur drama competitions
Andreyev, Leonid 47

Angels don't need Wings (Laurence Allan) 40
Ar y Groesffordd (R. G. Berry) 1, 36, 50, 51, 52
Archer, William 29, 32, 62
Aristotle 3, 4, 21, 22, 67, 71, 105, 123, 141, 142, 162 n19, 178 n6
Arnold, Matthew 137
Artaud, Antonin 15
'back to the land' 6, 20
Bacon, Francis 124
Ballad of the Mari Lwyd, The (Vernon Watkins) 34
Barrie, J. M. 29, 41, 46, 49, 50
Barry Amateur Dramatic Society 53, 55, 56
Bart, Jean 51
Beddau'r Proffwydi (W. J. Gruffydd) 50
Beerbohm, Max 129
Belloc, Hilaire 120, 124, 128, 129
Berkeley, Reginald 51
Berry, R. G. 1, 24, 31, 36, 43, 46, 47, 49, 50, 51, 52, 75, 129
Blackwood Amateur Dramatic Society 48, 55, 56
Blaengarw Amateur Dramatic Society 53, 56
Ble Ma Fa? (D. T. Davies) 1, 36, 66, 82, 98

INDEX

Booth, Wayne 3, 122, 158 n25
bourgeois tragedy (*bürgerliches Trauerspiel*, Gotthold Ephraim Lessing) 62
Bowen, Evelyn (organising secretary, Welsh National Theatre Company) 85–6
Brecht, Bertolt 15
Bridie, James 50
British Drama League of Community Drama Festival 104, 155

Candida (George Bernard Shaw) 50, 53
Čapek, Karel and Josef 41, 46, 51
Cardiff Municipal Officer's Dramatic Society 42
Carlyle, Thomas 124
Carroll, Noël 3, 100, 126, 172 n16
Carter, Winifred 51
Cartrefi Cymru (O. M. Edwards) 121
Casey, Edward 5, 6
Caste (Tom Robertson) 28, 68
Cathleen ni Houlihan (W. B. Yeats and Lady Gregory) 17, 34
Chapin, Harold 33, 37, 98
Chekhov, Anton Pavlovich 84
Cherry Orchard, The (Anton Chekhov) 84
Chesterton, G. K. 120, 124, 125–6, 127, 128, 129, 130, 135
Cloudbreak (A. O. Roberts) 83–4
Colli ac Ennill (W. Bryn Davies) 50
Colum, Padraic 33
comedy 3, 8, 13, 14, 22, 35, 39, 48, 53, 76, 77, 85, 86, 87, 88, 97, 107, 114, 117, 120, 166 n45
Comedy of Good and Evil, A (Richard Hughes) 8, 85–8
Common Reader, The (Virginia Woolf) 129
community drama, *also* community theatre 40, 44, 57, 100
community ethics 2, 19, 23, 103–4, 122, 143
community theatre, *see* community drama

Company We Keep, The (Wayne Booth) 3, 122, 123
contemplation 4, 22, 72, 74, 105–6, 134, 135
Corn is Green, The (Emlyn Williams) 35
Cove, Ernest George 44, 63
Creaking Chair, The (Allene Tupper Wilkes) 51
Currie, Gregory 3, 100
Cwm Glo (J. Kitchener Davies) 33, 45
Cwmni Trefriw 63
cydymdreiddiad tir ac iaith 18, 21, 139
Cyfrinach y Fasged Frwyn (D. Gwernydd Morgan) 50
Cymric Players (Ken Etheridge) 42
Cymru Fydd 7, 30, 71, 72
Cynon Amateur Dramatic Society (Aberdare) 56

Dancy, Jonathan 115, 118
Dane, Clemence 46, 49, 50
Darwin, Charles 141
Dau Wynne 137
Davies, Aneirin Talfan 91, 124
Davies, Betty Eynon 36
Davies, D. J. 43, 51
Davies, D. T. 1, 9, 11, 24, 30, 36, 43, 45, 46, 49, 51, 52, 64, 66, 69, 79, 80, 81, 82, 98
Davies, David 12, 14, 72
Davies, Henry Hubert 50
Davies, Idris 129
Davies, J. Kitchener 33, 43, 45, 47
Davies, Naunton 42, 48, 50, 51, 52, 65–6
Davies, Rhys 46, 49
Davies, W. Bryn 49, 50
de Montaigne, Michel 124
de Quincey, Thomas 124
de Walden, Lord Howard (T. E. Ellis) 1, 13, 30, 32, 36, 46, 54, 58, 63, 69, 70, 85
Deacon's Hat, The (Jeannette Marks) 35
Dear Brutus (J. M. Barrie) 50

INDEX

Death of a Salesman (Arthur Miller) 95
Defendant, The (G. K. Chesterton) 124, 128
Deirdre of the Shadows (W. B. Yeats) 17
Delaney, Shelagh 15
Delight (J. B. Priestley) 124
Descent of Man, The (Charles Darwin) 141
Devil's Disciple, The 51
Dewis Anorfod (Stanley Houghton, trans. *Hobson's Choice*) 51
Dicky Bach Dwl 6, 21, 40, 97, 100–1, 103–13, 119, 124, 172 n28
Dieithryn, Y (D. T. Davies) 36
Doctor er ei Waethaf (Saunders Lewis) 85
Dunsany, Lord 98
Dwywaith yn Blentyn (R. G. Berry) 51

East Moor Players (Cardiff) 42, 53
Ebbw Vale Amateur Dramatic Society 56
Edwards, Ada 44, 49
Edwards, O. M. (Owen Morgan) 7, 17, 20, 121
Eldest Son, The (John Galsworthy) 29
Ellis, T. E. *see* de Walden, Lord Howard
emotional knowledge 100
Ephraim Harris (D. T. Davies) 1, 36
Epidemic, The (Naunton Davies) 50
Ervine, St John 17, 25, 29, 46, 49, 50, 51, 53
Escape (John Galsworthy) 51, 53
essay, *also* personal essay 13, 22, 26, 79, 120, 122–31, 133–40, 143
Etheridge, Ken 42, 46
ethical literary criticism 3, 5, 6, 45, 60–1, 125
ethics of place 2, 3, 6, 23, 70, 96, 97, 106, 112, 122, 124, 141, 142, 143
eudaimonia 4, 71, 105 112, 178 n6
Evans, Caradoc 2, 33, 45, 46, 75, 76–8, 87, 90, 103, 143

Evans, George Ewart 2, 103
Evans, R. Rhys 49, 50

Fam, Y (Kate Roberts and Betty Eynon Davies) 36
Farmer's Wife, The (Eden Philpotts) 51
Fleure, H. F. 7, 17, 19, 20, 108, 111, 135, 139, 177 n73
Flight of the Queen, The (Lord Dunsany) 98
For Services Rendered (W. Somerset Maugham) 50
Four-Leaved Clover (Betty Eynon Davies) 36
Francis, J. O.
  biography 6–15
  essays
    'Against measuring heads' 135, 139–40
    'By the kitchen fire' 126
    'comment from Corwen, A' 126
    'followers of new lamps, The' 127
    'glory of Glamorgan, The' 120
    'In praise of Avon Wen' 128
    'Knickerbocker politics' 128, 131
    'lament of the Cambrian railway, A' 137, 140
    'legend of the Welsh, The' 123, 136–8, 140
    'London Welsh papers' 138–9, 140
    'On a dramatic entry' 127
    'Proselytes of the book' 139
    'railways of romance, The' 132, 137
    'village of merciful men, The' 123
    'village of the tides, The' 134, 138, 140
    'Welshman takes to the stage, The' 124
    '"Yr Adsain"' 134, 139

plays
- *Antony Settles Down* 11
- *Bakehouse, The*, also *Mrs Howells Intervenes* 10, 13, 16, 114–15, 116, 117
- *Beaten Track, The* 6, 7, 16, 21, 37, 78–84, 89, 96, 108, 117, 119, 139, 160 n58
- *Birds of a Feather* 13, 16, 51, 103, 104, 105–6, 160 n58
- *Bobl Fach Ddu, Y* 50
- *Change* 1, 2, 4, 7, 9, 10, 16, 20, 21, 34, 36, 37, 50, 61–71, 72, 75, 76, 78, 82, 83, 87, 88, 92, 94, 96, 105, 111, 114, 117, 120, 131
- *Cross-Currents* 7, 13, 14, 16, 22, 71–8, 81, 88, 91, 92, 93, 94, 96
- *Crowning of Peace, The* 14, 90
- *Dark Little People, The* 13, 16–17, 50, 104, 107–9, 114, 139, 160 n58
- *Deufor Gyfarfod* 75
- *Devouring Fire, The* (15, 16, 21, 83, 89, 91–5, 96, 131
- *For France* 11
- *His Shining Majesty* 97, 104, 160 n58
- *Howell of Gwent* 14, 16, 83, 85, 88–91, 96
- *Hunting the Hare* 7, 97, 104
- *King of the River* 103, 104, 106–7, 120, 139
- *Little Village* 114, 117–20, 139
- *Mrs Howells Intervenes*, see *The Bakehouse*
- *Nightbirds* 105
- *Poacher, The* 1, 10, 13, 14, 16, 21, 35, 48, 51, 82, 97, 100–5, 114, 115, 119, 160 n58
- *Potsier, Y* 14
- *Sewing Guild, The* 7, 115–17
- *Sheep and the Goats, The*, see *Tares in the Wheat*
- *Tares in the Wheat*, also *The Sheep and the Goats* 7, 39, 54, 104, 110–13, 166 n45, 172 n28
- *Things that are Caesar's, The* 160 n58
- *Whirligig: Comedy of Time's Revenges, The* 15, 39, 166 n45

work for radio
- *Beginners Please!* 124
- 'Johnnie Genteel' 124

French Leave (Reginald Berkeley) 51

Gallie, Menna 102
Galsworthy, John 14, 29, 34, 36, 37, 41, 46, 49, 51, 53, 64, 65, 66, 67, 69, 124
Garrick Dramatic Society (Mid-Rhondda) 55, 56
Gas Station Angel (Ed Thomas) 64, 95
Geddes, Patrick 19, 135
George, David Lloyd 1, 30, 70, 72, 109, 138
'Getting up on cold mornings' (Leigh Hunt) 124
Ghosts (Henrik Ibsen) 53
Goodwin, Geraint 102
Granville-Barker, Harley 27, 29, 34, 35, 66
Gregory, Lady Augusta 3, 17, 34, 35, 37, 99, 100, 104
Griffith, R. A. ('Elphin') 31, 32
Grovian Amateur Dramatic Society (Cardiff) 56
Gruffydd, W. J. 7, 43, 49, 50, 52, 166 n38
Grumpy (Horace Hodges and T. Wigney Percyval) 50
Guns of Victory, The (J. O. Francis) 11
Gwaelod-y-Garth Dramatic Society 46

Hardie, Keir 128, 131–2
Harding, Lyn 10–11
Harvest (Lennox Robinson) 33
Hauptmann, Gerhart 66, 68

Hawk Island (Howard Irving Young) 50
Hay, Ian and P. G. Wodehouse 48, 49, 50
Hazlitt, William 124
He Who Gets Slapped (Leonid Andreyev) 47
Heyday in the Blood (Geraint Goodwin) 102
Hodges and T. Wigney Percyval, Horace 49, 50
Honourable Society of Cymmrodorion 14, 138
Horeb Welsh Dramatic Society (Treherbert) 56
Houghton, Stanley 33, 37, 49, 50, 51
House of America (Ed Thomas) 64
Housman, Laurence 41
'How should one read a book?' (Virginia Woolf) 125
Howard de Walden Prize 30, 32, 35, 36, 70
Howell, Florence 46
Hsiung, S. I. (Hsiung Shih-I) 46–7, 49, 50
Hughes, John (translator) 13
Hughes, Mary (translator) 13
Hughes, Richard 8, 49, 83, 84–5, 86–8
Human Factor, The (Naunton Davies) 65–6
Hundred Years Old, A (Serafín and Joaquín Álvarez Quintero) 47, 50
Hunt, Leigh 124

Ibsen, Henrik 24, 25, 29, 36, 37, 41, 49, 51, 68, 69
identity 6, 7, 16, 28, 60, 74, 96, 111, 118, 121, 135, 136, 139, 140
  gwerin 65
  local 23, 98, 119–20
  national 3, 23, 33, 61, 97, 111, 122, 132–3, 136, 139, 140, 143
  Welsh 88, 108, 119–20, 121, 132, 136, 139, 140
Ifan, Wil 50
In Chancery (John Galsworthy) 14
In Sunshine and In Shadow (Alan Osborne) 64
In the Shadow of the Glen (J. M. Synge) 48, 104
Incorporated Stage Society 10, 63, 70
Inglis Jones, Elizabeth 2
'inn of tranquility, The' (John Galsworthy) 124
Insect Play, The (Karel and Josef Čapek) 46, 47, 51
Interference (Roland Pertwee and Harold Dearden) 50
interrelationship between people, place (and language) 15, 19, 20, 22, 60, 80, 84, 97, 122, 140
Intruder, The (Maurice Maeterlink) 83
Irish National Theatre, *see* Abbey Theatre
Irish National Theatre Company, *see* Abbey Theatre
It Pays to Advertise (Roi Cooper Megrue and Walter Hackett) 51

Jacobs, W. W. 51
Jennings, Gertrude 49
Joan Danvers, The (Frank Stayton) 48, 50
John a Jams (R. Brinley Jones) 51
John Bull's Other Island (George Bernard Shaw) 68
John Ferguson (St John Ervine) 50, 51, 53
John Gabriel Borkman (Henrik Ibsen) 51
Johnson, Philip 49
Jones, Henry Arthur 29, 44
Jones, Idwal 49
Jones, J. R. 18
Jones, J. Tywi, Rev. 49
Jones, Jack 46
Jones, R. Brinley 49, 51
Jones, T. Gwynn 7, 8, 14, 74, 130
Jones, Tom 16, 70, 130
Joneses, The (Laurence Cowen) 34
Journey's End (R. C. Sherriff) 51
Juno and the Paycock (Sean O'Casey) 14

Justice (John Galsworthy) 65

Keep, The (Gwyn Thomas) 64
King Lear (William Shakespeare) 50, 53

la Blanche, Vidal 18, 19, 20, 134
Laburnum Grove (J. B. Priestley) 48, 51
Lady Precious Stream (S. I. Hsiung) 47, 50
land ethic (Aldo Leopold) 17, 19, 91, 102
Land of Heart's Desire, The (W. B. Yeats) 86
landscapes, moral attributes of, *see* moral attributes of landscapes
Late Christopher Bean, The (Emlyn Williams) 46, 51
League of Young Actors (Abercwmboi) 44
Leave it to Psmith (Ian Hay and P. G. Wodehouse) 48, 50
Leopold, Aldo 19, 91
Lessing, Gotthold Ephraim 62
'Let Dogs Delight' (George Ewart Evans) 103
Lévinas, Emmanuel 3
Lewis, Saunders 13, 36, 85, 130
Little Miss Llewellyn (Frantz Fonson and Fernand Wicheler) 34, 63
Little Theatre Cardiff Company 56
London Little Theatre 84
London Welsh 11, 12, 123, 138–40
Look Back in Anger (John Osborne) 96
Look to the End (Jeannette Marks) 35
Lost Legacy, The (Rev. W. F. Phillips) 98–9
Love Letters (Jeannette Marks) 35
Love's Knowledge (Martha Nussbaum) 3, 158 n13
Lucas, E. V. 129

'Mabon's day' 16, 132
MacIntryre, Alasdair 4
Mackay and Robert Ord, Gayer 50
MacOwen, Norman 50

Maesymeillion (D. J. Davies) 51
Maeterlink, Maurice 83
Maid of Cymru, A (Dau Wynne) 137
Major Barbara (George Bernard Shaw) 29
Malleson, William Miles 41, 49
Man and Superman (George Bernard Shaw) 50
Man Who Stayed at Home, The (Lechmere Worrall and J. E. Harold Terry) 51
'Manchester school' of playwrights 33, 98
Mardy Amateur Dramatic Society 53, 55, 56, 104
Marks, Jeannette 35–6, 83, 98
Maugham, W. Somerset (William Somerset) 50
Megrue and Walter Hackett, Roi Cooper 51
Melting Pot, The (Israel Zangwill) 51
Merchant of Venice, The (William Shakespeare) 51
Merry, Merry Cuckoo, The (Jeannette Marks) 35, 98
Miles, Charles 9
Miller, Arthur 15, 95–6
Milne, A. A. 46, 49, 50, 129
Miss Sara Sampson (Gotthold Ephraim Lessing) 62
Mixed Marriage (St John Ervine) 17
'modest proposal, A' (Jonathan Swift) 125
Mollusc, The (Henry Hubert Davies) 50
Moloch (Winifred Carter) 51
Monkey's Paw, The (W. W. Jacobs) 51
Monologue for One, A (Naunton Davies) 50
Moore, George 1
moral attributes of landscapes 17–19
moral knowledge 66, 100, 116, 157 n9, 174–5 n21
moral particularism 4, 115, 118
Morgan and A. G. Prys-Jones, Trevor 49, 51
Morgan, D. Gwernydd 50
Morgan, Diana 46

Morgan, Magdalen (translator) 13
'mowing of a field, The' (Hilaire Belloc) 128
Mr Pim Passes By (A. A. Milne) 50
Murray, T. C. 51
My People (Caradoc Evans) 2, 45

naive realism (Jane Bennett) 133–4
nation, *also* national *and* Welsh nation 1–2, 6, 14, 16, 18, 20, 24, 27, 30, 31, 33, 34, 36, 37, 40, 43, 44, 45, 47, 48, 55, 61, 64, 68, 69, 70, 72, 74, 75, 77, 79, 80, 84, 85, 87, 88, 89, 91, 98, 119, 123, 136, 137, 138, 139, 143
national, *see* nation
National Drama in Wales (J. O. Francis) 57, 95
National Drama Week (1914) 1, 2, 11, 61, 70
national identity, *see* identity
nationalism 7, 13, 17, 71, 72–4, 75, 119, 142
Neath Little Theatre, *also* Neath Little Theatre Company 42, 48, 71, 100
Neath Little Theatre Company, *see* Neath Little Theatre
Negative Dialektik, Die (Theodor W. Adorno) 133
new drama, *also* new Welsh drama 3, 22, 24, 25, 28–31, 34, 35, 37, 61, 69, 96
New Tenant, The (Norman MacOwen) 50
New Theatre (Cardiff) 1, 11
Newport High School Old Girls' Dramatic Society 42
Nicomachean Ethics (Aristotle) 71, 123
Night Must Fall (Emlyn Williams) 46
No Damage Done (Trevor Morgan and A. G. Prys-Jones) 51
Nonconformism 16, 17, 24, 25, 26, 31, 32, 61, 77, 98, 103, 111, 113, 119, 128, 130, 132, 143
Noson o Farrug (R. G. Berry) 50

Nussbaum, Martha 3, 4, 60–1, 67, 100, 158 n13

O'Casey, Sean 14
Odyssey Theatre 40
Old Students' Association (University College of Wales, Aberystwyth) 9, 70
'On Ely' (Hilaire Belloc) 124
'On going a journey' (William Hazlitt) 124
'On murder considered as one of the fine arts' (Thomas de Quincey) 124
On the Study of Celtic Literature (Matthew Arnold) 137
One-act play 3, 10, 11, 35, 54, 83, 84, 91, 97, 98–100, 104, 120
Onesimus (Wil Ifan) 50
Osborne, Alan 64
Osborne, John 15, 96
Othello (William Shakespeare) 50, 53
Outward Bound (Sutton Vane) 50

Paddy the Next Best Thing (Gayer Mackaye and Robert Ord) 50, 53
Parry-Williams, T. H. (Thomas Herbert) 130
Parry, J. Eddie 43, 46, 51, 52, 75, 88, 90, 101
Payne, Ffransis G. 130
Peate, Iorwerth 20, 130
Pelenni Pitar (D. T. Davies) 51
Pen y Daith (J. Ellis Williams) 51
Penarth Amateur Dramatic Society 56
personal essay, *see* essay
Pertwee and Roland Dearden, Roland 50
Phillips, John 49, 51
Phillips, Rev. W. F. 98
Philosopher of Butterbiggins, The (Harold Chapin) 98
Philpotts, Eden 49, 51
phronēsis, *see* practical wisdom
'piece of chalk, A' (G. K. Chesterton) 125–6, 135
Pinero, Arthur Wing 29
Piscator, Erwin 15

place 2–3, 6, 7, 16, 17–18, 20–1, 22, 23, 60–3, 67, 73–4, 79, 80, 95, 113, 118, 119, 121, 123, 124, 127, 131, 132, 133, 134–6, 137, 139–40, 141–3
Plaid Cymru 7, 20, 120
Plato 28, 31, 125, 162 n19
play of Welsh life 3, 15, 17, 24, 30, 32, 33, 34, 35, 36, 39, 44, 47, 54, 59, 78, 83, 98, 99
Playboy of the Western World, The (J. M. Synge) 17
Pobun 58, 85
Points (J. Eddie Parry) 51
Pont Orewyn (T. E. Ellis) 1
Pontardawe Dramatic Society 55, 56
Pontlottyn Dramatic Society 53
Port Talbot Rep 56
Port Talbot YMCA Dramatic Society 53, 56
Posner, Richard 45
practical wisdom, *also* phronēsis 21, 100, 105–6, 162n85, 175 n22
Priestley, J. B. 48, 49, 51, 53, 124
Pwyllgor, Y (D. T. Davies) 44, 82
Pwyllgorddyn, Y (J. Ellis Williams) 50

Quintero, Serafín and Joaquín Álvarez 47, 49, 50

R.U.R. (Rossum's Universal Robots) (Karel and Josef Čapek) 47
Raine, Allen 2, 107
Raphaelson, Sampson 50
Rattigan, Terence 96
Rawls, John 72, 73
realism, *also* realist *and* realistic 2, 3, 8, 15, 17, 22, 24, 25, 27, 28, 29, 30, 31, 32, 33, 34, 35, 44, 45, 47, 59, 60, 61, 62, 63, 64, 67, 70, 75, 76, 77, 78, 80, 83, 84, 86, 87, 88, 89, 90, 92, 96, 98, 99, 105, 116, 143
realist, *see* realism
realistic, *see* realism
Rhoscomyl, Owen (Arthur Owen Vaughan) 1, 2, 32, 46

Rhys Lewis 63
Riders to the Sea (J. M. Synge) 48, 99–100
Rising of the Moon, The (Lady Gregory) 104
Rivals, The (Richard Brinsley Sheridan) 44
Roberts, A. O. 83, 84
Roberts, Kate 36, 130
Roberts, R. Silyn 7, 13
Robertson, Tom 28, 68
Robinson, Lennox 33
Robinson, Percy 50
rooted, *see* roots
rootedness, *see* roots
roots, *also* rootedness *and* rooted 3, 18, 74, 75, 79, 80, 81, 83, 107–9, 119, 135, 136, 140
Royal Court Theatre (London) 17
Royal Welch Fusiliers 11
Ruskin, John 124

Sacred Flame, The (W. Somerset Maugham) 50
St Simeon Stylites (F. Sladen-Smith) 98
Saints and Sinners (Henry Arthur Jones) 44
Sauer, Carl 18–19
Schmidt, Arno 125
Seccombe's Dramatic Society (Cardiff) 42
School for Scandal, A (Richard Brinsley Sheridan) 10
Serch Hudol (Ada Edwards) 44
Sesame and Lilies (John Ruskin) 124
Shadow of the Glen (J. M. Synge) 48
Shakespeare, William 46, 49, 50, 51
Shaw, George Bernard 24, 25, 27, 29, 30, 34, 36, 37, 41, 46, 49, 50, 51, 68
Sheridan, Richard Brinsley 10, 44
Sherriff, R. C. 51
Ship, The (St John Ervine) 50, 53
'Signs of the times' (Thomas Carlyle) 124
Sisters' Tragedy, The (Richard Hughes) 84

INDEX

Skin Game, The (John Galsworthy) 51
Sladen-Smith, F. 98
Soar Amateur Dramatic Society (Pontygwaith) 56
Society (Tom Robertson) 28
'Souvenirs from Erin' (Idris Davies) 129
Sowerby, Githa 33, 68
Spreading the News (Lady Gregory) 100
Squall, The (Jean Bart) 51
Stanislavski, Constantin 15
Stapledon, George 19
Stayton, Frank 46, 48, 49, 50
Steppin' Westward (Jeannette Marks) 35
Stevenson, Robert Louis 124, 127, 129
Strife (John Galsworthy) 64, 65, 69
Strike for a Kingdom (Menna Gallie) 102
Swansea Little Theatre 41, 42, 46, 54, 104
Swansea Stage Society 41–2, 53, 56
Swansea YMCA Amateur Dramatic Society 56
Swift, Jonathan 125
Synge, J. M. 17, 33, 36, 37, 48, 83, 99–100, 104

Taffy (Caradoc Evans) 33, 45, 76–8
Tân y Hydref (trans. of *Autumn Fire*, T. C. Murray) 51
Taylor, Tom 26
Theory of Justice, A (John Rawls) 72
Thomas, Ed 64, 95
Thomas, Gwyn 2, 64
Thomas, R. S. 79
Those Who Wait (Ernest George Cove) 44
Tinker's Wedding, The (J. M. Synge) 104
To What Red Hell (Percy Robinson) 50
Tobias and the Angel (James Bridie) 50

Tonypandy Unemployed Club Dramatic Society 42
tradition 21, 24, 25, 34, 35, 60, 64, 65, 66, 67, 79, 80, 82, 83, 89, 96, 97, 108, 111, 113, 117, 118, 119, 120, 121, 126, 127, 128, 143
tragedy 60, 62, 84, 90, 91
Trecynon Amateur Dramatic Society 53, 55, 56, 104, 110, 117
Treharris and District Amateur Dramatic Society 56
Tress of Hair, A (Jeannette Marks) 35
'Triton mit dem Sonnenschirm: Überlegungen zu einer Lesbarmachung von *Finnegans Wake* von James Joyce, Der' (Arno Schmidt) 125
Twelfth Night (William Shakespeare) 50
Twm o'r Nant 30

University College of South Wales and Monmouthshire Dramatic Society 44

Vane, Sutton 46, 50
Vaughan, Hilda 2
Vickery, Frank 37
Village Wizard, The (Naunton Davies) 51
virtue, *also* virtuous 3–5, 6, 12, 16, 18, 21–2, 23, 27, 37, 67, 72, 74, 76, 78, 81, 89, 105–6, 111, 112, 115, 116, 118, 119, 123, 126, 134, 141–2
virtue ethics (Aristotelian) 3–4, 5, 158 n13
virtuous, *see* virtue

Wales (periodical) 34, 123, 129
Wallace, Edgar 53
Wasps (Caradoc Evans) 90
Waste (Harley Granville-Barker) 29, 66
Watkins, Vernon 34
Way Things Happen, The (Clemence Dane) 50

Weavers, The (Gerhart Hauptmann) 66, 68
Wedekind, Frank 68
Weil, Simone 80
Wells, H. G. 127
Welsh Honeymoon (Jeannette Marks) 35
Welsh identity, *see* identity
Welsh nation, *see* nation
Welsh national drama movement, *also* Welsh national theatre movement 10–11, 30, 31, 34, 44, 46, 58–9, 64, 70, 85, 143
Welsh National Drama Week (New Theatre, Cardiff, 1914) 61, 70
Welsh National Theatre Company 14, 85–6, 87
Welsh national theatre movement, *see* Welsh national drama movement
Welsh Outlook, The (periodical) 12, 16, 20, 21, 24, 27, 34, 67, 72, 82, 99, 123, 126, 129, 130, 138
Welsh Players, *also* Ystwyth Players 10, 17

Welsh Witch (Allen Raine) 107
Wiliam (John Phillips) 51
Wilkes, Allene Tupper 49, 51
Williams, Emlyn 11, 35, 46, 49, 51
Williams, J. Ellis 49, 50, 51
Williams, Meriel 85
Williams, Tennessee 15, 95–6
Williamstown Social Centre Players 42
Woolf, Virginia 125, 129
Workhouse Ward, The (Lady Gregory) 17
Worrall and J. E. Harold Terry, Lechmere 51

Yeats, W. B. 17, 33, 34, 79, 86
Ymadawedig, Yr (Stanley Houghton, trans. *The Dear Departed*) 50
Young, Howard Irving 50
Ysgrifau (T. H. Parry-Williams) 130
Ystwyth Players, *see* Welsh Players

Zangwill, Israel 51